T0140542

Communications
in Computer and Information Science   2050

Rationale

The CCIS series is devoted to the publication of proceedings of computer science conferences. Its aim is to efficiently disseminate original research results in informatics in printed and electronic form. While the focus is on publication of peer-reviewed full papers presenting mature work, inclusion of reviewed short papers reporting on work in progress is welcome, too. Besides globally relevant meetings with internationally representative program committees guaranteeing a strict peer-reviewing and paper selection process, conferences run by societies or of high regional or national relevance are also considered for publication.

Topics

The topical scope of CCIS spans the entire spectrum of informatics ranging from foundational topics in the theory of computing to information and communications science and technology and a broad variety of interdisciplinary application fields.

Information for Volume Editors and Authors

Publication in CCIS is free of charge. No royalties are paid, however, we offer registered conference participants temporary free access to the online version of the conference proceedings on SpringerLink (http://link.springer.com) by means of an http referrer from the conference website and/or a number of complimentary printed copies, as specified in the official acceptance email of the event.

CCIS proceedings can be published in time for distribution at conferences or as post-proceedings, and delivered in the form of printed books and/or electronically as USBs and/or e-content licenses for accessing proceedings at SpringerLink. Furthermore, CCIS proceedings are included in the CCIS electronic book series hosted in the SpringerLink digital library at http://link.springer.com/bookseries/7899. Conferences publishing in CCIS are allowed to use Online Conference Service (OCS) for managing the whole proceedings lifecycle (from submission and reviewing to preparing for publication) free of charge.

Publication process

The language of publication is exclusively English. Authors publishing in CCIS have to sign the Springer CCIS copyright transfer form, however, they are free to use their material published in CCIS for substantially changed, more elaborate subsequent publications elsewhere. For the preparation of the camera-ready papers/files, authors have to strictly adhere to the Springer CCIS Authors' Instructions and are strongly encouraged to use the CCIS LaTeX style files or templates.

Abstracting/Indexing

CCIS is abstracted/indexed in DBLP, Google Scholar, EI-Compendex, Mathematical Reviews, SCImago, Scopus. CCIS volumes are also submitted for the inclusion in ISI Proceedings.

How to start

To start the evaluation of your proposal for inclusion in the CCIS series, please send an e-mail to ccis@springer.com.

Miguel Botto-Tobar ·
Marcelo Zambrano Vizuete ·
Sergio Montes León · Pablo Torres-Carrión ·
Benjamin Durakovic
Editors

International Conference on Applied Technologies

5th International Conference on Applied Technologies, ICAT 2023
Samborondon, Ecuador, November 22–24, 2023
Revised Selected Papers, Part II

Editors
Miguel Botto-Tobar
Eindhoven University of Technology
Eindhoven, The Netherlands

Sergio Montes León
Universidad Rey Juan Carlos
Madrid, Spain

Benjamin Durakovic 🕩
International University of Sarajevo
Sarajevo, Bosnia and Herzegovina

Marcelo Zambrano Vizuete
Universidad Técnica del Norte
Ibarra, Ecuador

Pablo Torres-Carrión
Universidad Técnica Particular de Loja
Loja, Ecuador

ISSN 1865-0929   ISSN 1865-0937 (electronic)
Communications in Computer and Information Science
ISBN 978-3-031-58952-2   ISBN 978-3-031-58953-9 (eBook)
https://doi.org/10.1007/978-3-031-58953-9

This Springer imprint is published by the registered company Springer Nature Switzerland AG
The registered company address is: Gewerbestrasse 11, 6330 Cham, Switzerland

If disposing of this product, please recycle the paper.

Preface

The 5th International Conference on Applied Technologies (ICAT) was held on the main campus of the Universidad Espíritu Santo, in Samborondón, Ecuador during November 22 until 24, 2023, and it was organized jointly by Universidad Espíritu Santo in collaboration with GDEON. The ICAT series aims to bring together top researchers and practitioners working in different domains in the field of computer science to exchange their expertise and to discuss the perspectives of development and collaboration. The content of this volume is related to the following subjects:

- Intelligent Systems

ICAT 2023 received 250 submissions written in English by 435 authors coming from 12 different countries. All these papers were double-blind peer-reviewed by the ICAT 2023 Program Committee consisting of 183 high-quality researchers. To assure a high-quality and thoughtful review process, we assigned each paper at least three reviewers. Based on the peer reviews, 66 full papers were accepted, resulting in a 26% acceptance rate, which was within our goal of less than 40%.

We would like to express our sincere gratitude to the invited speakers for their inspirational talks, to the authors for submitting their work to this conference, and to the reviewers for sharing their experience during the selection process.

November 2023

Miguel Botto-Tobar
Marcelo Zambrano Vizuete
Sergio Montes León
Pablo Torres-Carrión
Benjamin Durakovic

Organization

General Chair

Miguel Botto-Tobar   Eindhoven University of Technology,
                            The Netherlands

Program Committee Chairs

Miguel Botto-Tobar   Eindhoven University of Technology,
                            The Netherlands
Marcelo Zambrano Vizuete   Universidad Técnica del Norte, Ecuador
Sergio Montes León   Universidad Rey Juan Carlos, Spain
Pablo Torres-Carrión   Universidad Técnica Particular de Loja, Ecuador
Benjamin Durakovic   International University of Sarajevo,
                            Bosnia and Herzegovina

Organizing Chairs

Miguel Botto-Tobar   Eindhoven University of Technology,
                            The Netherlands
Marcelo Zambrano Vizuete   Universidad Técnica del Norte, Ecuador
Sergio Montes León   Universidad Rey Juan Carlos, Spain
Pablo Torres-Carrión   Universidad Técnica Particular de Loja, Ecuador
Benjamin Durakovic   International University of Sarajevo,
                            Bosnia and Herzegovina

Steering Committee

Miguel Botto-Tobar   Eindhoven University of Technology,
                            The Netherlands
Angela Díaz Cadena   Universitat de València, Spain

Program Committee

A. Bonci	Marche Polytechnic University, Italy
Ahmed Lateef Khalaf	Al-Mamoun University College, Iraq
Aiko Yamashita	Oslo Metropolitan University, Norway
Alejandro Donaire	Queensland University of Technology, Australia
Alejandro Ramos Nolazco	Instituto Tecnólogico y de Estudios Superiores Monterrey, Mexico
Alex Cazañas	University of Queensland, Australia
Alex Santamaria Philco	Universitat Politècnica de València, Spain
Allan Avendaño Sudario	Escuela Superior Politécnica del Litoral, Ecuador
Alexandra González Eras	Universidad Politécnica de Madrid, Spain
Ana Núñez Ávila	Universitat Politècnica de València, Spain
Ana Zambrano	Escuela Politécnica Nacional, Ecuador
Andres Carrera Rivera	University of Melbourne, Australia
Andres Cueva Costales	University of Melbourne, Australia
Andrés Robles Durazno	Edinburgh Napier University, UK
Andrés Vargas Gonzalez	Syracuse University, USA
Angel Cuenca Ortega	Universitat Politècnica de València, Spain
Ángela Díaz Cadena	Universitat de València, Spain
Angelo Trotta	University of Bologna, Italy
Antonio Gómez Exposito	University of Sevilla, Spain
Aras Can Onal	TOBB University of Economics and Technology, Turkey
Arian Bahrami	University of Tehran, Iran
Benoît Macq	Université Catholique de Louvain, Belgium
Benjamin Durakovic	International University of Sarajevo, Bosnia and Herzegovina
Bernhard Hitpass	Universidad Federico Santa María, Chile
Bin Lin	Università della Svizzera italiana, Switzerland
Carlos Saavedra	Escuela Superior Politécnica del Litoral, Ecuador
Catriona Kennedy	University of Manchester, UK
César Ayabaca Sarria	Escuela Politécnica Nacional, Ecuador
Cesar Azurdia Meza	University of Chile, Chile
Christian León Paliz	Université de Neuchâtel, Switzerland
Chrysovalantou Ziogou	Chemical Process and Energy Resources Institute, Greece
Cristian Zambrano Vega	Universidad de Málaga, Spain/Universidad Técnica Estatal de Quevedo, Ecuador
Cristiano Premebida	University of Coimbra, Portugal
Daniel Magües Martinez	Universidad Autónoma de Madrid, Spain
Danilo Jaramillo Hurtado	Universidad Politécnica de Madrid, Spain

Darío Piccirilli	Universidad Nacional de La Plata, Argentina
Darsana Josyula	Bowie State University, USA
David Benavides Cuevas	Universidad de Sevilla, Spain
David Blanes	Universitat Politècnica de València, Spain
David Ojeda	Universidad Técnica del Norte, Ecuador
David Rivera Espín	University of Melbourne, Australia
Denis Efimov	Inria, France
Diego Barragán Guerrero	Universidad Técnica Particular de Loja, Ecuador
Dimitris Chrysostomou	Aalborg University, Denmark
Domingo Biel	Universitat Politècnica de Catalunya, Spain
Doris Macías Mendoza	Universitat Politècnica de València, Spain
Edwin Rivas	Universidad Distrital de Colombia, Colombia
Ehsan Arabi	University of Michigan, USA
Emanuele Frontoni	Università Politecnica delle Marche, Italy
Emil Pricop	Petroleum-Gas University of Ploiesti, Romania
Erick Cuenca	Université Catholique de Louvain, Belgium
Fabian Calero	University of Waterloo, Canada
Fan Yang	Tsinghua University, China
Fariza Nasaruddin	University of Malaya, Malaysia
Felipe Ebert	Universidade Federal de Pernambuco, Brazil
Fernanda Molina Miranda	Universidad Politécnica de Madrid, Spain
Fernando Almeida	University of Campinas, Brazil
Fernando Flores Pulgar	Université de Lyon, France
Firas Raheem	University of Technology, Iraq
Francisco Calvente	Universitat Rovira i Virgili, Spain
Francisco Obando	Universidad del Cauca, Colombia
Freddy Flores Bahamonde	Universidad Técnica Federico Santa María, Chile
Gabriel Barros Gavilanes	INP Toulouse, France
Gabriel López Fonseca	Sheffield Hallam University, UK
Gema Rodriguez-Perez	LibreSoft/Universidad Rey Juan Carlos, Spain
Ginger Saltos Bernal	Escuela Superior Politécnica del Litoral, Ecuador
Giovanni Pau	Kore University of Enna, Italy
Guilherme Avelino	Universidade Federal do Piauí, Brazil
Guilherme Pereira	Universidade Federal de Minas Gerais, Brazil
Guillermo Pizarro Vásquez	Universidad Politécnica de Madrid, Spain
Gustavo Andrade Miranda	Universidad Politécnica de Madrid, Spain
Hernán Montes León	Universidad Rey Juan Carlos, Spain
Ibraheem Kasim	University of Baghdad, Iraq
Ilya Afanasyev	Innopolis University, Russia
Israel Pineda Arias	Chonbuk National University, South Korea
Jaime Meza	Universiteit van Fribourg, Switzerland
Janneth Chicaiza Espinosa	Universidad Técnica Particular de Loja, Ecuador

Javier Gonzalez-Huerta	Blekinge Institute of Technology, Sweden
Javier Monroy	University of Malaga, Spain
Javier Sebastian	University of Oviedo, Spain
Jawad K. Ali	University of Technology, Iraq
Jefferson Ribadeneira Ramírez	Escuela Superior Politécnica de Chimborazo, Ecuador
Jerwin Prabu	BRS, India
Jong Hyuk Park	Korea Institute of Science and Technology, South Korea
Jorge Eterovic	Universidad Nacional de La Matanza, Argentina
Jorge Gómez Gómez	Universidad de Córdoba, Colombia
Juan Corrales	Institut Universitaire de France et SIGMA Clermont, France
Juan Romero Arguello	University of Manchester, UK
Julián Andrés Galindo	Université Grenoble Alpes, France
Julian Galindo	Inria, France
Julio Albuja Sánchez	James Cook University, Australia
Kelly Garces	Universidad de Los Andes, Colombia
Kester Quist-Aphetsi	Center for Research, Information, Technology and Advanced Computing, Ghana
Korkut Bekiroglu	SUNY Polytechnic Institute, USA
Kunde Yang	Northwestern Polytechnic University, China
Lina Ochoa	CWI, The Netherlands
Lohana Lema Moreta	Universidad de Espíritu Santo, Ecuador
Lorena Guachi Guachi	Yachay Tech, Ecuador
Lorena Montoya Freire	Aalto University, Finland
Luis Galárraga	Inria, France
Luis Martinez	Universitat Rovira i Virgili, Spain
Luis Urquiza-Aguiar	Escuela Politécnica Nacional, Ecuador
Manuel Sucunuta	Universidad Técnica Particular de Loja, Ecuador
Marcela Ruiz	Utrecht University, The Netherlands
Marcelo Zambrano Vizuete	Universidad Técnica del Norte, Ecuador
María José Escalante Guevara	University of Michigan, USA
María Reátegui Rojas	University of Quebec, Canada
Mariela Tapia-Leon	University of Guayaquil, Ecuador
Marija Seder	University of Zagreb, Croatia
Marisa Daniela Panizzi	Universidad Tecnológica Nacional – Regional Buenos Aires, Argentina
Marius Giergiel	KRiM AGH, Poland
Markus Schuckert	Hong Kong Polytechnic University, China
Matus Pleva	Technical University of Kosice, Slovakia
Mauricio Verano Merino	Technische Universiteit Eindhoven, The Netherlands

Miguel Botto-Tobar	Eindhoven University of Technology, The Netherlands
Miguel Gonzalez Cagigal	Universidad de Sevilla, Spain
Miguel Murillo	Universidad Autónoma de Baja California, Mexico
Miguel Zuñiga Prieto	Universidad de Cuenca, Ecuador
Mohamed Kamel	Military Technical College, Egypt
Mohammad Al-Mashhadani	Al-Maarif University College, Iraq
Mohammad Amin	Illinois Institute of Technology, USA
Muneeb Ul Hassan	Swinburne University of Technology, Australia
Nam Yang	Technische Universiteit Eindhoven, The Netherlands
Nathalie Mitton	Inria, France
Nayeth Solórzano Alcívar	Escuela Superior Politécnica del Litoral, Ecuador/Griffith University, Australia
Noor Zaman	King Faisal University, Saudi Arabia
Omar S. Gómez	Escuela Superior Politécnica del Chimborazo, Ecuador
Óscar León Granizo	Universidad de Guayaquil, Ecuador
Oswaldo Lopez Santos	Universidad de Ibagué, Colombia
Pablo Lupera	Escuela Politécnica Nacional, Ecuador
Pablo Ordoñez Ordoñez	Universidad Politécnica de Madrid, Spain
Pablo Palacios	Universidad de Chile, Chile
Pablo Torres-Carrión	Universidad Técnica Particular de Loja, Ecuador
Patricia Ludeña González	Universidad Técnica Particular de Loja, Ecuador
Paulo Chiliguano	Queen Mary University of London, UK
Pedro Neto	University of Coimbra, Portugal
Praveen Damacharla	Purdue University Northwest, USA
Priscila Cedillo	Universidad de Cuenca, Ecuador
Radu-Emil Precup	Politehnica University of Timisoara, Romania
Ramin Yousefi	Islamic Azad University, Iran
René Guamán Quinche	Universidad de los Paises Vascos, Spain
Ricardo Martins	University of Coimbra, Portugal
Richard Ramirez Anormaliza	Universitat Politècnica de Catalunya, Spain
Richard Rivera	IMDEA Software Institute, Spain
Richard Stern	Carnegie Mellon University, USA
Rijo Jackson Tom	SRM University, India
Roberto Murphy	University of Colorado Denver, USA
Roberto Sabatini	RMIT University, Australia
Rodolfo Alfredo Bertone	Universidad Nacional de La Plata, Argentina
Rodrigo Barba	Universidad Técnica Particular de Loja, Ecuador
Rodrigo Saraguro Bravo	Universitat Politècnica de València, Spain

Ronnie Guerra	Pontificia Universidad Católica del Perú, Peru
Ruben Rumipamba-Zambrano	Universitat Politècnica de Catalanya, Spain
Saeed Rafee Nekoo	Universidad de Sevilla, Spain
Saleh Mobayen	University of Zanjan, Iran
Samiha Fadloun	Université de Montpellier, France
Sergio Montes León	Universidad Rey Juan Carlos, Spain
Stefanos Gritzalis	University of the Aegean, Greece
Syed Manzoor Qasim	King Abdulaziz City for Science and Technology, Saudi Arabia
Tenreiro Machado	Polytechnic of Porto, Portugal
Thomas Sjögren	Swedish Defence Research Agency (FOI), Sweden
Tiago Curi	Federal University of Santa Catarina, Brazil
Tony T. Luo	A*STAR, Singapore
Trung Duong	Queen's University Belfast, UK
Vanessa Jurado Vite	Universidad Politécnica Salesiana, Ecuador
Waldo Orellana	Universitat de València, Spain
Washington Velasquez Vargas	Universidad Politécnica de Madrid, Spain
Wayne Staats	Sandia National Labs, USA
Willian Zamora	Universidad Laíca Eloy Alfaro de Manabí, Ecuador
Yessenia Cabrera Maldonado	University of Cuenca, Ecuador
Yerferson Torres Berru	Universidad de Salamanca, Spain/Instituto Tecnológico Loja, Ecuador
Zhanyu Ma	Beijing University of Posts and Telecommunications, China

Organizing Institutions

Sponsoring Institutions

Collaborators

Contents – Part II

Intelligent Systems

Neural Network Model to Classify a Tweet According to Its Sentiment

Luis Diaz-Armijos⬤, Omar Ruiz-Vivanco(✉)⬤, and Alexandra González-Eras⬤

Universidad Técnica Particular de Loja, Loja, Ecuador
oaruiz@utpl.edu.ec

Abstract. This research presents a recurrent neural network model that analyzes tweets and classifies them according to three categories: "positive", "neutral" and "negative", in order to identify supporting phrases in the semantic context of the topic under analysis. To do this, the Tweet Sentiment Extraction dataset and the LSTM neural model are used to train the network and evaluate, through network performance measurements and expert analysis, the precision and sensitivity of the model.

The results allow us to classify the sentiment behind a specific tweet with 86.78% accuracy, which shows that the network has a high level of precision, in relation to the expert's assessment and comparing it with other works that have analyzed the sentiment. Dataset using Sentiment Analysis, Topic Modeling among other techniques. Additionally, a web dashboard is presented, which integrates the model analysis flow and allows the visualization of the results of the tweet classification.

In this way, the work offers a tool that can be used to classify the large amount of information on Twitter according to its polarity, recognizing and classifying patterns according to the semantic meaning of the terms. The applications of the model are many, for example, for understanding the characteristics of the personality of the public on social networks, the perception of customers in relation to products, services; which allows us to recognize opportunities to adjust marketing strategies, which benefit both clients and companies in general.

Keywords: Neural Networks · Sentiment Analysis · Tweet Sentiment Extraction dataset · LSTM neural model

1 Introduction

The growing popularity of social media has given rise to an immensity of data generated by users around the world. Among these platforms, Twitter stands out as an inexhaustible source of textual information, where users share their thoughts, opinions and emotions in real time. This constant avalanche of data presents a unique challenge and opportunity to understand the communicative intent behind tweets and analyze public mood and opinion at an unprecedented level. The review of each of the tweets to determine trends in the communication intention demands time and resources for those organizations that need to know these details for their particular purposes. Sentiment analysis through

M. Botto-Tobar et al. (Eds.): ICAT 2023, CCIS 2050, pp. 3–17, 2024.
https://doi.org/10.1007/978-3-031-58953-9_1

a tweet is very useful since through this process it will be possible to understand the expressed attitudes, opinions, emotions and feelings, which allows us to understand general public opinion on different types of topics [1] The sentiment analysis of the tweets that a personal or commercial brand receives helps determine the perception of its users and makes decisions aimed at improving the reception of the image that is intended to be achieved [2].

This research focuses on the classification of communicative intent in tweets using a combination of NLP and neural network techniques. The objective is to develop a model capable of automatically discerning and categorizing tweets into three fundamental classes: "positive," "neutral," and "negative." To address this task, this research draws on the latest advances in the field of NLP and neural networks, taking inspiration from previous work in related areas such as text classification and sentiment analysis [3, 4]. Keyphrase extraction is also integrated, a technique that has been shown to be effective in identifying relevant text segments in long documents [5].

The dataset used comes from the Kaggle competition: "Tweet Sentiment Extraction" [6]. Data cleaning and subsequent class balancing are performed, allowing the artificial neural network model to generalize correctly for all possible classes [7], n this case, positive, neutral or negative tweets. Balancing is obtained by adjusting to the amount of data from the majority class or, in turn, adjusting to the amount of data from the minority class. The learning algorithm consists of a bidirectional LSTM (Long ShortTerm Memory), which is a type of recurrent artificial neural networks that allows information to be kept in memory for long periods of time [8]. Likewise, this algorithm is used in problems that involve text classification and, above all, sentiment analysis [9].

Using the balanced classes, two experiments are developed testing different parameterization, with a majority class with 100 epochs and with a batch_size of 250 for each training, 86.78% is obtained; while with the minority class with 70 epochs and a batch_size of 32 the resulting value is 83.61%, being a high assessment in relation to related works and the evaluation by expert.

The remainder of this article explains in detail the materials and method, model development, and model results in comparison to existing approaches. Finally, the final conclusion of this article is shown and possible extensions are provided as future work is carried out.

1.1 Current Status

Recurrent Neural Networks (RNN) have been used for sentiment analysis on Twitter [10]. Sentiment analysis is a popular research field that aims to extract opinions, attitudes, and emotions from social media platforms like Twitter [11]. Twitter is a significant tool for sharing and acquiring peoples' opinions, emotions, views, and attitudes towards particular entities [12]. In the proposed architecture, a gated attention recurrent network (GARN) is used for sentiment analysis on the sentiment 140 dataset [13]. The GARN architecture combines recurrent neural networks (RNN) and attention mechanisms to classify sentiment classes such as positive, negative, and neutral [14]. Neural network models have been found to outperform traditional classification methods like logistic regression and random forest for sentiment classification of tweets. The performance of the neural network model achieved an accuracy of approximately 90%.

Table 1 shows a reference of the main related works, which have been used as a basis for Twitter sentiment analysis. The reference has been organized according to the perspective of each work, considering the methods, results and conclusions. Analyzing the results, we can see that the accuracy values for predicting sentiments on Twitter are in a range of 76% to 90%.

Table 1. Related works.

Work	Perspective	Method	Result	Conclusion
Sentiment Analysis of Twitter [22]	Sentiment analysis is a technique that uses machine learning to determine the sentiment or emotion expressed in text	- Logistic regression for binary classification problems - Twitter API, Tweepy, and Textblob for real-time análisis	83.98% accuracy	- Proposed tool detects hate speech with 83.98% accuracy. - Tool is free and available for public use
Sentiment Analysis with NLP on Twitter Data [14]	Sentiment analysis can automatically extract subjective information from textual data, allowing for the extraction of summary opinions and sentiment details from large datasets	- Traditional machine learning methods - Natural Language Processing (NLP) with ensemble methods	77.26% accuracy	- Sentiment analysis is widely used in various fields. - Traditional machine learning methods are biased towards a specific class
Twitter Sentiment Analysis Using Recurrent Neural [10]	The paper does not mention the use of bidirectional recurrent neural networks for sentiment analysis	RNN used for sentiment classification	76% accuracy	- RNN model achieved 76% accuracy in sentiment classification

(continued)

Table 1. (*continued*)

Work	Perspective	Method	Result	Conclusion
Comparison of Neural Network and Traditional Classifiers [12]	The performance of neural network models is compared with traditional classifiers for sentiment analysis in Twitter	- Sequential neural network with dense layers - Logistic regression and random forest	- Neural network: 90% accuracy – -Logistic regression: 90% accuracy, -random forest: 83% accuracy	- Neural network model outperforms logistic regression and random forest models - Neural network achieves an accuracy of approximately 90%

2 Method

We use the KDD (Knowledge Discovery in Databases) data mining methodology [15] that analyzes the different stages of the tweet processing flow. First, data selection is carried out, where the "Tweet Sentiment Extraction" dataset is chosen, then comes data preparation, where the dataset is transformed so that it is processed appropriately by the neural model. The third phase is model development, where advanced natural language processing techniques and recurrent neural networks are used to train the neural network to classify tweets into sentiment categories, such as "positive," "neutral," and "negative." "This process involves selecting appropriate network architectures, training strategies, and evaluating model performance.

2.1 Data Selection

The data set used is obtained from the Kaggle competition [6] called "Tweet Sentiment Extraction", under the Creative Commons Attribution 4.0 international license. They are presented in ".csv" format and are composed of a total of 27480 observations or rows and 4 variables or columns. The initial structure of the file (see Fig. 1) is described below:

- "textID", unique ID for each tweet.
- "text", text of the tweet;
- "selectedText", text that supports the sentiment of the tweet;
- "sentiment", general polarity of the tweet.

	textID	text	selected_text	sentiment
0	cb774db0d1	I'd have responded, if I were going	I'd have responded, if I were going	neutral
1	549e992a42	Sooo SAD I will miss you here in San Diego!!!	Sooo SAD	negative
2	088c60f138	my boss is bullying me...	bullying me	negative
3	9642c003ef	what interview! leave me alone	leave me alone	negative
4	358bd9e861	Sons of ****, why couldn't they put them on t...	Sons of ****,	negative
5	28b57f3990	http://www.dothebouncy.com/smf - some shameles...	http://www.dothebouncy.com/smf - some shameles...	neutral
6	6e0c6d75b1	2am feedings for the baby are fun when he is a...	fun	positive
7	50e14c0bb8	Soooo high	Soooo high	neutral
8	e050245fbd	Both of you	Both of you	neutral
9	fc2cbefa9d	Journey!? Wow... u just became cooler. hehe....	Wow... u just became cooler.	positive

Fig. 1. Initial structure of the Tweet Sentiment Extraction dataset.

2.2 Data Preparation

This phase focuses on dataset cleaning according to the considerations proposed in Table 2, using four Python packages: "gensim" which contains a set of word vectorization tools [16], "NLTK" Natural Language Toolkit, package for natural language processing [17], "re" that provides regular expression matching operations, string: which already contains native functions for text strings [18].

Table 2. Considerations for data cleaning

Negative aspects	Variables	Mitigation actions
Data that does not provide relevant information	textID	Remove columns that do not provide relevant information
Linked data	selectedText	Remove links
Data with special characters	selectedText	Remove special characters such as signs, symbols, etc
Stopwords	selectedText	Remove empty words that have no meaning
upper and lower case	selectedText	Convert all records to lowercase
unbalanced data between polarities	Sentiment	Apply data balancing techniques

The number of variables is reduced to 2 and the "positive" polarity is represented by the value of "1", the "neutral" polarity by "0" and the "negative" polarity by "−1", the number of records passes from 27480 to 27350 (see Fig. 2) and the class balancing is carried out towards the majority class with the maximum value of 11108 using the "RandomOverSampler" technique [19], which works using the nearest neighbor algorithm, duplicating the lowest classes until a balancing of each is achieved. One of the polarities, this technique does not provide new tweets and does not affect the performance of the artificial neural network model, and towards the minority class with the minimum value of 7673, using the "UnderSam-pling" technique [19].

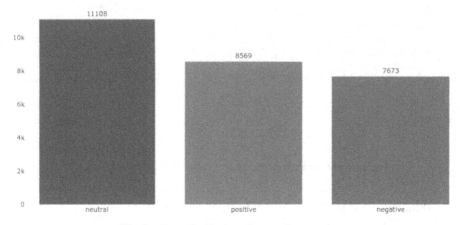

Fig. 2. Class distribution after word processing

In the majority class the number of records is equal to the value of 11108, therefore, the "positive polarity" goes from 8569 to 11108, an increase of approximately 22.9%, and the "negative polarity" goes from 7673 to 11108 increasing approximately 30.9%. The construction of the tokenized data set is carried out through the tokenization of the words and using the Keras tokenizer, which is a text preprocessing package of the TensorFlow [21] platform (see Fig. 3). The value for max_word is equal·to 17609 and that of max_len is equal to 134.

	selected_text	tokenized_text
0	id have responded if were going	[273, 16, 7575, 72, 124, 46]
1	sooo sad	[382, 54]
2	bullying me	[5008, 12]
3	leave me alone	[314, 12, 566]
4	sons of	[2365, 11]
5	some shameless plugging for the best rangers f...	[75, 7576, 5009, 9, 2, 122, 5010, 3835, 14, 1898]
6	fun	[58]
7	soooo high	[434, 521]
8	both of you	[395, 11, 4]
9	wow just became cooler	[206, 21, 2734, 3164]

Fig. 3. Extract of the tokenized text of the dataset's majority class

In the minority class the number of records is equal to the value of 7673, when applying the UnderSampling class balancing technique, therefore, the "neutral polarity" goes from 11108 to 7673, a decrease of approximately 44.8%, and, the "positive polarity" goes from 8569 to 7673, decreasing approximately 12.9%. In the same way, the tokenized data set is constructed using the Keras tokenizer (see Fig. 4). The values for max_words and max_len are set to 14699 and 134 respectively.

	selected_text	tokenized_text
0	sooo sad	[386, 53]
1	bullying me	[5621, 12]
2	leave me alone	[340, 12, 508]
3	sons of	[2390, 11]
4	dangerously	[5622]
5	lost	[226]
6	uh oh am sunburned	[1563, 91, 66, 1735]
7	sigh	[719]
8	sick	[116]
9	onna	[5623]

Fig. 4. Extract of the tokenized text of the dataset's minority class

2.3 Model Development

In the development of the model, the collaborative environment of Google Colaboraty [20] is used together with the TensorFlow platform and the Python programming language, the "Sequential" recurrent neural network algorithm provided by Keras is used, which uses a deep learning model. Bidirectional LTSM.

The first layer of the algorithm (see Fig. 5) is the "Input" or "encoder" layer, which converts the text into a sequence of indexes. "TextVectorization" layer, the "Embedding" layer stores sequences of vectors for each index, which are used to train the model. The "Bidirectional" layer propagates each of the inputs forward and backward and then concatenates the final output, allowing the signal from the beginning of the input not to need to be processed to the end at each time step to affect the output [16]. In the end, the Dense layer performs some final processing and converts that vector representation into a single classification output in the Classification layer (see Table 3).

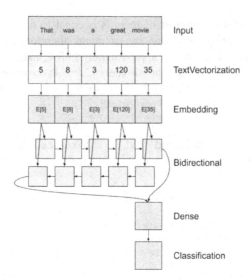

Fig. 5. LSTM neural network diagram [16]

Table 3. LSTM configuration model.

Layer	Parameter	Set value	Description
Incrustación	input_dim	max_words	Size of the vocabulary to be processed
	output_dim	40	Dimension size of the output data
	input_lenght	max_len	Length of input sequences
Bidireccional	hidden_layer	LSTM	Hidden layer that allows the algorithm to remember the best performance from all training phases
Densidad	Input	3	Number of polarity classes to be analyzed
	activation	Softmax	Activation function

2.4 Model Training

The data set is divided into 70% for training and 30% for model evaluation. It is important to mention that each of the defined values are established taking as reference the related work detailed in [23] and after multiple experiments where said values are those that maximize the performance of the artificial neural network model (see Fig. 6).

```
model = keras.Sequential([
    keras.layers.Embedding(
        max_words,
        40,
        input_length = max_len
    ),
    keras.layers.Bidirectional(
        keras.layers.LSTM(
            20,
            dropout = 0.6
            )
        ),
    keras.layers.Dense(
        3,
        activation = 'softmax'
    )
])

model.compile(
    optimizer = 'rmsprop',
    loss = 'categorical_crossentropy'
    metrics = ['accuracy']
)
```

Fig. 6. Model configuration

Two experiments are considered, one for the majority class and the other with the minority class, each experiment is carried out with the exchange of parameters between the parameters: "epochs" and "batch_size" (see Table 4).

Table 4. Parameters for experiments.

Parameter	Description	Values
Epochs	Número de veces que se reentrenará el algoritmo	10, 30, 50, 70, 100
batch_size	Fracción de datos que tomará del total de datos de entrenamiento	auto (32), 100, 250, 500

3   Discussion of Results

In this section we present the practical implementation of the recurrent neural network model designed to analyze supporting phrases in tweets and classify them into sentiment categories, considering the decisions made for the creation of balanced classes with the objective of providing a comparative between both experiments, determining the best alternative to address the inherent challenges in sentiment analysis on social networks such as Twitter. In addition, we show the web application that allows the management of the entire tweet analysis process. Finally, the evaluation of the model is carried out, making a comparison against related works and the evaluation of experts.

3.1 Tweet Classification Model

Table 5 presents the results of the LSTM model for classifying the polarity of tweeter phrases. For each class, 5 cases are presented with different values of epochs and batch_size. For the majority class, the best result is 86.78% precision, the result of applying the algorithm with 100 epo-chs and 250 batch_size, while the best result for the minority class is 83.61% obtained with 70 epochs. And 32 batch_size.

Table 5. Results of tweet classification model

		batch_size			
Experiment	Epochs	auto (32)	100	250	500
E1	10	0.8500	0.8444	0.8508	0.8454
	30	0.8668	0.8632	0.8584	0.8561
	50	0.8664	0.8635	0.8653	0.8483
	70	0.8632	0.8598	0.8665	0.8594
	100	0.8625	0.8603	**0.8678**	0.8632
E2	10	0.8293	0.8296	0.8273	0.7827
	30	0.8241	0.8282	0.8222	0.8087
	50	0.8300	0.8290	0.8194	0.8119
	70	**0.8361**	0.8277	0.8171	0.8186
	100	0.8299	0.8238	0.8135	0.8134

3.2 Architecture of the Web Application

To build the web application, development tools are used to accelerate the development process in projects that involve interaction with artificial intelligence models (see Table 6). The web application is made up of two main modules:

- Statistics display: Allows you to view statistical graphs of all the tweets that have been recorded up to the current date in the web application.
- Classification of tweets: Allows the entry of a new tweet and the visualization of the polarity predicted by the artificial neural network model.

A model, view, controller (MVC) architecture is implemented, where the user interface and the data access layer and interaction with the artificial neural network model will be combined in a single project. This architecture allows structuring the web application as a collection of modules, so that portions of code can be reused in similar tasks and above all allows the application to scale easily in the future (see Fig. 7).

Table 6. Web application development tools.

Tools	Use
Git	Web application versioning system
GitHub	Web application source code repository
GitHub Actions	Continuous integration, compilation and deployment platform of new versions of the web application
HTML5	Used for the layout of the web application
CSS3	Language used for the styles of each of the components of the web application
JavaScript	Programming language for interaction between client and server
Python	Server-side programming language that interacts with the artificial neural network model
Flask	Python programming language framework that allows interpreting the requests made by the client
Insomnia	REST type client that allows you to run tests on each of the end-points of the web application
Heroku	Platform used for the deployment of the web application in a productive environment

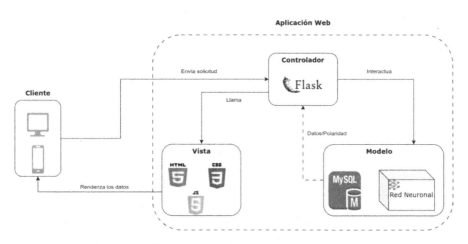

Fig. 7. Web application architecture

The web application can be accessed from any device with a web browser, it consists of a main screen (see Fig. 8) that allows users to view a dashboard with statistical data and graphs up to the current date on the classified tweets and their polarities predicted by the artificial neural network model.

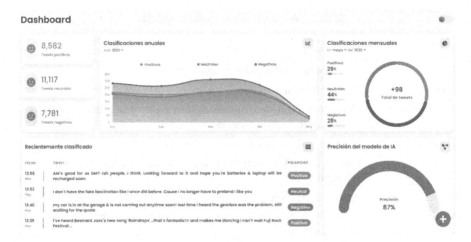

Fig. 8. Main screen of the web application

3.3 Model Evaluation

The evaluation of the model is carried out by comparing the results of related works, mentioning that the tweet classification model, the result of this work, is positioned competitively with the reference models, indicating that the results of the experimentation are significant with respect to the correct classification of the polarity of tweets (see Table 7).

Table 7. Comparison with related works.

N°	Models	Método	Accuracy
1	Twitter Sentiment Analysis Using Recurrent Neural	RNN used for sentiment classification	76%
2	Sentiment Analysis with NLP on Twitter Data	- Traditional machine learning methods - Natural Language Processing (NLP) with ensemble methods	77.26%
3	Comparison Of Neural Network and Traditional Classifiers	- Random forest	83%
4	This work	- Sequential neural network with minority class, 70 epochs and 32 batch_size	83,61%

(continued)

Table 7. (*continued*)

N°	Models	Método	Accuracy
5	Sentiment Analysis of Twitter	- Logistic regression for binary classification problems - Twitter API, Tweepy, and Textblob for real-time análisis	83.98%
6	This work	- Sequential neural network with majority class, 100 epochs and 250 batch_size	86.78%
7	Comparison Of Neural Network and Traditional Classifiers	- Sequential neural network with dense layers	90%
8	Comparison Of Neural Network and Traditional Classifiers	- Logistic regression	90%

A comparison is made of the results obtained by the tweet classification model against the verification of a professional in Psychology, for this a sample of 20 tweets of each polarity is taken, according to the label of the original Kaggel dataset, 60 in total, which are evaluated by both methods. Table 8 shows the aforementioned results, of the 20 positive tweets, RNN Sequential classifies 18 as positive, 2 as neutral and 1 as negative, resulting in a reliability level of 90%. On the other hand, of the 20 neutral tweets, 1 is classified as positive, 17 as neutral and 2 as negative, generating 85% reliability. Finally, of the 20 negative tweets, 1 tweet was predicted as positive, 1 tweet as neutral and 17 tweets as negative, generating a reliability level of 85%.

Table 8. Comparison of the evaluation by both methods

		Positive	Neutral	Negative
Our model	Positive	18	1	1
	Neutral	2	17	1
	Negative	1	2	17
Expert	Positive	19	1	0
	Neutral	1	17	2
	Negative	0	2	18

4 Conclusions

In this study, a recurrent neural network model has been developed to analyze the sentiment behind supportive phrases in tweets and classify them into three categories: "positive," "neutral," and "negative." The implementation of this model in an intuitive web interface provides companies and organizations with a valuable tool to understand public perception on social networks, which can be essential for making strategic decisions in areas such as marketing, customer service. Customer service, image crisis management and identification of improvement opportunities.

The accuracy of the model stands out, reaching 86.78% when classifying sentiment in tweets. This accuracy is a strong indication of the model's ability to perform sentiment analysis effectively on a wide variety of tweets. This makes it easier to use the model in mass classification of tweets, saving time and resources by eliminating the need to review each tweet individually.

There are opportunities for future research and improvements in this area, exploring advanced natural language processing techniques and more complex neural network architectures to further improve model accuracy. Additionally, adapting the model to deal with regional dialects and Twitter-specific slang could be a useful improvement. The inclusion of a larger and more diverse data set could improve the model's ability to understand and classify feelings in different contexts and topics. Handling multiple languages would allow for broader application on a global platform like Twitter. Real-time social media monitoring applications could be an interesting direction for future research, allowing for faster response to events and trends.

References

1. Jaso-Hernández, M., Pinto, D., C. Lucero, D.V.: Analisis de sentimientos en Twitter: impacto de las caracteristicas morfológicas (2018)
2. Castro, J., Alfaro, R., Allende, H.: Análisis de sentimiento y clasificación de texto mediante Adaboost Concurrente (2018)
3. Kim, Y.: Convolutional neural networks for sentence classification. In: Proceedings of the 2014 Conference on Empirical Methods in Natural Language Processing (EMNLP) (2014)
4. Vaswani, A.: Attention is all you need. In: Advances in Neural Information Processing Systems (NeurIPS) (2017)
5. Mikolov, T.: Distributed representations of words and phrases and their compositionality. In: Advances in Neural Information Processing Systems (NeurIPS) (2013)
6. Kaggle: Tweet Sentiment Extraction Homepage. https://www.kaggle.com/c/tweet-sentiment-extraction. Accessed 20 Apr 2023
7. Kharwal, A.: Class Balancing in Machine Learning (2021). [En línea]. https://thecleverprogrammer.com/2021/04/25/class-balancing-in-machine-learning/
8. AWS|Elastic compute cloud (EC2) de capacidad modificable en la nube Homepage. https://aws.amazon.com/es/ec2/. Accessed 20 Jun 2022
9. Mystery, V.: Complete Guide to Bidirectional LSTM (With Python Codes) (2021). [En línea]. https://analyticsindiamag.com/complete-guide-to-bidirectional-lstm-with-python-codes/
10. Parveen, N., Chakrabarti, P., Hung A., Shaik, B.T.: Twitter sentiment analysis using hybrid gated attention recurrent network. J. Big Data 10(1), 50 (2023). https://doi.org/10.1186/s40537-023-00726-3
11. Mishra, J.K.: Twitter sentiment analysis. Indian Sci. J. Res. Eng. Manag. (2023). https://doi.org/10.55041/ijsrem24071
12. Guo, H.: Comparison of neural network and traditional classifiers for twitter sentiment analysis. Highlights Sci. Eng. Technol. 38, 1062–1070 (2023). https://doi.org/10.54097/hset.v38i.5996

13. Jagadeesan, M., Saravanan, T., Selvaraj, P., Asif Ali, U., Arunsivaraj, J., Balasubramanian, S.: Twitter Sentiment Analysis with Machine Learning, pp. 681–686 (2022). https://doi.org/10.1109/ICACRS55517.2022.10029114
14. Brindha, K., Senthilkumar, M., Singh, A.K.: Sentiment Analysis with NLP on Twitter Data (2022). https://doi.org/10.1109/SMARTGENCON56628.2022.10084036
15. Shu, X., Ye, Y.: Knowledge discovery: methods from data mining and machine learning. Soc. Sci. Res. **102817**, 110 (2023)
16. Haider, M.M., Hossin, M.A., Mahi, H.R., Arif, H.: Automatic text summarization using Gensim Word2Vec and K-means clustering algorithm. In: 2020 IEEE Region 10 Symposium, TENSYMP 2020, pp. 283–286 (2020) https://doi.org/10.1109/TENSYMP50017.2020.9230670
17. González-Eras, A., Aguilar, J.: Determination of professional competencies using an alignment algorithm of academic profiles and job advertisements, based on competence thesauri and similarity measures. Int. J. Artif. Intell. Educ. **29**, 536–567 (2019)
18. González-Eras, A., Aguilar, J.: Esquema para la actualización de Ontologías de Competencias en base al Procesamiento del Lenguaje Natural y la Minería Semántica. Revista Ibérica de Sistemas e Tecnologias de Informação **E17**, 433–447 (2019)
19. Imbalanced-learn documentation Homepage. https://imbalanced-learn.org/stable/index.html. Accessed 12 May 2023
20. Google Colaboraty Homepage. https://colab.research.google.com/?utm_source=scs-index. Accessed 11 Jun 2023
21. TensorFlow | Clasificación de texto con un RNN | Text | TensorFlow, Homepage. https://www.tensorflow.org/text/tutorials/text_classification_rnn?hl=es-419. Accessed 20 Jan 2023
22. Prathamesh, N.K.: Sentiment analysis of twitter. Int. J. Sci. Technol. Eng. (2021). https://doi.org/10.22214/ijraset.2022.47954
23. Vira-Honda, S.: Homepage. https://github.com/sergiovirahonda/TweetsSentimentAnalysis. Accessed 20 Jul 2023

Virtual Assistant for the Registration of Clinical Histories Using Natural Language Processing in the Health Sector

Alexis Campos(✉) [ID], Bradd Suarez[ID], and Juan-Pablo Mansilla[ID]

Universidad Peruana de Ciencias Aplicadas, Lima, Peru
{u201517792,u20171d467,pcsijman}@upc.edu.pe

Abstract. Medicine has evolved over time, utilizing technology to automate its relevant processes and expedite healthcare delivery. A notable example is electronic medical records, which would facilitate a doctor's task when recording them, as it often becomes cumbersome and involves wasted time. However, many healthcare specialists with a higher age demographic find it challenging to adapt to digital or virtual environments for the completion of these medical records, which would streamline their documentation. Therefore, the focus of this present study is on a virtual assistant that, employing natural language processing, will serve the purpose of resolving the described problem, all through voice commands. The system was validated through a testing scenario with a sample of thirty users, using a success indicator that measures the percentage reduction in the time required to complete a medical history. Consequently, an average reduction of 54.1% in the time required for medical history recording was achieved. Additionally, 70% of the participants perceived that the virtual assistant would contribute to the optimization of medical history recording. Likewise, 80% considered the user interface to be pleasant and intuitive.

Keywords: Virtual Assistant · Medical Records · Natural Language Processing · Chatbots · Artificial Intelligence

1 Introduction

Currently, many healthcare centers employ a highly deficient care system due to a shortage of human resources, equipment, and the capacity to address patients' issues, resulting in the absence of medical records [24]. This leads to a waste of time for both the physician and the patient due to the excessive time spent on medical record documentation. Many healthcare service provider institutions (IPRESS) have relied on physical medical record keeping, which has seen incidents of data loss due to the vast amount of documentation that lacks proper management or storage organization. Furthermore, these institutions that maintain physical medical record formats continue to provide an extended care service, even in emergency areas. In a 2016 case study at Rebagliati Hospital, it is

M. Botto-Tobar et al. (Eds.): ICAT 2023, CCIS 2050, pp. 18–30, 2024.
https://doi.org/10.1007/978-3-031-58953-9_2

highlighted that medical records in the emergency area are manually created and subsequently sent to an on-duty data entry specialist who records the information into a statistical system. Therefore, this transition in medical record keeping can impact the time it takes to allocate the patient's destination to address their health problem [23].

The strategy employed by the government to mitigate the initial problem was the creation of Law No. 30024 (Law establishing the National Electronic Medical Records Registry), wherein this proposal simplifies the issues associated with physical medical records, both in terms of legibility and organization, by recording patient data using a computer. However, healthcare centers require trained personnel for the proper registration of electronic medical records, with a particular emphasis on medical specialists. These specialists are the only ones authorized to complete the registration of a medical record, whether it be physical or electronic. Nevertheless, there exists a digital divide where many doctors with years of experience struggle to adapt to technology, including virtual and digital environments. Consequently, they prefer the manual method despite the inconveniences or issues posed by physical medical records during emergencies [22]. In summary, the issue addressed by this present study is the deficiency in the quality of electronic medical record-keeping in the healthcare sector. Therefore, the development of a virtual assistant is proposed to facilitate the registration of new medical records through natural language processing.

2 Related Works

In this section, articles related to projects involving virtual assistants or artificial intelligence implemented in healthcare environments will be reviewed. Emphasis will be placed on the contributions of these projects, and many of them will serve as references and examples for subsequent milestones.

The study conducted by [7] aims to employ a chatbot that enables communication with a computer not only through clicking on icons or entering text but, conversely, has the capability to interact in human terms. The primary outcome revealed that the chatbot successfully maintained good participation in communication at the sentence level with humans. Therefore, the interpretation of input data facilitated efficient interaction between humans and computers.

The authors [25] propose the use of four voice assistants in a postpartum clinical environment, including Apple Siri, Amazon Alexa, Google Assistant, and Microsoft Cortana, in order to assess verbal responses regarding postpartum depression. The primary result obtained was that virtual assistants recognize human colloquial speech with an acceptable level of accuracy, but they do not maintain effectiveness at a precise level for such human language recognition.

[18] conducted a study in the field of medicine that emphasizes learning through clinical practices to gain experience in future surgical work. As a result, the study with this solution demonstrates the potential role of integrating artificial intelligence and virtual reality simulation in surgical and medical education.

Furthermore, through the validation process using algorithms, it reveals the feasibility of using the framework to build an objective and automated feedback platform for a neurosurgical task.

According to [5] virtual assistants on mobile devices such as Google Assistant, Siri, Cortana, and Echo require at least one, two, five, or even ten seconds to interpret user input. This is because they search for sentences that cannot be semantically interpreted. The primary result highlights that such an intelligent voice assistant can provide a better personalized service compared to others available in mobile applications on the market.

The authors [17] conducted an analysis of chatbots to determine their potential utility in addressing sensitive health issues. To this end, a test scenario and surveys were employed to gather sample data and assess the acceptability of such chatbots among medical specialists. The primary outcome revealed that chatbots are not perceived as a desirable health intervention, and further research is needed to identify the level of interaction that is more acceptable.

A study conducted by the authors [15] highlights that many physicians may make incorrect diagnoses due to an overload from simultaneously processing complex information they must manage and the overwhelming amount of relevant data that can be missed in the clinical decision-making process. Therefore, the study presents results such as resolving inconsistencies to identify controversial cases, making data-driven decisions, and standardized interpretation, and classifying the clinical characteristics of each patient.

According to [4] the increasing number of female breast cancer cases raises concerns about women's health insurance. Therefore, a chatbot was implemented to help women communicate regarding female breast cancer symptoms (FBC) and then consult with doctors at different clinics in the region for the respective diagnosis and early treatment. The primary outcome indicated that the chatbot effectively handles user inquiries with a high degree of precision to confirm the absence of FBC symptoms.

The authors [13] propose a detailed study aimed at developing a computational model using AI to accurately predict patient outcomes using data available in most emergency department classification systems. The primary result shows that the developed model efficiently predicts hospital admissions using only a few metrics collected in the triage stations, which will reduce waiting times and decrease emergency department classification errors.

According to [21] they propose a virtual assistant to remind diabetes patients to take their medication, which can be monitored by healthcare professionals. Additionally, the study aims to analyze medication possession ratios and measure glycosylated hemoglobin levels to evaluate changes in patients before and after the study. The main result shows a significant improvement in participants' average glycosylated hemoglobin (HbA1c) test results, and in-person medical appointments decreased by 0.7% per month, supporting the potential use of the application.

[12] proposes using artificial intelligence to develop virtual assistants like Siri, Alexa, and Cortana for visually impaired senior citizens, as most of them use

traditional devices with keyboards. The proposed solution optimizes costs and functionality to be user-friendly. The primary result indicates that the proposed artificial intelligence-based virtual assistant solution is sufficiently developed to perform basic tasks, such as removing items from a shopping list, through voice recognition without the need for touching the device screen.

[16] propose underlying technologies and theoretical background for a healthcare platform dedicated to providing medical assistance to individuals with mobility disabilities and offering advanced monitoring capabilities in hospital and home settings. The primary result of the study involves the design, demonstration, and implementation of key indicators and guidelines to measure and evaluate the platform's effects on patients, promoting natural communication between machines and relevant humans for patients currently in rehabilitation or recovery.

[3] propose designing and implementing a chatbot to provide updates on the virus, preventive measures, and psychological support for patients living in remote areas. The main result of the proposed solution is to offer patients access to virtual doctors for communication, not only for COVID-19 but also for other diseases.

According to [19] they propose implementing a text and voice-based virtual assistant with artificial intelligence for an online learning platform that assists teachers in creating video lectures and providing course information to students. The primary result shows that AI has been successful in education, where teachers have started working with the virtual assistant to achieve better learning outcomes for their students.

[20] propose a study to develop a chatbot that can provide support to patients with chronic conditions. The chatbot's architecture is designed to allow the addition of new services and tools over time. The main result of the proposed solution offers flexibility, modularity, and expandability advantages in a virtual assistant scenario, enabling the chatbot to be customized to the specific needs of patients with different medical conditions.

[14] propose a study that provides an overview of various AI methods applied to electronic health record (EHR) data in the field of ophthalmology. The main result is that the applied technique has improved the clinical diagnosis of eye diseases, assessing risks, and predicting disease progression.

[10] propose a study in which AI can classify diseases, stratify patients, and identify the best treatment for precision medicine, contributing to intensive care units (ICU). The primary result is that the ICU team benefits from high-precision models for research and clinical practice, helping them visualize and analyze large amounts of information.

[2] conducted a study reviewing the current literature on health-related chatbots in the context of COVID-19. The main result identified five key applications of current health chatbots, including disseminating health information and knowledge, personal risk assessment and self-triage, exposure monitoring and notifications, symptom tracking and COVID-19 health aspects, and combating misinformation and fake news.

According to [1] they propose an artificial intelligence model to convert regular hospital rooms into isolation units to reduce the spread of COVID-19. The primary result suggests that the MLPNN model decided to choose a prefabricated approach, saving 43

[6] propose developing an artificial intelligence technique to enhance human activity recognition (HAR) processes. The primary result demonstrates that the proposed technique outperforms recent methods under various measures in experimental results.

According to [8] they propose a new artificial intelligence data processing method to assess, predict, and classify osteoporosis risk factors in clinical data for men and women separately. The main result indicates that applying AI algorithms in a clinical setting helps primary care providers classify patients with osteoporosis and improve treatment by recommending appropriate exercise programs.

[11] conducted a study proposing a quick and accurate decision-making system to identify high-risk patients for clinical deterioration following COVID-19 infection, avoiding unnecessary hospital admissions. The primary result suggests that the methods potentially reduce the number of patients transferred to the hospital without an increase in adverse COVID-19 outcomes.

According to the study by [26] they aim to understand the risk factors associated with adverse events during exchange transfusion (TE) in severe neonatal hyperbilirubinemia. The main result indicates that XAI achieved better performance in predicting adverse events during TE and helped doctors gain deeper insights into non-linear relationships and practical knowledge generation.

3   Methods

3.1   Methodology

This project was developed using the Scrum methodology, employing Sprints during specific weeks to better manage the work. The project has specific objectives in place to maintain the quality of its execution. Firstly, research was conducted to analyze AI-based technologies for natural language processing that facilitate patient clinical records within the healthcare system. Secondly, physical and logical architectures were designed to maintain a mapping of IT artifacts and the type of mobile device to be used. Subsequently, a mobile application was developed and implemented to enhance usability for medical specialists. Thirdly, upon completing all application functionalities, a validation process was conducted to assess the effectiveness of these functions through a test scenario in order to gather sample data for success indicators. Lastly, a Continuity Plan is proposed to demonstrate the application's scalability and its future prospects. Finally, the research and project development are summarized with final conclusions.

3.2   Integrated Architecture

In this research, a user-friendly mobile application was proposed to enable medical specialists to create new medical records and access them based on data collected during medical consultations. As part of this proposed solution, an integrated architecture was devised to support the final deliverable, which is the mobile application. Furthermore, this architecture represents the relationship between the front-end and back-end processes of the mobile application, which will be developed for Android devices with internet access, as detailed in the architecture. Next, we will present the developed and certified architecture (Fig. 1).

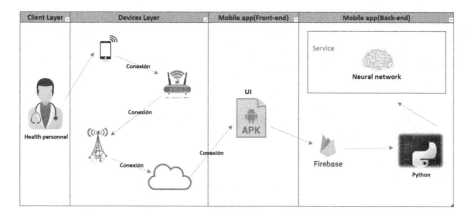

Fig. 1. Integrated architecture

3.3   Programming

During the research work, bench-marking was conducted, which involved comparing tools that provide a natural language processing algorithm based on criteria such as "contribution to AI solution," "programming advantage," and "ease of use." These tools were rated on a 5-point Likert scale, which assigns a score on a scale from 1 to 5, where "1" represents low value and "5" represents high value for each criterion [9]. As a result, React Native emerged as the tool of choice for developing artificial intelligence projects. In comparison to other tools, it offers open-source libraries that facilitate its development to incorporate the required functionalities. To implement natural language processing techniques, the "Voice" function from the "react-native-voice/voice" library was imported. This function incorporates a voice recognition algorithm that facilitates communication between machine and human. Therefore, its get to run the program on an Android mobile device. Which will be able to recognize the sound word of the medical specialist to record the necessary data.

3.4   Mobile Application Interface

Login Interface. The initial interface of the solution is depicted in Fig. 2a, where the fields to be entered by the medical specialist are visible. These fields represent the email and password credentials previously registered in the application.

Registration Interface. The main interface of the solution, as depicted in Fig. 2b, displays the attributes of a new clinical record where the medical specialist can input data using the microphone button. This button activates the virtual assistant that performs voice recognition through natural language processing techniques.

Clinical History Viewing Interface. The final interface of the mobile application, as depicted in Fig. 2c, displays all the data recorded in the mobile application's database following the registration process shown in Fig. 2b. Therefore, the solution meets the expected resolution.

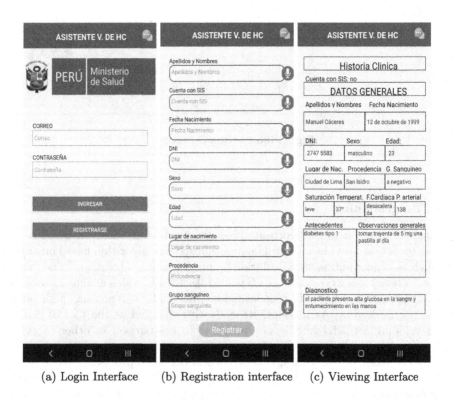

(a) Login Interface   (b) Registration interface   (c) Viewing Interface

Fig. 2. Login, Data Registration, and Data Viewing Interfaces

4   Experiments and Results

In this section, will be discussed the experiments the project has undergone, what is needed to replicate these experiments, and a discussion of the results obtained after this process.

4.1   Preparation Protocol

Programming Environment. This environment was created using React Native in the Visual Code program, which contains all the necessary components for implementing the mobile application. Both the back-end and front-end were developed in JavaScript and JSON format was used to facilitate storage in the Firebase database.

Database Connection. The Firebase cloud storage domain was used, since it had security rules to prevent third parties from accessing the confidential information of the medical records. In addition, to make the connection, a configuration section is needed in the coding so that the apikey, authdomain, projectid, storagebucket, messagingSenderId and appId are contemplated. The latter make up the variables of the firebase script for interconnection with the mobile application solution.

4.2   Definition of Indicators

Success indicators were defined to analyze the validation results of the project in order to gather information for improvement opportunities (Table 1).

Table 1. INDICATORS

IND 1	Percentage reduction in medical record registration time
IND 2	Percentage of medical specialist satisfaction

4.3   Test Scenario

To validate the project, a test scenario was employed at the 'Trebol Azul' healthcare center located in Lima, Peru. A total of 30 participants, who were medical specialists, used their Android mobile devices to conduct the respective tests. This generated sample data represented in Table 2 regarding the time spent on registrations, both in the context of the electronic medical records issue and the mobile application. Additionally, the percentage reduction in registration time for each participant was also obtained.

Table 2. SAMPLE DATA

Medical User	Medical record registration time	Application Solution	Reduction time percentage
1	21 min	11 min	47.6 %
2	36 min	13 min	63.9 %
3	30 min	17 min	43.3 %
4	40 min	15 min	62.5 %
5	35 min	15 min	57.1 %
6	26 min	12 min	53.8 %
7	44 min	20 min	57.1 %
8	44 min	19 min	54.5 %
9	28 min	15 min	46.4 %
10	35 min	14 min	60.0 %
11	38 min	12 min	68.4 %
12	29 min	15 min	48.2 %
13	27 min	16 min	40.7 %
14	26 min	12 min	53.8 %
15	41 min	17 min	58.5 %
16	36 min	16 min	55.5 %
17	35 min	17 min	51.4 %
18	38 min	15 min	60.5 %
19	35 min	15 min	57.1 %
20	30 min	17 min	43.3 %
21	31 min	11 min	64.5 %
22	40 min	18 min	55.0 %
23	34 min	17 min	50.0 %
24	30 min	13 min	56.6 %
25	30 min	14 min	53.3 %
26	32 min	16 min	50.0 %
27	34 min	15 min	55.8 %
28	33 min	15 min	54.5 %
29	33 min	17 min	48.4 %
30	29 min	14 min	51.7 %

4.4   Evaluation of Indicators

Indicator 1 - Percentage Reduction in Medical Record Registration Time. Given the quantitative data obtained from the medical record registration times, two variables were proposed for both the electronic medical record registration time and the mobile application registration time to obtain the result of the mentioned success indicator. An equation was formulated to calculate the reduction in medical record registration time, as shown in the following formula.

$$100 - (\frac{x * 100}{y}) = z \tag{1}$$

x = Time for medical record registration using the proposed mobile application solution

y = Electronic medical record registration time

z = Percentage reduction in medical record registration time

Indicator 2 - Percentage of Medical Specialist Satisfaction. Given the interfaces and functionalities defined in the mobile application solution, the User Experience (UX) design process was used to validate the usability, efficiency, and user interface of the application, aiming to establish a satisfactory relationship between the user and the final product.

5   Analysis and Discussion of Results

In this section, we will present the results obtained by the proposed indicators according to the validation process employed for the project solution.

After obtaining the percentage reductions in registration time, it was verified that the required goal was achieved. Therefore, an arithmetic mean was calculated for all the percentage reductions, resulting in an average effectiveness of 54.1% through the mobile application. This can be seen in the graph in Fig. 3, where the separation threshold represents the aforementioned percentage.

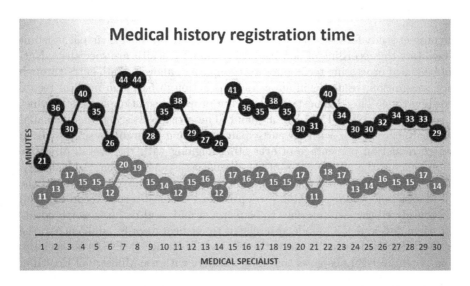

Fig. 3. Percentage reduction in clinical history recording time

With a greater focus on UX design, it was possible to obtain and verify that the majority of medical specialists had a good level of satisfaction with the solution provided in the mobile application used on their Android mobile devices. This can be corroborated in Fig. 4, which shows that there was an 80% level of usability correctness and 20% for improvement. Similarly, it is observed that there was a 70% level of efficiency correctness and 30% for improvement. Furthermore, it is confirmed that there is an 80% level of correct interface design and 20% for improvement.

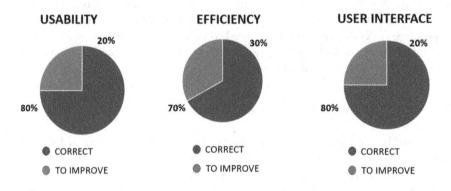

Fig. 4. Percentage of satisfaction of the medical specialist

6   Conclusions

The present study focused on the development of a mobile device virtual assistant to facilitate the recording of new medical records by healthcare specialists. Natural language processing techniques were employed, allowing data entry through voice recognition, resulting in an average reduction of 54.1% in medical record recording time. This demonstrated that the proposed solution successfully met its scope and resolved the issue at hand. The virtual assistant was validated in a healthcare center with 30 participants, yielding favorable results with an average reduction percentage of over 50%, aligning with the overall objective and enhancing the effectiveness of the virtual assistant solution. Additionally, 80% of participants found the application to be user-friendly, 70% believed the virtual assistant would contribute to optimizing medical record recording, and 80% considered the user interface to be pleasant and intuitive. It is worth noting that when developing a mobile app related to medical records, adherence to the technical standards established by the Ministry of Health (MINSA) is crucial to avoid potential legal obstacles that may interfere with the Ministry of Health in Peru.

Furthermore, it should be emphasized that the proposed solution can be scaled up, as it is currently targeted at MINSA healthcare centers in Lima, Peru. It can be expanded to include other national departments or even international contexts, accommodating various languages. This expansion aims to automate and enhance clinical processes, ensuring that both patients and healthcare specialists reap greater benefits.

Financing. Universidad Peruana de Ciencias Aplicadas/UPC-EXPOST-2023-2.

Acknowledgment. The authors thank the evaluators for their important suggestions that have allowed a significant improvement of this work. Likewise, to the Research Department of the Universidad Peruana de Ciencias Aplicadas for the support provided to carry out this research work through the UPC-EXPOST-2023-2 incentive.

References

1. Ahmed, K.S., Ali, M.R., Lashin, M.M., Sherif, F.F.: Designing a new fast solution to control isolation rooms in hospitals depending on artificial intelligence decision. Biomed. Signal Process. Control (2022). https://doi.org/10.1016/j.bspc.2022.104100
2. Almalki, M., Azeez, F.: Health chatbots for fighting COVID-19: a scoping review. Acta Inform. Med. **28**(4), 241–247 (2020). https://doi.org/10.5455/AIM.2020.28.241-247
3. Battineni, G., Chintalapudi, N., Amenta, F.: AI chatbot design during an epidemic like the novel coronavirus. Healthcare (Switzerland) **8**(2), 154 (2020). https://doi.org/10.3390/healthcare8020154
4. Chen, J.-H., et al.: Online textual symptomatic assessment chatbot based on Q&A weighted scoring for female breast cancer prescreening. Appl. Sci. **11**(11), 1–15 (2021). https://doi.org/10.3390/app11115079
5. Po-Sheng, C., Chang, J.-W., Lee, M.-C., Chen, C.-H., Lee, D.-S.: Enabling intelligent environment by the design of emotionally aware virtual assistant: a case of smart campus. IEEE Access (2020). https://doi.org/10.1109/ACCESS.2020.2984383
6. Dhiravidachelvi, E., et al.: Intelligent deep learning enabled human activity recognition for improved medical services. Comput. Syst. Sci. Eng. **44**(2), 961–977 (2022). https://doi.org/10.32604/csse.2023.024612
7. Duncker, D.: Chatting with chatbots: sign making in text-based human-computer interaction. Sign Syst. Stud. **48**(1), 79–100 (2020). https://doi.org/10.12697/SSS.2020.48.1.05
8. Fasihi, L., Tartibian, B., Eslami, R., Fasihi, H.: Artificial intelligence used to diagnose osteoporosis from risk factors in clinical data and proposing sports protocols. Sci. Rep. **12**(1), 18330 (2022). https://doi.org/10.1038/s41598-022-23184-y
9. Granat, L., Andersson, S., Hadziabdic, E., Brännström, M., Sandgren, A.: Translation, adaptation, and validation of the Self-efficacy in Palliative Care scale (SEPC) for use in Swedish healthcare settings. BMC Palliat. Care (2022). https://doi.org/10.1186/s12904-022-00940-5
10. Greco, M., Caruso, P.F., Cecconi, M.: Artificial Intelligence in the Intensive Care Unit. Semin. Respir. Crit. Care Med. (2020). https://doi.org/10.1186/s13054-020-2785-y
11. Hasan, M., et al.: Pre-hospital prediction of adverse outcomes in patients with suspected COVID-19: development, application and comparison of machine learning and deep learning methods. Comput. Biol. Med. (2022). https://doi.org/10.1016/j.compbiomed.2022.106024
12. Ho, D.K.-H.: Voice-controlled virtual assistants for the older people with visual impairment. Eye (Basingstoke). (2018). https://doi.org/10.1038/eye.2017.165

13. Jung, L., Hsieh, C., Chih, L., Yu, L., Chung, K.: Prediction of hospitalization using artificial intelligence for urgent patients in the emergency department. Sci. Rep. (2021). https://doi.org/10.1038/s41598-021-98961-2
14. Lin, W., Chen, J., Chiang, M., Hribar, M.: Applications of artificial intelligence to electronic health record data in ophthalmology. Transl. Vis. Sci. Technol. **9**(2), 13 (2020). https://doi.org/10.1167/tvst.9.2.13
15. Macchia, G., et al.: Multidisciplinary tumor board smart virtual assistant in locally advanced cervical Cancer: a proof of concept. Front. Oncol. **11**, 797454 (2022). https://doi.org/10.3389/fonc.2021.797454
16. Mavropoulos, T., et al.: A context-aware conversational agent in the rehabilitation domain. Future Internet **11**(11), 231 (2019). https://doi.org/10.3390/fi11110231
17. Miles, O., West, R., Nadarzynski, T.: Health chatbots acceptability moderated by perceived stigma and severity: a cross-sectional survey. Digital Health **7**, 20552076211063012 (2021). https://doi.org/10.1177/20552076211063012
18. Mirchi, N., Bissonnette, V., Yilmaz, R., Ledwos, N., Winkler-Schwartz, A., Rolando, F.: The virtual operative assistant: an explainable artificial intelligence tool for simulation-based training in surgery and medicine. PLOS ONE **15**(2), e0229596 (2020). https://doi.org/10.1371/journal.pone.0229596
19. Nguyen, T.-H., Tran, D.-N., Vo, D.-L., Mai, V.-H., Dao, X.-Q.: AI-powered university: design and deployment of robot assistant for smart universities. J. Adv. Inf. Technol. **13**(1), 79–93 (2022). https://doi.org/10.12720/jait.13.1.78-84
20. Roca, S., Sancho, J., García, J., Alesanco, Á.: Microservice chatbot architecture for chronic patient support. J. Biomed. Inform. **102**, 103305 (2020). https://doi.org/10.1016/j.jbi.2019.103305
21. Roca, S., Lozano, M.L., García, J., Alesanco, Á.: Validation of a virtual assistant for improving medication adherence in patients with comorbid type 2 diabetes mellitus and depressive disorder. Int. J. Environ. Res. Public Health **18**(22), 12056 (2021). https://doi.org/10.3390/ijerph182212056
22. Rojas Mezarina, L., Cedamanos Medina, C., Vargas Herrera, J.: Registro Nacional de Historias Clinicas Electronicas en Peru (2015)
23. Rolando Vasquez, A., Amado Tineo, J., Ramirez Calderon, F., Velasquez Velasques, R., Huari Pastrana, R.: Sobredemanda de atención médica en el servicio de emergencia deadultos de un hospital terciario. Lima, Perú (2016)
24. Soto, A.: Barreras para una atencion eficaz en los hospitales de referencia del ministerio de salud del Peru: Atendiendo a pacientes en el siglo XXI con recursos del siglo XX. (2019)
25. Yang, S., Lee, J., Emre, S., Jeffrey, B., Simon, L.: Clinical advice by voice assistants on postpartum depression: cross-sectional investigation using apple Siri, Amazon Alexa, Google Assistant, and Microsoft Cortana. JMIR mHealth uHealth **9**(1), e24045 (2021). https://doi.org/10.2196/24045
26. Zhu, S., Zhou, L., Feng, Y., Zhu, J., Shu, Q., Li, H.: Understanding the risk factors for adverse events during exchange transfusion in neonatal hyperbilirubinemia using explainable artificial intelligence. BMC Pediatr. **22**(1), 567 (2022). https://doi.org/10.1186/s12887-022-03615-5

Physicochemical and Microbiological Characterization of Drinking Water from the Luz de América parish, Ecuador: Statistical Approach

Nahir Dugarte-Jimenez[1]([✉]) [iD], Fernando Vinueza-Escobar[1] [iD],
Sandra Armijos-Hurtado[1] [iD], Rodrigo Bastidas-Chalán[1,2] [iD],
and Mayckel Calero-Silva[1] [iD]

[1] Departamento de Ciencias Exactas, Universidad de las Fuerzas Armadas ESPE.
Sede Santo Domingo, Vía Santo Domingo-Quevedo km 24, Santo Domingo de los
Tsáchilas, Ecuador
{nydugarte,nfvinueza,smarmijos1,rvbastidas,mscalero1}@espe.edu.ec,
rvbastidasc@itsjapon.edu.ec
[2] Instituto Superior Tecnológico Japón, Av. Galápagos y Cuenca, Santo Domingo de
los Tsáchilas, Ecuador

Abstract. The present research was performed in the community of
Luz de America, Santo Domingo de los Tsáchilas, Ecuador, during
March-April (rainy season) and October (dry season) of 2022. The study
assessed the quality of the drinking water consumed in the parish by collecting 176 samples in each season, as there have been no studies on water
quality in the area. Physicochemical and microbiological parameters were
analyzed according to the NTE INEN 1108 standard. The percentage of
compliance with the standard was determined on the basis of the water
source (well, user's tap) and the municipalities under evaluation. The
highest levels of non-compliance were found for residual chlorine and
total coliforms in both seasons, while turbidity showed low compliance
only in the rainy season. To determine the influence of seasonality, the
Wilcoxon-Pratt Signed-Rank test was applied to the variables analyzed,
all of which presented a p-value < 0.05, meaning that the medians of
the difference between the two seasons for each variable were different,
except for total coliforms (p-value $= 0.092$). Kendall's correlation matrix
was used to analyze the correlation between physicochemical and microbiological variables, showing 14 significant correlations in each climatic
season, of which Turbidity-Colour was the highest for both rainy and
dry seasons. Finally, a website was created for the stakeholders and the
public, presenting the geo-referenced results obtained in the laboratory,
ensuring compliance with the main water quality parameters for the benefit of the community.

Keywords: Kendall's correlation · Wilcoxon-Pratt test ·
Physicochemical characterization · water quality

© The Author(s), under exclusive license to Springer Nature Switzerland AG 2024
M. Botto-Tobar et al. (Eds.): ICAT 2023, CCIS 2050, pp. 31–43, 2024.
https://doi.org/10.1007/978-3-031-58953-9_3

1 Introduction

Safe drinking water is a global concern related to human health and covers all surface and groundwater in use or potentially destined to be consumed worldwide by the seven billion and a half people of the planet [1]. Based on this the United Nations established Sustainable Development Goals to reduce the percentage of population without access to safe drinking water [2], despite the higher demand.

Lack of strict water sanitation treatments cause gastroenteric diseases, and approximately 1.6 million children die annually due to diarrheas, cholera, hepatitis, dysentery, among other gastrointestinal infections [1]. If the levels of safe water increased, 361,000 deaths, per year could be avoided [2].

Lack of access to sufficient and safe drinking water, particularly in low- and middle-income nations, has a significant negative impact on human health [3]. In Ecuador, water is essential for the three dimensions of sustainable development: social, economic, and environmental. The Andes represent 99% of the world's tropical glaciers, distributed into fragile ecosystems due to complex interaction among climate, geomorphology, and environmental changes caused by people [4].

The province of Santo Domingo has enough freshwater sources like ponds, wells, rivers, lakes, groundwater, and aquifers all over its territory, however, the residents of Santo Domingo city in terms of health, as the rest of the residents of the country, are at risk, since Ecuador is ranked one of the highest in terms of being at risk when it comes to safe, clean water. According to The State of Drinking water in Ecuador. Study and analysis about dIstribution, infraestructural and Social Issues [5].

Luz de América is a small settlement located in the south, where its population is mainly engaged in agricultural, livestock, and commercial activities. These activities have reduced the quality of water being El Esfuerzo -another rural parish in the neighborhood- the newer supplier affecting its own inhabitants. In urban areas, the water supply is monitored and treated regularly, while rural areas are not included. This is why this study focuses on the compliance of the NTE INEN 1108 standards, in Luz de America community. The study is complemented by analyzing the influence of two climate conditions -rainy and dry- respect to the physicochemical and microbiological variables. Finally, the research examines whether there is a correlation between the variables, under the following hypotheses:

H1: The median of the differences of each pair of data, between rainy and dry seasons, is zero. Median(differences)=0.
H2: There is a correlation between the analyzed variables within each climatic season.

2   Materials and Methods

2.1   Study Area

Luz de América parish is located 23 km south of Santo Domingo, has a total area of 310.30 km^2 (Fig. 1). The highway that connects Santo Domingo with Quevedo crosses the parish, which elevation reaches 327 m in average. The climate is humid and tropical, ranging between 23°C to 26°C. The rainy season extends from January to May, while the dry goes for the rest of the year.

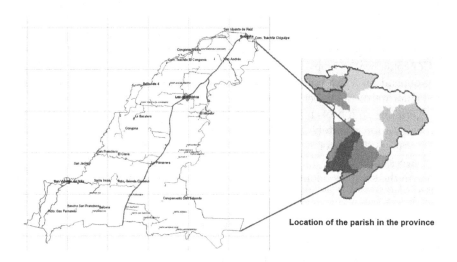

Location of the parish in the province

Fig. 1. Map of Luz de América parish.

The research has included Luz de América, this main settlement gives name to a larger region, El Nila, El Cóngoma, and 30 de Noviembre, all small settlements, for samples collection, which are managed and supplied by a Water Committee, an entity responsible for the safe water distribution. La Primavera was considered for sampling since is not covered by any water committee. The main source of water for Luz de America, is El Esfuerzo River. El Nila is supplied from a deep well and Nila River. The El Cóngoma and 30 de Noviembre get water supply from a spring and La Primavera, primarily relies on wells self-constructed by each dwelling.

2.2   Data Collection

This work was divided into two phases. The first phase explored the conditions of accessibility to the vital liquid based on the responses given to a questionnaire which also tried to know the concepts of the service provided. The survey involved 858 people interviewed directly by the team. The number of questions was six, combining multiple choice and open ended.

The second one consisted of a process of gathering 352 samples of water, from the previously interviewed households, half on rainy and the other half in dry season. Samples were taken from the water taps of the network, treatment pools, and tanks. When was impossible to have access to the public water network, wells used as sources for consumption were part of the samples, to gain firsthand and original insights into this research.

The sampling was divided into five groups based on the areas covered by the four water boards, and the supplied by wells. In the populated center of Luz de América, water samples were collected from the households receiving treated water. The treatment process in this area involves sedimentation and chlorination using tablets. The Nila water board draws water from a deep well and does not have a treatment plant, although, by adding hypochlorite solution to the flow they believe are fulfilling the need for safe water. On the other hand, the Cóngoma water board does not treat its water nor apply chlorine. They solely depend on a full trust using a storage tank. The 30 de Noviembre water board chlorinates the water but does not follow a proper procedure. Lastly, the Primavera due to a broken storage tank, residents in that area consumed water from wells, approximately 20 m depth.

A total of 352 water samples were collected from the selected sites based on its accessibility. The number of users per community gave the method to distribute the samples, along with the water source in both seasons, as shown in Table 1:

Table 1. Distribution of samples by Water Committees

Water Committees	User tap	Water source	Well	Overall total
Luz de América	101	14	N/A	115
Nila	23	2	3	28
Cóngoma	13	3	N/A	16
Primavera	N/A	N/A	10	10
30 de noviembre	6	1	N/A	7
Overall total	143	20	13	176

2.3   Physicochemical and Microbiological Assays

The samples were collected in plastic bottles according to the specifications of the Standard Methods for Examination of Water and Wastewater, 1060 [6]. They were kept refrigerated at 4°C throughout the sampling process, transported to the laboratory less than 4 h after the gathering, and stored under the same conditions. The samples for microbiological analysis were taken in single-use sterile plastic containers.

The following parameters were measured during the sampling process: temperature, hydrogen potential (pH), and residual chlorine. The temperature and pH parameters were measured using Cobra4 brand PHYWE meters, while the residual chlorine was measured using HI 701 Chlorine field colorimeters from Hanna Instruments [7]. The latter parameter was determined only in the treated water samples.

The physical-chemical tests conducted in the laboratory included turbidity, color, and concentration of nitrates and nitrites, following standardized methods for water analysis [6]. For the color assay, a HI727 colorimeter from Hanna Instruments was used. The determination of turbidity was performed using a PT-2000 turbidimeter from Yoke. The concentration of nitrites and nitrates was determined using the Shimadzu 1240 UV-VIS spectrophotometer.

The multiple tube fermentation technique (9221 E) [6] along with Neogen's Lauryl Sulfate and MUG broth (Neogen, s.f.) was utilized to calculate the density of Total Coliforms (TC). To confirm the findings brilliant green bile broth according to method 9221 B [6] was used. Then, in the multiple tube fermentation technique, three sets of, 5 tubes each, were utilized, plus 10 ml of double-strength medium, 1 ml, and 0.1 ml of inoculated sample, respectively. The density will give the most probable number per 100 ml. (MPN/100 ml).

2.4   Data Analysis

Due to its unlikely incidence of random factors or by chance, the statistical significance or p value chosen is 0.05, a threshold that represents the maximum risk tor making a false positive announcements during the conclusion stage.

Version 4.2.1, RStudio on Windows 10 was utilized for this analysis, after an exploratory study of the data, gathered by box plots. The normality assumption was validated by the improved Kolmogorov-Smirnov test known as Lilliefors. The Wilcoxon Pratt Signed Rank test allowed to analyze medians of the variables under control, and by this way all existing correlations were taken into account. The results inferred are based on the coefficient Kendall's Tau.

3   Results and Discussions

Table 1 shows the places and communities studied along with the sources of safe water consumed. At this point, is worth encouraging the fact that conventional treatment plants are unavailable in most of them. They count with some points to water collection, treated by means of chlorination, not performed in an adequate and a technical manner. The dosing is "played by ears" and irregularly, due to the lack of personnel trained, nor a chronogram to specify when and where place tablets and the number of them to dose water treatments. Regulations emanated by authorities are not implanted.

As a result of phase 1 data collection, respondents reported having suffered from some illness during the last 6 months as a result of drinking water at home. The main diseases are summarized in Fig. 2.

As observed in Fig. 2, the right column indicates that 157 drinkers, an 18% of the sample reported gastrointestinal diseases, while 230 users, representing

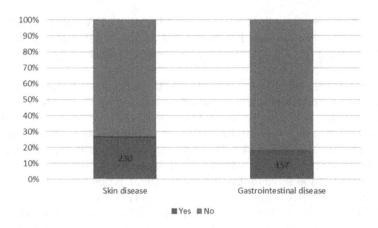

Fig. 2. Diseases reported by consumers of the drinking water service.

26% of the 858 water service users, have reported skin diseases. These illnesses are originated by contaminants microbial activities present in the water consumed [8]. Generally, pathogens such as viruses, bacteria, and protozoa are the leading causes of gastroenteritis, and 50% of these cases are attributed to the consumption of unsafe water with the presence of human and animal feces, with its respective biotoxins.

Table 2 presents values that were obtained from each parameter, including averages, medians, minimums, and maximums values compared with the national quality drinking water levels and based on the INEN 1108 standards.

Table 2. Physicochemical and microbiological parameters analyzed during the rainy and dry seasons.

Parameter	Rainy season data				Dry season data				INEN 1108
	Aver	Min	Max	Median	Aver	Min	Max	Median	
Residual chlorine (mg/L)	0.5889	0.00	2.5000	0.5000	0.2918	0	2.27	0.17	0.3 a 1.5
pH (UpH)	7.6590	5.80	9.6000	7.7150	7.299	5.6	8.4	7.49	6.5–8.0
Turbidity (NTU)	14.832	0.00	212.400	8.996	6.775	0	116.3	2.885	5
Color (UPt/Co)	20.57	0.00	500.00	5.00	6.52	0	150	0	15
Nitrate (mg/L)	9.041	0.00	173.860	1.391	0	0	41.043	4.936	50.0
Nitrite (mg/L)	0.20375	0.00	10.0000	0.09211	0	0	0.4158	0	3.0
Total coliforms (NMP/100 ml)		< 1.1	>2400	14.5		< 1.1	1600	7.8	<1.1
Temperature (ọC)	25.18	21.30	33.50	25.10	23.69	20.30	28.00	23.80	*

The temperature is an unregulated parameter according to the INEN 1108 standard.

It is evident that the concentration of residual chlorine increases significantly during the rainy season, may be attributed to the lack of accurate dosing practices. The higher flow and water source leads to arbitrary increase in the amount of chlorine used, particularly in the Luz de América main area. In the province the rainy season coincides with high temperatures dissolving and diffusing chlorine tablets in the water rapidly causing higher chlorine concentrations.

In Table 2, above, a comparative presentation of turbidity and color parameters show higher levels during the first season of the year, due by the fact of rainfall washing away sediments and suspended particles from surrounding areas, while eroding soils and discomposing organic matter transferred to rivers, lakes, and reservoirs. These factors increase turbidity, cloudy water, leading to increase potential soluble substances, giving the characteristic color of the samples. Similar circumstances were analyzed and divulged in a study conducted in Salta, Argentina, in a research [9].

As well the first season shows higher concentrations of nitrates and nitrites, due to higher temperature and the solubility of nitrate and nitrite compounds are part of the fertilization processes of the soils, along with the reception of runoff water from livestock activities, that brings also levels of nitrogen in the water, as mentioned in the study by [10].

It is also, in this season when the concentration of Total Coliforms (TC) is higher, since rainwater carries H2O from livestock activities, and the infiltration of runoff water into the ground causes cross contamination by coliform in water sources. The second season of the year exceeds the standard but at lower concentrations respect to the rainy season.

Comparing total coliforms against residual chlorine is evident that there is a tremendous need to implement a chlorine dosing method in the area. Teaching and training personnel in good practices for dosing will eliminate bacterial activities and will avoid its concentrations, to obtain safe water and better quality of life. This is crucial, as mentioned in the 2016 study by [11].

Table 3. Compliance Percentage by Community (Rainy season)

RAINY SEASON						
Parameter	Luz de América	Nila	Cóngoma	Primavera	30 de Noviembre	Total
Residual chlorine	79.13%	28.57%	0.00 %	20.00%	14.29%	57.95%
pH	72.17%	67.86%	87.50%	20.00%	100%	71.02%
Total Coliform	46.09%	3.57%	12.50%	20.00%	57.14%	35.23%
Nitrate	98.26%	100.00%	100.00%	100.00%	100.00%	98.86%
Nitrite	99.13%	100.00%	100.00%	90.00%	100.00%	98.86%
Color	100.00%	75.00%	76.52%	89.29%	100.00%	80.68%
Turbidity	0,00%	12,50%	26,09%	7,14%	10,00%	19,89%

In Table 3 and Table 4, shows the compliance percentage for each parameter concerning the samples taken, allowing to identify and prioritize the needs of each community, with the intention to promote the teaching and training and the how to cope future emergencies and reach the maximum level of compliance to the INEN 1108 standard.

Table 4. Compliance Percentage by Community (Dry season)

Parameter	Luz de América	Nila	Cóngoma	Primavera	30 de Noviembre	Total
			DRY SEASON			
Residual chlorine	50.88%	3.85%			14.29%	35.09%
pH	92.11%	96.15%	100.00%	10.00%	100.00%	88.89%
Total Coliform	0%	0%	35.71%	100.00%	0%	8.77%
Nitrate	100.00%	100.00%	100.00%	100.00%	100.00%	100.00%
Nitrite	100.00%	100.00%	100.00%	100.00%	100.00%	100.00%
Color	92.98%	100.00%	100.00%	80.00%	100.00%	94.15%
Turbidity	71,05%	100,00%	100,00%	80,00%	100,00%	79,53%

The compliance respect to residual chlorine is 57.95% during the rainy season, and 35.03% during the dry. It is important to highlight that Nila, 30 de Noviembre, and Primavera had a compliance percentage of less than 30%. Additionally, it should be noted that the community of Cóngoma does not chlorinate its water. These results emphasize the need to implement and improve the disinfection of the water, kill harmful bacteria and viruses by means of an efficient chlorination according to the standards issued.

The previous factor has all to do with the very low compliance percentage for total coliforms since during the rainy is 35.23%, while dry season is just a poor 8.77%.

Below, Table 5, shows the compliance percentage per parameter based on the type of water sources. This table allows to identify which one has the highest non-compliance and in which parameters relevant deviations from the standard curve occur.

Table 5. Compliance by Parameter and Water Source

Parameter	RAINY SEASON (%)				DRY SEASON (%)			
	Tap water	Well water	Raw water	Total	Tap water	Well water	Raw water	Total
Residual chlorine	45.00	62.94	23.08	57.95	38.03	0.00	40.00	35.09
pH	70.00	74.13	38.46	71.02	93.66	28.57	100.0	88.89
Total Coliform	45.00	35.66	15.38	35.23	2.82	71.43	6.67	8.77
Nitrate	100.0	98.60	100.0	98.86	100.0	100.0	100.0	100.0
Nitrite	100.0	99.30	92.31	98.86	100.0	100.0	100.0	100.0
Color	90.00	77.62	100.0	80.68	94.37	85.71	100.00	94.15
Turbidity	50.00	16.78	7.69	19.89	78.17	85.71	86.67	79.53

There is a higher non-compliance of quality parameters during the collection of rainfall, followed by well water, and tap water, which, by the way, shows the highest level of compliance in the first season of the year. In contrast, during the dry season, it can be observed that well water has the highest non-compliance, followed by tap water, and finally, catchment water shows the highest level of compliance, due to the drastic reduction in rainfall.

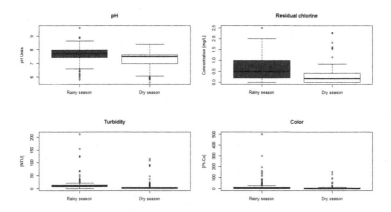

Fig. 3. Box plots by climatic season for the analyzed variables.

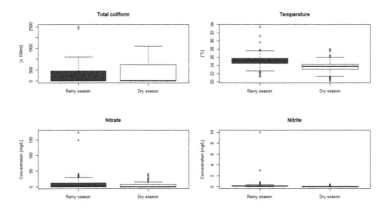

Fig. 4. Box plots by climatic season for the analyzed variables.

A comparison of the laboratory results obtained from the 176 samples gathered during each season is shown in Fig. 3 and Fig. 4 using box plots. This information provides an initial understanding of the data distribution for eight physicochemical variables analyzed: pH, chlorine, turbidity, apparent color, most probable number, temperature, nitrites, and nitrates.

The box plots show a greater amount of atypical data during the rainy season, mainly, turbidity, apparent color, nitrites, and nitrates. Also, in the dry season, there is the presence of atypical data, in this case, color, turbidity, and nitrates. The outliers visualized far from the box plot represent an alert to the researcher, which were verified as possible real values generated in the process of sampling and analysis in the laboratory within two periods of study.

To validate whether the variables obtained in the rainy or dry seasons tend to have a normal distribution, the Kolmogorov-Smirnov normality test applied Lilliefors correction to the whole set of variables. As it was said before, the significance level chosen was 0.05. The result of using the test reveals that all variables have a p-value of less than 0.05, which means that all of them have a non-normal distribution, making it convenient to use non-parametric statistics to develop the hypothesis tests proposed.

H1: The median of the differences of each pair of data, between rainy and dry seasons, is zero. Median(differences)=0

The Wilcoxon signed-rank test is a non-parametric statistical test, applicable for paired data when the distribution is not normal. It facilitates knowing whether there is a significant difference between the medians of the two groups compared, or not. In the case of the study of the set of physicochemical and microbiological variables, the results obtained are presented in Table 6.

Table 6. Results of normality test and comparison of means for the differences

Variable	Lilliefors Normality test (D)	Lilliefors Normality test (p-value)	Wilcoxon-Pratt Signed-Rank test (Z)	Wilcoxon-Pratt Signed-Rank test (p-value)
Residual chlorine	0.16952	6.47E-11	7.5870	3.40E-16
pH	0.10112	0.001037	5.9312	7.18E-10
Total coliform	0.22263	2.20E-16	0.0948	0.92510
Turbidity	0.29845	2.20E-16	6.7567	1.03E-12
Color	0.31656	2.20E-16	4.9306	4.07E-07
Nitrate	0.21098	2.20E-16	2.5578	0.01025
Nitrite	0.36681	2.20E-16	9.4362	2.20E-16
Temperature	0.20911	2.20E-16	9.6739	2.20E-16

The test confirms that the assumed distribution probability occurrence is less than 0.05, indicating that do not follow a normal distribution, or in other words, the statistical test rejects the null hypothesis. Except for the variable total coliform (p-value = 0.9252). This complements other research studies in which the effect of the climatic season on the analyzed variables was not considered [2].

H2: There is a correlation between the analyzed variables within each climatic season.

Regarding the relationship between the studied variables, the Kendall's Tau coefficient was used to analyze the association between the set of variables for both the rainy and dry seasons.

Figure 5, shows the correlation matrix per season, where 14 correlations were statistically significant, taking into account variables between turbidity and color, with a correlation value of 0.29. Respect to residual chlorine and nitrites exists a correlation of -0.22, having the both of them a low level of correlation which suggest a low association between them [12]. Most correlations between variable pairs exhibit a very low level of correlation. Correlations that were not statistically significant are represented by an "X".

Figure 6 shows the dry season matrix, where the statistically significant correlations are displayed. Notably, the turbidity-color pair exhibits a moderate positive correlation of 0.44, while the residual chlorine - total coliform pair shows

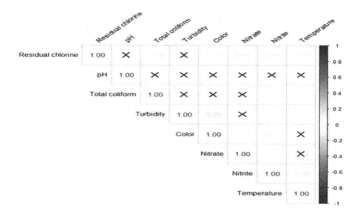

Fig. 5. Kendall's correlation matrix for the rainy season.

a negative correlation of 0.37, so is viable to infer that exists a low or weak level of association. Correlations that were not statistically significant are represented by an "X".

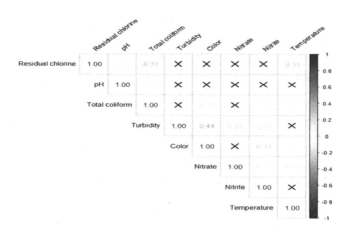

Fig. 6. Kendall's correlation matrix for the dry season.

This separate analysis for each climatic season complements other similar research studies that do not consider the effect of climatic season on the correlation of the analyzed variables [2], being this aspect one of the contribution of this study.

4   Conclusions

Under the umbrella of the current NTE INEN 1108 regulations, this study identified for the first time, in the Luz de América rural parish, the parameter of total coliforms, (TC), is the most critical point, due to its frequency since it exceeds the permissible limits for both seasons. El Cóngoma showed 0% compliance in terms of residual chlorine. It indicates the need for proper methods of chlorination to be applied to all water to avoid morbidity caused by microbiological contamination and to ensure safe water distribution in the Luz de América rural parish. Additionally, the median differences between the rainy and dry seasons for each of the analyzed variables yielded a p-value less than 0.05. Therefore the medians differ between each climatic season for all the studied physicochemical variables, except for Total coliform, where no significant difference was observed (p-value = 0.92).

Significant correlations were obtained for 14 variables chosen to be studied during in each climatic season, evaluating the respective correlation between physicochemical and microbiological variables. The highest correlations for the rainy season were observed between Turbidity-Color and Color-Nitrite. In the dry season, the highest correlations were found between Turbidity-Color and Residual chlorine - Total coliform.

Finally, this research is available for stakeholders and the general public, by mans of a website http://educaciondigital.espe.edu.ec:8081/ProyectoVinculacionLuzAmerica/ containing all information on the compliance of key water quality parameters. The website's objective is to enable responsible parties to plan improvement actions regarding water quality standards for the benefit of the community.

Acknowledgment. The authors thank the ESPE - Universidad de las Fuerzas Armadas for providing resources and access to laboratory facilities. Also, special acknowledgement to the authorities of the parish, Luz de América, and the Water Committees consulted. Their collaboration with logistics and personnel to carry out the field phase was vital to achieve the expected results. Finally, last but not the least, thank the students who contributed with great sense of responsibility for the sake of the execution of this study.

References

1. Fernández-Luqueño, F., et al.: Physicochemical and microbiological characterisation for drinking water quality assessment in southeast Coahuila, Mexico. Int. J. Environ. Pollut. **59**(1), 78–92 (2016)
2. Sánchez-Gutiérrez, R., Benavides-Benavides, C., Chaves-Villalobos, M., Quirós-Vega, J.: Calidad del agua para consumo humano en una comunidad rural: caso corral de piedra, guanacaste, costa rica. Revista Tecnología en Marcha **33**(2), 3–16 (2020)
3. Kayser, G.L., Amjad, U., Dalcanale, F., Bartram, J., Bentley, M.E.: Drinking water quality governance: a comparative case study of Brazil, Ecuador, and Malawi. Environ. Sci. Policy **48**, 186–195 (2015)

4. Choque-Quispe, D., et al.: Insights from water quality of high Andean springs for human consumption in Peru. Water **13**(19), 2650 (2021)
5. Rice, C., Simpson, M.: The state of drinking water in Ecuador (2020). https://storymaps.arcgis.com/stories/74d9240654f54f598e6465f7517a0c16
6. Rice, E.W., Baird, R.B., Eaton, A.D.: Standard methods for the examination of water and wastewater. In: 23rd ed. American Water Works Association (2017)
7. Hanna Instruments. https://hannainst.ec/descargas/. n.d
8. Cevallos, E.S.P., Cano, J.R.M., Ayala, M.A.G., Jaramillo, M.E.N.: Enfermedades transmitidas por el consumo de Agua Contaminada. METANOIA: REVISTA DE CIENCIA, TECNOLOGÍA E INNOVACIÓN **4**(6), 211–222 (2018)
9. Rodriguez-Alvarez, M.S., Moraña, L.B., Salusso, M.M., Seghezzo, L.: Caracterización espacial y estacional del agua de consumo proveniente de diversas fuentes en una localidad periurbana de salta. Revista argentina de microbiología **49**(4), 366–376 (2017)
10. Vitoria, I., Maraver, F., Sánchez-Valverde, F., Armijo, F.: Contenido en nitratos de aguas de consumo público españolas. Gac. Sanit. **29**(3), 217–220 (2015)
11. Tarqui-Mamani, C., Alvarez-Dongo, D., Gómez-Guizado, G., Valenzuela-Vargas, R., Fernandez-Tinco, I., Espinoza-Oriundo, P.: Calidad bacteriológica del agua para consumo en tres regiones del perú. Revista de Salud Pública **18**, 904–912 (2016)
12. Helsel, D.R., Hirsch, R.M., Ryberg, K.R., Archfield, S.A., Gilroy, E.J.: Statistical methods in water resources: us geological survey techniques and methods. Book **4**, 458 (2020)

Machine Learning Models for Identifying Patterns in GNSS Meteorological Data

Luis Fernando Alvarez-Castillo, Pablo Torres-Carrión$^{(\boxtimes)}$ (iD),
and Richard Serrano-Agila

Universidad Técnica Particular de Loja, Loja 1101608, Ecuador
{lfalvarez2,pvtorres,rgserrano}@utpl.edu.ec

Abstract. This research is centered on the comprehensive analysis of meteorological data sourced from strategically positioned Global Navigation Satellite System (GNSS) stations located in Ecuador. Meteorological data of LJEC, PLEC, CUEC, and GZEC was collected and analyzed. For each station, three years (2017–2019) meteorological data recorded throughout each year at one-second intervals were analyzed. Data mining techniques are employed for in-depth analysis, utilizing machine learning algorithms to discern these stations behavior patterns. A machine learning model has been meticulously developed and fine-tuned to harmonize with the data's underlying structure, thereby yielding precise results with a minimal margin of error. After model development and requisite testing, a satisfaction rate of 90% has been achieved, affirming formulated hypotheses validation.

Keywords: Machine Learning · Meteorological Data · Data Mining · GNSS Network · Ecuador

1 Introduction

Machine learning is a procedure in which computational systems acquire knowledge from data and employ algorithms to perform tasks without specific programming [1, 2]. Advanced data analysis techniques, including machine learning, have evolved into essential instruments for uncovering concealed patterns and deducing correlations that conventional analytical methods may struggle to address due to limitations or challenges [3].

Machine learning holds significance across diverse domains, encompassing meteorological analyzes [4], weather [5–7], agricultural practices [8], environmental sciences [9, 10], weather forecasting [11–15], data intelligence model [16, 17], ocean dynamic [18], disaster mitigation [19], rainfall [20]. Consequently, the systematic scrutiny and analysis of meteorological data bear paramount importance in addressing distinct challenges. Machine learning offers a novel approach to addressing tropical cyclone forecast challenges, whether through purely data-driven models or enhancing numerical models through machine learning integration [21]. Their approach hinges on a decision tree algorithm-based model, yielding precise and reliable.

M. Botto-Tobar et al. (Eds.): ICAT 2023, CCIS 2050, pp. 44–55, 2024.
https://doi.org/10.1007/978-3-031-58953-9_4

Machine learning can be categorized into two principal groups: supervised algorithms and unsupervised algorithms. Supervised algorithms [22, 23] operate with the advantage of a designated training dataset, which includes predefined correct responses. This training dataset allows them to generate accurate responses for all potential inputs based on the patterns observed in the training examples. In contrast, unsupervised algorithms [24] are not furnished with predefined correct responses. Instead, they excel in identifying intrinsic similarities among input data and subsequently grouping items that exhibit shared characteristics. This clustering process aids in revealing hidden structures within data.

Meteorological data, frequently employed in weather forecasting, extends its significance to domains necessitating insights into rainfall and humidity levels [25]. For instance, [26] employs electronic instrumentation to gauge meteorological parameters, thereby mitigating diseases in avocado cultivation. Outcomes. These applications exemplify the versatility of meteorological information beyond weather prediction.

A compelling application of meteorological data resides in its capacity to enhance and optimize pre-existing systems, as demonstrated by [27] in the domain of automated crop irrigation. Their approach leverages machine learning algorithms, specifically Partial Least Squares Regression (PLSR), to anticipate periods devoid of precipitation and subsequently initiate automated irrigation processes. This research endeavor is meticulously organized into distinct sections, encompassing methodology, results, discussion, and conclusions, providing a structured framework for comprehensive exploration and analysis.

Historically, Global Navigation Satellite Systems (GNSS) and meteorological observation systems operated as discrete entities. Artificial intelligence is approaching to GNSS data [28]. Nonetheless, contemporary trends underscore the advantages stemming from the fusion of GNSS data processing and meteorological studies, exemplifying their synergistic potential. GNSS stations systematically amass data throughout the calendar year. The dataset harbors invaluable climatic insights, underscoring the primary objective of applying data mining methodologies, in conjunction with machine learning algorithms. The overarching aim is to unveil latent patterns within the data and foresee its behavioral trends.

This work has been developed and structured based on the following sections: methodology, results, discussion and conclusions.

2 Methodology

The dataset utilized in this investigation was sourced from the Geoportal of the Ecuadorian Military Geographic Institute. Presently, Ecuador maintains a comprehensive network of 40 meteorological stations dispersed across the entire national landscape. From this network, four specific stations denoted by their respective codes PLEC, LJEC, GZEC, CUEC, corresponding to the geographical locations of Palanda, Loja, Gualaquiza, and Cuenca, were meticulously chosen for inclusion in this study. These strategically positioned stations are primarily concentrated in the southern region of the country (refer to Fig. 1). The dataset selected for analysis encompasses meteorological observations spanning a three-year period from 2017 to 2019, recorded at one-second intervals. The dataset comprises critical meteorological parameters, including temperature (TD), atmospheric pressure (PR), and relative humidity (HR), which constitute the focal elements of the study.

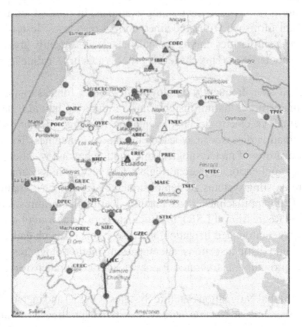

Fig. 1. Geographical Distribution of Stations in Ecuador, adapted from (Continuous GNSS Monitoring Network of Ecuador - REGME | REGME, 2013)

This research is grounded in the Cross Industry Standard Process for Data Mining (CRISP-DM) methodology, which offers a systematic framework delineating the standard lifecycle of a data analysis project. The CRISP-DM methodology comprises a well-structured sequence of phases, including Data Analysis, Data Preparation and Feature Selection, Experimentation and Modeling, Results Evaluation, and Deployment, rendering a standardized and comprehensive roadmap for the progression of the study.

In pursuit of model development, we have formulated and intend to empirically validate three hypotheses during the modeling phases, with temperature as the primary variable of interest:

- Hypothesis 1 (H1): Temperature can be effectively predicted based on relative humidity.
- Hypothesis 2 (H2): Temperature can be effectively predicted based on a combination of relative humidity and atmospheric pressure.
- Hypothesis 3 (H3): Temperature can be effectively predicted with consideration of historical observation data as a reference point.

These hypotheses serve as the foundational constructs guiding the subsequent stages of modeling and analysis, facilitating the assessment of temperature prediction accuracy.

The research was conducted utilizing the Python programming language, a selection driven by its proficiency and the availability of robust libraries that facilitate the modeling process. The scikit-learn library, renowned for its machine learning capabilities, served as the principal tool for the implementation of machine learning algorithms.

The initial stage involved meticulous data cleaning and integration procedures. This necessity arose due to the initial dataset being fragmented and compressed, necessitating consolidation into a singular, more manageable file format, specifically CSV.

After data consolidation, rigorous data cleansing procedures were undertaken, entailing the removal of null data points, extraneous attributes, and the imputation of missing data values. The culmination of these endeavors yielded a comprehensive dataset, comprising a total of 7,423,581 records and encompassing 9 distinct columns (refer to Fig. 2). Furthermore, recognizing the disparate attribute ranges, data normalization and scaling techniques were diligently applied to ensure homogeneity within the dataset.

	Year	Month	Day	Hour	Min	Seg	PR	TD	HR
0	19	1	1	0	0	3	789.4	16.3	63.1
1	19	1	1	0	0	5	789.4	16.3	63.0
2	19	1	1	0	0	6	789.4	16.3	63.1
3	19	1	1	0	0	8	789.4	16.3	63.1
4	19	1	1	0	0	9	789.4	16.3	63.1
5	19	1	1	0	0	10	789.4	16.3	63.1
6	19	1	1	0	0	12	789.4	16.3	63.2
7	19	1	1	0	0	13	789.4	16.3	63.2
8	19	1	1	0	0	15	789.4	16.3	63.2
9	19	1	1	0	0	16	789.3	16.3	63.2
10	19	1	1	0	0	18	789.3	16.3	63.2

Fig. 2. Overview of Integrated Dataset

The dataset was partitioned into a training set comprising 70% of the data and a testing set encompassing the remaining 30%. For the initial two hypotheses, the temporal component was excluded from consideration. Consequently, the attributes of focus consisted of temperature (TD), atmospheric pressure (PR), and relative humidity (HR). Notably, the central variable under scrutiny, The primary objective of this study was the prediction of temperature (TD), which remained the central target variable throughout the analysis.

In the pursuit of hypothesis validation, distinct machine learning algorithms were employed. For the assessment of H1, both linear regression and decision tree algorithms were selected. The rationale behind the choice of linear regression lay in the presence of a discernible inverse correlation (−0.83) between two of the variables, namely temperature (TD) and relative humidity (HR), rendering this algorithm suitable for the task. In this context, temperature served as the dependent variable, while humidity assumed the role of an independent variable.

Transitioning to H2, the same algorithms, linear regression, and decision trees, were leveraged, albeit with the incorporation of atmospheric pressure (PR) as an additional independent predictor variable. Consequently, this scenario entailed the application of multiple linear regression and decision tree algorithms.

In the context of H3, temporal considerations were introduced to ascertain the potential dependence of current temperature behavior on past observations spanning multiple years. To rigorously evaluate this hypothesis, neural networks, specifically Multilayer Perceptron, were deployed as the chosen algorithm.

3 Results

To rigorously assess the first hypothesis, a series of experiments were meticulously executed, employing the simple linear regression approach due to the inherent involvement of merely two variables. After model training with the designated percentage of data, specifically 70%, predictions were meticulously generated using the reserved test data constituting the remaining 30%. The evaluation of the model's performance was undertaken through a suite of meticulously selected metrics (Table 1).

Table 1. Assessment Metrics for the Simple Linear Regression Model

Measures	Results
Scoring function	0.6882251284793326
Mean square error (mse)	2.0614041432648618
Mean absolute error (mae)	1.0693085373649418
Coefficient of determination (r2)	0.6885513216364018

In Fig. 3, a line and scatter plot graphically represents the prediction results, facilitating a comprehensive visual juxtaposition with the actual observed values. This representation provides an effective means of assessing the algorithm's predictive performance, aligning the projected outcomes with the real-world data points that constituted the anticipated targets for prediction.

Subsequently, the decision tree regression algorithm was employed. Analogous to the linear regression approach, 70% of the dataset was allocated for training the model, while the remaining portion facilitated testing and validation. Upon rigorous testing and analysis, the ensuing results were ascertained (refer to Table 2).

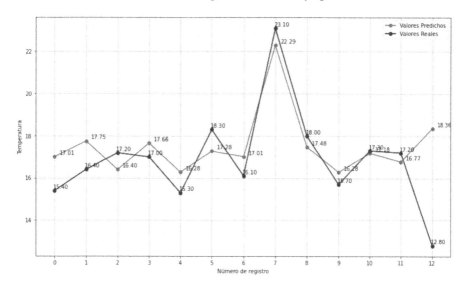

Fig. 3. Graphical Representation of Simple Linear Regression Results

Table 2. Evaluation Metrics for the Decision Tree Algorithm

Measures	Results
Scoring function	0.7448954414331792
Mean square error (mse)	1.6863457907486519
Mean absolute error (mae)	0.9135479580389311
Coefficient of determination (r2)	0.7452172736196919

Below, a graphical representation (Fig. 4) provides a visual depiction of the predictive outcomes derived from the decision tree algorithm.

To assess the second hypothesis, the identical algorithms as those employed previously were utilized. However, in this instance, atmospheric pressure was incorporated as an additional predictor variable. The initial algorithm applied was multiple linear regression, and the outcomes are elucidated in Table 3.

For facilitating a more nuanced juxtaposition of the algorithm's outcomes, a corresponding line and dot graph depicting the predictions has been meticulously generated (refer to Fig. 5).

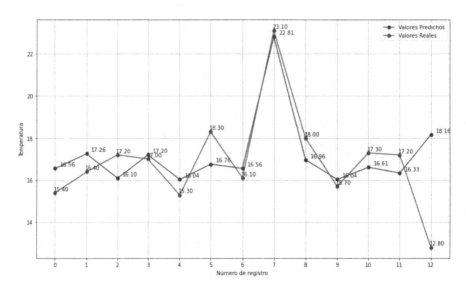

Fig. 4. Decision Tree Results

Table 3. Assessment Metrics for Multiple Linear Regression Algorithm

Measures	Results
Scoring function	0.7132295909259432
Mean square error (mse)	1.895577077124412
Mean absolute error (mae)	1.022106570164799
Coefficient of determination (r2)	0.7136054192305581

To evaluate the second hypothesis, the same algorithms as before were employed, but in this instance, atmospheric pressure (PR) was incorporated as an additional independent variable. The initial algorithm employed was the multiple linear regression, and the ensuing results are delineated in Table 4.

Similarly, a graph has been generated for visualizing the prediction results of the multiple linear regression algorithm in contrast to the actual values, providing a clear depiction of the model's performance (see Fig. 6).

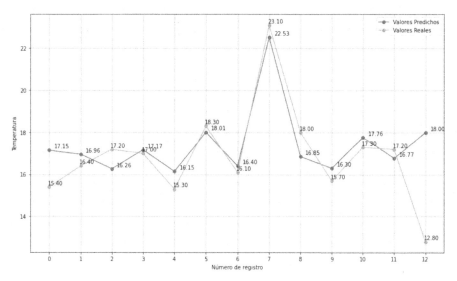

Fig. 5. Multiple Linear Regression Results

Table 4. Evaluation Metrics for the Decision Tree Algorithm

Measures	Results
Scoring function	0.7760705557563674
Mean square error (mse)	1.4798498467572674
Mean absolute error (mae)	0.8600687949536094
Coefficient of determination (r2)	0.7764158569026871

The third hypothesis incorporated the Multilayer Perceptron algorithm, with consideration for the time variable. To discern the relationship between current and past observations, an investigation was conducted, revealing a notable correlation between hours. This revelation indicated that the temperature at the current hour was contingent upon the temperature at the previous hour. Consequently, the two most recent past hours were selected as predictor variables due to their pronounced correlation. Following the model's configuration and subsequent testing, the ensuing results were attained (see Table 5).

The results revealed an impressive coefficient of determination, reaching 90%. This accomplishment signifies precise predictions characterized by minimal error percentages. To further illustrate the model's performance, a graph depicting the model's predictions in comparison to the actual values is presented (see Fig. 7).

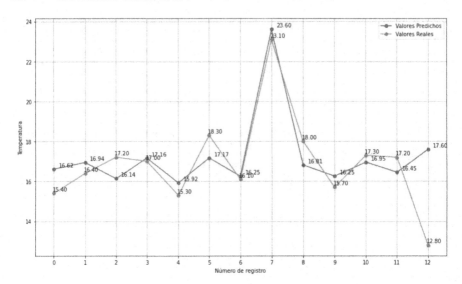

Fig. 6. Tree Results Decision

Table 5. Evaluation Metrics for the Multilayer Perceptron Algorithm

Measures	Results
Scoring function	0.9031513667213553
Mean square error (mse)	0.5237729771944719
Mean absolute error (mae)	0.5494806159203439
Coefficient of determination (r2)	0.9031513667213553

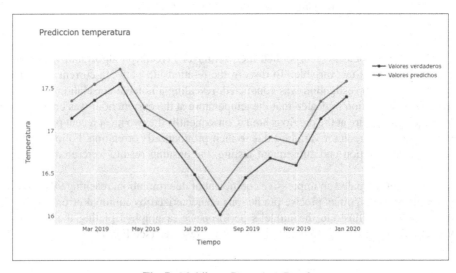

Fig. 7. Multilayer Perceptron Results

4 Discussion

The results of hypothesis testing merit detailed consideration. In the case of Hypothesis 1, the employed algorithms exhibited prediction accuracies of 68% and 74%. These figures exhibit a notable resemblance to the research conducted by Ramírez-Gil et al. (2018), where a parallel evaluation encompassing temperature, humidity, and rainfall variables, utilizing regression algorithms, yielded accuracy rates of 69.8% and 75.8%.

Moving on to Hypothesis 2, the multiple linear regression and decision tree algorithms yielded prediction accuracies of 71% and 77%, respectively. These outcomes closely resemble those achieved by Shobha & Asha (2019), who applied multiple linear regression to temperature, pressure, wind, and rainfall variables, culminating in correct clustering outcomes falling within the range of 74.5% to 80%. In a similar vein, Hernandez et al. (2019) harnessed the decision tree algorithm, achieving results exceeding 55% accuracy for variables such as temperature, pressure, wind, rain, and dew.

The discoveries stemming from Hypothesis 3 are particularly striking, unveiling an impressive accuracy level of 90% by incorporating past observations as predictor variables. It is noteworthy that Choudhary et al. (2019) embarked on a related trajectory, employing an ARIMA model to forecast future values predicated on historical data, culminating in commendable results with an accuracy rate of 83%.

5 Conclusions

- Linear regression, decision trees, and neural networks demonstrate robust efficacy when applied to this dataset. These algorithms effectively conform to the dataset's inherent structure and yield results characterized by low error rates.
- The incorporation of time as a predictor variable significantly enhances the accuracy of the algorithms. This augmentation is attributed to the observed direct correlation between future observations and their historical counterparts. Notably, both humidity and pressure variables exert a noteworthy influence on temperature prediction.
- These variables exhibit varying degrees of impact on the behavior of temperature, rendering them indispensable considerations in the modeling process.

References

1. Janiesch, C., Zschech, P., Heinrich, K.: Machine learning and deep learning. https://doi.org/10.1007/s12525-021-00475-2/Published
2. Khan, S.: Advancements in machine learning: from theory to practice (2023)
3. Chkeir, S., Anesiadou, A., Mascitelli, A., Biondi, R.: Nowcasting extreme rain and extreme wind speed with machine learning techniques applied to different input datasets. Atmos. Res. **282** (2023). https://doi.org/10.1016/j.atmosres.2022.106548
4. Kohail, S.N., El-Halees, A.M.: Implementation of data mining techniques for meteorological data analysis. J. Inf. Technol. (2011). http://www.esjournals.org
5. Chauhan, D., Thakur, J.: Data mining techniques for weather prediction: a review. Int. J. Recent Innov. Trends Comput. Commun. (2014). http://www.ijritcc.org

6. Zeyad, M., Hossain, M.S.: A comparative analysis of data mining methods for weather prediction. In: 2021 International Conference on Computational Performance Evaluation, ComPE 2021, Institute of Electrical and Electronics Engineers Inc., pp. 167–172 (2021). https://doi.org/10.1109/ComPE53109.2021.9752344

7. Laim, B.R.: Data mining techniques for weather forecasting. https://www.researchgate.net/publication/371469933

8. Amini, M., Rahmani, A.: Agricultural databases evaluation with machine learning procedure. https://ssrn.com/abstract=4331902

9. Zhong, S., et al.: Machine learning: new ideas and tools in environmental science and engineering. Environ. Sci. Technol. **55**(19), 12741–12754 (2021). https://doi.org/10.1021/acs.est.1c01339

10. Jaber, M.M., et al.: Predicting climate factors based on big data analytics based agricultural disaster management. Phys. Chem. Earth **128** (2022). https://doi.org/10.1016/j.pce.2022.103243

11. Laim, B.R.: Enhancing weather forecasting through data mining techniques. https://www.researchgate.net/publication/371417707

12. Hannachi, A.: Patterns Identification and Data Mining in Weather and Climate. Springer Atmospheric Sciences. Springer, Cham (2021). https://doi.org/10.1007/978-3-030-67073-3. http://www.springer.com/series/10176

13. Marquez, P.: Weather prediction: improving accuracy using data mining and forecasting techniques (2020). https://scholarworks.utep.edu/open_etd

14. Wang, Z., Mazharul Mujib, A.B.M.: The weather forecast using data mining research based on cloud computing. J. Phys. Conf. Ser. (2017). https://doi.org/10.1088/1742-6596/910/1/012020

15. Ali, M.F.M., Asklany, S.A., El-Wahab, M.A., Hassan, M.A.: Data mining algorithms for weather forecast phenomena: comparative study (2019). https://www.researchgate.net/publication/337797654

16. Khosravi, K., et al.: Meteorological data mining and hybrid data-intelligence models for reference evaporation simulation: a case study in Iraq. Comput. Electron Agric. **167** (2019). https://doi.org/10.1016/j.compag.2019.105041

17. Kareem, F.Q., Abdulazeez, A.M., Hasan, D.A.: Predicting weather forecasting state based on data mining classification algorithms. Asian J. Res. Comput. Sci., 13–24 (2021). https://doi.org/10.9734/ajrcos/2021/v9i330222

18. Romero Alvarez, F.E., Vélez-Langs, O.E.: Data mining in the analysis of ocean-atmosphere dynamics in Colombia's central Caribbean ocean. In: Pichardo-Lagunas, O., Miranda-Jiménez, S. (eds.) Advances in Soft Computing. LNCS (LNAI), vol. 10062, pp. 413–424. Springer, Cham (2017). https://doi.org/10.1007/978-3-319-62428-0_33

19. Linardos, V., Drakaki, M., Tzionas, P., Karnavas, Y.L.: Machine learning in disaster management: recent developments in methods and applications. Mach. Learn. Knowl. Extr. **4**(2), 446–473 (2022). https://doi.org/10.3390/make4020020

20. Saubhagya, S., Tilakaratne, C., Mammadov, M., Lakraj, P.: An application of ensemble spatiotemporal data mining techniques for rainfall forecasting, 6 (2023). https://doi.org/10.3390/engproc2023039006

21. Chen, R., Zhang, W., Wang, X.: Machine learning in tropical cyclone forecast modeling: a review. Atmosphere **11**(7) (2020). https://doi.org/10.3390/atmos11070676

22. Nasteski, V.: An overview of the supervised machine learning methods. Horizons B **4**, 51–62 (2017). https://doi.org/10.20544/horizons.b.04.1.17.p05

23. Osisanwo, F.Y., Akinsola, J.E.T., Awodele, O., Hinmikaiye, J.O., Olakanmi, O., Akinjobi, J.: Supervised machine learning algorithms: classification and comparison. Int. J. Comput. Trends Technol. **48** (2017). http://www.ijcttjournal.org

24. Verkerken, M., D'hooge, L., Wauters, T., Volckaert, B., De Turck, F.: Towards model generalization for intrusion detection: unsupervised machine learning techniques. J. Netw. Syst. Manag. **30**(1) (2022). https://doi.org/10.1007/s10922-021-09615-7
25. Sharma, D., Sharma, P.: Design and implementation of rainfall prediction model using supervised machine learning data mining techniques. Indian J. Data Mining **1**(2), 20–26 (2021). https://doi.org/10.54105/ijdm.B1615.111221
26. Ramírez-Gil, J.G., Martínez, G.O.G., Morales Osorio, J.G.: Design of electronic devices for monitoring climatic variables and development of an early warning system for the avocado wilt complex disease. Comput. Electron. Agric. **153**, 134–143 (2018). https://doi.org/10.1016/j.compag.2018.08.002
27. Choudhary, S., Gaurav, V., Singh, A., Agarwal, S.: Autonomous crop irrigation system using artificial intelligence. Int. J. Eng. Adv. Technol. **8**(5s), 46–51 (2019). https://doi.org/10.35940/ijeat.E1010.0585S19
28. Pierdicca, R., Paolanti, M.: GeoAI: a review of artificial intelligence approaches for the interpretation of complex geomatics data. Geosci. Instrum. Methods Data Syst. **11**(1), 195–218 (2022). https://doi.org/10.5194/gi-11-195-2022

Development of Animal Morphology Measurement Tool with Convolutional Neural Networks and Single-View Metrology Algorithms

Ricardo Loor Párraga$^{(\boxtimes)}$ and Marco Sotomayor Sánchez

Universidad Espíritu Santo, Samborondón 092301, Ecuador
{ricardoloor,mvinicio}@uees.edu.ec

Abstract. Research aimed at obtaining physical measurements of animals in the wild generally makes use of chemical immobilizers to manipulate the object of study, which can be detrimental to the latter. This is why the present research of quantitative approach performs an experimental study that proposes the union of single-view metrology algorithms with the implementation of convolutional neural networks proposed in the YOLO model to develop a web application with two-layer architecture that can classify and take measurements of animals photographed with monocular camera traps in open spaces. This study returned positive results by allowing the development of a web page capable of taking measurements on 2D images with a margin of error of 0.55 cm in 0.49 s and classifying animals with an effectiveness of 93.85%, thus fulfilling the main objective of the study and contributing to the research gap.

Keywords: Single view metrology · convolutional neural networks · YOLO · web application

1 Introduction

Since ancient times, human beings, eager to deepen their knowledge related to the world around them, have conducted research that seeks to clarify and provide answers to their doubts, and the field of fauna analysis has been no exception. The disadvantage of this lies in the fact that; A clear example of this is the study by Cote, Festa-Bianchet and Fournier (1998) who explained the negative effects of chemical immobilization for research purposes in mountain goats, where it was discovered that a large number of females examined significantly decreased their reproductive effectiveness or even abandoned their offspring, which reduced the probability that the latter would survive. It is because of this and many other factors that researchers such as Brager (1999), Durban (2006) or Mahendiran (2017) have tried to provide a definitive solution to this issue, since the negative effects brought about by the handling of animals is not a problem that is limited to a certain number of species.

M. Botto-Tobar et al. (Eds.): ICAT 2023, CCIS 2050, pp. 56–68, 2024.
https://doi.org/10.1007/978-3-031-58953-9_5

It is at this point where ideas begin to emerge of methodologies that allow the study of fauna in their natural ecosystem without having to manipulate or affect in any way the integrity of the object of study, and to be able to photograph the environment without being detected by the animals or without having to be still for hours in one place, they employed the use of monocular camera traps, same that have a motion sensor that activated the trigger in the presence of an animal. With these images available to the researchers, the only thing missing was a way to process these photographs in order to obtain as much information as possible from them, photogrammetry techniques were considered (Dawson & Stoolen, 1999), laser measurement (Durban, 2006), and even specific machines were developed (Tazdemir et al., 2011) and environment mapping techniques with special cameras were considered (Pezzuoloa, Guarinob, Sartoria, González, & Marinello, 2018), but none of these could be commercialized or became a standard, either because of cost, because they were very species-specific or because they simply did not generate the desired success rate, but such uncertainty ceased when success cases involving applications of artificial intelligence and computer vision techniques in animal ecology emerged, and an example of this is Van Horn et al. (2015) with their implementation of Deep learning in a bird species recognition application or McDowall and Lynch (2017) who used the same technology but focused on mapping penguin colonies.

Pimm et al. (2015) state that, in order to reduce the costs, labor, and logistics involved in studying wildlife, ecologists are increasingly turning to greater automation to locate, count, and identify organisms in natural environments. This is why it was decided to continue along the line of using digital analysis technologies to process images captured from monocular camera traps, for this the YOLO (You Only Look Once) algorithm (2015) will be used, which focuses on the task of object detection based on a single convolutional neural network to improve response times while allowing a low detection error. Coupled with this, the algorithms proposed by Criminisi, Reid and Zisserman (2000) that have been widely used in the area of object measurement in 2D images captured with monocular cameras will be implemented, since such algorithms are based on applications of geometry and algebraic representations, which minimizes the amount of input information needed about the image.

Despite the number of existing studies related to the use of new technologies to eradicate the manipulation of animals present in field studies, methodologies that simultaneously implement the techniques present in the YOLO methodology (based on convolutional neural networks) and the "single-view metrology" algorithms proposed by Antonio Criminisi to measure the morphology of free-ranging animals photographed with camera traps have not yet been addressed.

The present work aims to develop a tool that implements convolutional neural networks combined with the YOLO (You Only Look Once) algorithm and single-view metrology algorithms to classify species and measure the morphology of animals in the wild, photographed with monocular camera traps. In order to achieve this objective, a convolutional neural network based on the YOLO study will be developed and trained to analyze an image as an input parameter and to distinguish the exact location of a specific object, as well as to perform an accurate classification that allows the user to observe the species to which the photographed animal belongs. Subsequently, "single-view metrology" algorithms will be implemented to obtain a precise measurement of the objects shown in the images. All this can be accessed through a GUI that allows the user to upload the photos obtained from the camera traps, and the GUI will be in charge of processing them with the help of the implemented algorithms. Finally, the error rate of the system will be analyzed through comparisons with real measurements of the animals.

2 Theoretical Framework

In order to understand in depth the previously exposed problem, this theoretical framework will chronologically address the efforts made by other researchers who intended to establish a standard in the area of non-invasive animal measurement methods, to later cover the technologies that will be used in this project in order to provide a solution to the research gap using 3D measurement algorithms from 2D images and convolutional neural networks.

2.1 Related Studies

For more than two decades, methodologies have been developed to promote the study of animals with the aim of preserving species and their ecosystems. One of the first works carried out with the aim of embracing this approach was done by Brager and Chong (1999), who, with the help of photogrammetry techniques (a technique that uses mathematical functions to process images with the purpose of reconstructing or mapping objects (Baltsavias, 1999)), were able to carry out short-range studies of white-headed dolphins. It should be noted that this study was not the first to implement photogrammetry techniques to study animal behavior (previously, Best and Ruther (1992) used this same technique to study whales Australis), but it was the first to implement this technique focusing on the preservation of the species. Two months after Brager and Chong's study, another research was proposed by the above mentioned together with Dawson and Slooten (1999), who decided to carry out the same research on the same dolphins, but this time with an improved methodology; since this time they decided to implement a combined system of stereo photogrammetry (use of two or more cameras to capture the image from different angles) in addition to an underwater video system. This gave them better results, but it was concluded that this technique only worked in controlled spaces and with little tide.

Several years passed and Durban (2006) proposed a different approach by implementing laser metrics (which consisted of attaching parallel lasers to a DLSR camera) to determine the morphological measurements of free-ranging whales by analyzing images captured at long distances. This methodology was considered viable, but only when a user captures hundreds of photos in short time lapses and selects the ones with the best angle of the whale in order to take the corresponding measurements with the smallest possible margin of error.

Up to this point, most of the related studies were carried out in aquatic species, since their capture was much more complicated than in terrestrial species, nevertheless, the capture of terrestrial animals for later study continued to be a problem, since; as Pelletier (2003) expresses: "Chemical immobilization affects the combat and social dominance of terrestrial animals". This is why Bergerón (2007) decided to apply a technique similar to that of Durban (2006) by using parallel lasers to determine the measurements of the horns of mountain goats. This research yielded excellent results with a margin of error of 2 mm.

Despite the trend that was being generated to use the two previously mentioned techniques (photogrammetry and parallel lasers) pioneers began to emerge in the area of animal morphology measurement; this is the case of Tazdemir, Urkmez and Inal (2011), who proposed a system composed of 4 cameras, a scale platform and a body reflection sensor that together allowed obtaining accurate measurements of bovine morphology and weight. The results were as expected with a 97% success rate, but the complexity and cost of the system made it a non-viable methodology, and this was reflected in the little use that has been made of it, since in later works the techniques mentioned at the beginning of this section continued to be used, such as Berger (2012) and Willisch (2013) who decided to use the photogrammetry technique to take measurements of animals in their habitats, or Barrickman (2015) who used the technique of parallel lasers to remotely measure the body dimensions of mantled howler monkeys.

The area of computer science has also contributed in the study of non-invasive analysis of animal behavior and measurement, as an example we have the work proposed by Fernandes et al. (2018), who used computer vision image segmentation techniques in conjunction with the xbox Kinect camera to map the environment and estimate the weight and morphological measurements of pigs, which resulted in a mean absolute error of 3.5%, which is considered satisfactory for an automated system that does not require further human intervention. It is worth mentioning that this was not the first study that implemented computer vision and Deep learning techniques to study animal behavior, as there are studies such as: the one by McDowall and Lynch (2017) that used the structure-through-motion technique to map penguin colonies; or the study by Peixoto et al. (2019) that analyzed the behavior of mice using the YOLO convolutional neural network-based algorithm, which has been used in countless studies and applications, as it is considered one of the most reliable and fastest algorithms for detecting objects in images. This tells us that the approach of combining methodologies and techniques related to computation such as: Deep learning, neural networks or computer vision with the non-invasive study of free species in their natural habitat is feasible, mainly because of the automation that the previously mentioned techniques bring with them. In addition to this, 3D scene reconstruction techniques can be implemented from a single image, as seen in the work proposed by Zhu et al (2020), who implemented single-view metrology algorithms (proposed by Criminisi in 2002) on a set of images to test whether these algorithms satisfied the scalar reconstruction of the objects present, a study that yielded promising results, to the point of being considered "state of the art" results on specific datasets.

Recent studies have involved the use of camera traps, which blend in with the environment and capture photos when they detect movement. Based on these devices, Tarugara, Clegg, Gandiwa, Muposhi, and Wenham (2019) decided to bait a log so that their object of study, Panthera pardus, would be photographed by camera traps. For this study to be completed, the log in question had to comprise two nails with a specific measurement; so that, when analyzing the image in the selected software (imageJ), the distance between nails would be taken as a reference, which gave promising results (mean error of 2 cm). Other researchers (Cui et al, 2020) also make use of camera traps, but this time they process the images obtained with the help of photogrammetric estimation and a measuring stick that is placed in the same place where the animal passed, which allowed them to have an average error of 5 cm, which, although not better than Tarugara's work, is an advantage in being able to apply this technique to more species (unlike Tarugara's, which focuses its objective on carnivorous animals).

One of the main problems encountered by the aforementioned researchers when trying to process 2D images captured with camera traps was depth prediction (which would allow them to determine the space between the camera and its target), and this is why they had to implement other types of methodologies, But this depth estimation problem could have been solved by applying some of the Single View Metrology algorithms proposed by Crimsini (2002), which reconstruct 3D scenes from purely 2D measurements by taking into account 2D properties such as fading lines or the location of objects in order to determine the relationship between the objects present in the scene.

As could be appreciated in this review of related studies, there are many efforts that try to establish a definitive methodology to eradicate wildlife measurement experiments that involve the manipulation of their objects of study; and although, some of them approached the conception of an efficient and marketable technique, there is still a margin in which to work to improve the processing of the captured images, since; as mentioned above, a good approach that can be given to the study proposed by Tarugara et al. (2019) is to apply Single View Motrology algorithms to perform an efficient measurement of the animal without the need to assemble a scenario, not to mention the fact that this measurement algorithm stands out from the others by the fact that it does not need detailed information from the camera to be able to perform calculations of objects placed at different distances since all the information it uses is the one found in the geometry of the image, And to this we can add the YOLO algorithm so that it is in charge of delimiting the position of the object and at the same time classifying the species of the photographed animal, something that is not observed in any of the studies previously covered.

3   Conceptual Framework

3.1   YOLO (You Only Look Once)

It is an algorithm that offers a new approach to the already well-known object detection techniques. Proposed by Redmon, Divvala, Girshick, and Farahdi (2016) YOLO frames object detection as a regression program to spatially separated bounding boxes and associated class probabilities rather than reusing classification algorithms to detect objects. A single neural network predicts bounding boxes and class probabilities directly from complete images in an evaluation.

YOLO implements convolutional neural networks that initially extract features from an image in order to perform classification while the rest of the layers focus on predicting the probability of the output and its coordinates. The YOLO architecture is based on the "GoogleLeNet" image classification model, with the difference that YOLO uses 1×1 reduction layers followed by 3×3 convolutional layers, giving us a total of 24 convolutional layers followed by 2 fully connected layers (Redmon et al., 2016).

3.2 Trap Cameras

Trap cameras are used in the technique called "camera trapping", which consists of the use of remotely activated cameras that automatically take images or videos of animals or other subjects that pass in front of them. These tools have been widely used around the world, especially in the study of mammals and birds (Rovero, Zimmermann, Berzi, & Meek, 2013).

The advantage of using camera traps lies in the fact that they are a non-invasive methodology that generally causes little disturbance to the target species. Camera traps can be left unattended in the field for weeks at a time, and are therefore ideal for studying animals that usually escape from humans. This great advantage of camera traps over other methods is that the photographs provide objective records or evidence of the presence and identity of the animals (Rovero, 2009).

3.3 Single View Metrology Algorithms

A set of algorithms that describe how measurements of 3D objects can be calculated from a single perspective view of a scene with minimal geometric information determined from the image. This minimal information is usually the vanishing line of a reference plane or a vanishing point for a direction that is not parallel to the plane. It is shown that the structure of the affine scene can be determined from the image, without knowledge of the internal calibration of the camera (e.g., focal length), nor of the explicit relationship between camera and world (pose).

These algorithms base the measurement between parallel planes on 2 fundamental theorems:

Theorem 1: "Given the vanishing line of a reference plane and the vanishing point of a reference direction, then the distances from the parallel reference plane to the reference direction can be computed from their endpoints in the image to a common scaling factor. The scaling factor can be determined from a known reference length."

Theorem 2: "Given a set of linked parallel planes, the distance between any pair of planes is sufficient to determine the absolute distance between any other pair, the link being provided by a chain of point correspondences between the set of planes." (Criminisi, 2002).

4 Methodology

The present research comprises a sequential and evidential development in which a rigorous order is followed, starting from the conception of an idea that is developed with the help of the chosen techniques and culminates with the elaboration of the report of the results obtained, which is why the approach on which this study is based is quantitative; since, as expressed by Hernández, Collado and Baptista (2010) this approach measures phenomena, uses statistics and analyzes the quantitative results of the hypothesis tested.

The development of this project will be carried out on a laptop that has 16 GB of RAM, a 500 GB solid state hard drive, an NVIDIA RTX 2070 graphics card, an Intel core i7-9750H processor and works with the Windows 10 64-bit operating system.

Regarding the research design, it was decided to apply an experimental approach composed of 5 stages, which are:

Stage 1: Data Selection

In this stage, the type of data (in this case images and data) required to train the convolutional neural network will be determined. Once the necessary characteristics have been defined, we will proceed to inquire about the entities, sites or institutions capable of providing such information, to proceed to make the respective data requests and try to obtain as much information as possible, to subsequently make an exhaustive selection of the images that meet all the requirements previously proposed.

Stage 2: Data Preprocessing

In this stage we will use the technique of noise identification, segmentation and morphology (edge smoothing) of images as a basis to have a clean dataset that allows us to work without major complications when implementing the processing algorithms.

Stage 3: Data Transformation

The discrete cosine transform (DCT) technique will be applied, which represents an image as a sum of sinusoids of different magnitudes and frequencies. The DCT has the property that, for a typical image, most of the visually significant information about the image is concentrated in a few coefficients of the image. This is why this technique is used in image compression applications.

Stage 4: Data Integration

For the data integration part, the common storage methodology will be used, where a copy of the original source data will be kept in the system and processed so that we can obtain a unified view. However, the data will remain in its original source. Data integration would finalize the stages concerning data collection and processing in order to proceed to implementation.

Stage 5: Implementation

In this phase we proceeded to develop the web application that would contain the combination of the YOLO implementation with the single view metrology algorithms.

5   Development

In this section all the stages proposed in the methodology will be addressed, this is done in order to document all the steps that constituted the development of the prototype of the animal morphology measurement tool, which began with data processing based on the KDD process to subsequently develop the tool focusing on the evolution of its deliverables in the agile SCRUM methodology.

5.1 Stage 1: Data Selection

The first thing that was done in the conception of this stage was the delimitation of the types of data to be analyzed and the information they should contain, with this it was agreed that such data would be images of animals captured with camera traps in different scenarios, these images should be of dimensions 4624×3648 pixels, which matches the image captured by a Bushnell Trophy Cam hd camera of 16 megapixels, camera that was available in this project.

After an arduous search through the most recognized animal life databases worldwide, it was concluded that none of them included the necessary data for the present research, since most of these data sets sought to provide the necessary attributes for species classification, but not for animal morphology measurements, so the format needed for this project (image + measurements) could not be found.

This is why it was decided to have 2 types of datasets to work with:

1: Datasets obtained from external resources (such as the Animal-10N Dataset, the CIFAR-10 or the Wildlife Insights classification dataset) in order to perform animal classification and train the YOLO convolutional neural network.
2: Images of objects or animals of known measurements captured manually with the Bushnell Trophy Cam hd camera trap in order to implement the Single View Metrology algorithms.

5.2 Stage 2: Data Preprocessing

The preprocessing of the data obtained from the previous stage was divided into 5 phases that were to be applied to all the present images collected to ensure that these are consistent in terms of quality. These phases are:

Read the Image: In this step the images of the datasets in arrays were loaded.

Resize the Image: The "process" function was created, which allowed, with the help of the "resize" function of cv2, to scale the images.

Remove Noise (Denoise): Within the "process" function previously created, the necessary code was added to apply the Gaussian blur technique (specific to cv2) in order to display the image with a blur and thus improve the structure of the images at different scales.

Segmentation: In this step, continuing with the additions in the "process" method, the separation of the background of the image with what is present in the foreground was implemented. For this, we started by creating a gray instance of the image, to later apply the "threshold" function and thus perform the segmentation.

Morphology (Edge Smoothing): Although, up to this point we already had the required properties to be able to work with the images, it was decided to improve them by blurring, and the morphologyEx method was applied to improve the strokes of the image.

Finally, markers were applied to delimit the different scenes present in the images.

5.3   Stage 3: Data Transformation

Given the limited space available on the computer with which we worked, we decided to apply a transformation algorithm to the images in order to minimize their disk size, this was done using the compression technique called DCT.

In order to implement this algorithm, the fttpack package from the scipy library was used. This package contains the "dct" and "idct" methods (idct to perform the inverse of the DCT); these methods have 6 possible input parameters, of which only 2 were used: "x" to represent the array comprising the image and "norm" to represent the normalization mode, which in our case was "ortho"; normalization mode corresponding to the following equation (Fig. 1):

$$f = \begin{cases} \frac{1}{2}\sqrt{\frac{1}{N-1}} & \text{if } k = 0 \text{ or } N-1, \\ \frac{1}{2}\sqrt{\frac{2}{N-1}} & \text{otherwise} \end{cases}$$

Fig. 1. Function corresponding to orthonormalization. Source: (scipy library documentation, 2020).

Since the previously mentioned method serves only to transform one-dimensional arrays, the implementation of "dct" and "idct" was performed twice per method (the method was called within the method), since the images are represented as two-dimensional arrays of pixels.

5.4   Stage 4: Data Integration

In this stage we used the Python scripts developed for the preprocessing and transformation of the images so that their output would be stored in a single folder in which all the preprocessed and normalized images from different sources would be stored. With this, the objective of keeping a copy of the data in its original source (each of the acquired datasets) and a preprocessed copy stored in a unified folder was achieved.

5.5   Stage 5: Implementation

In order to carry out this implementation we delved into the concepts covered by SVM algorithms and discovered that: In order to be able to compute the real height of a 2D object, the height of another object present in the image needs to be known, as well as the parallel lines and the depth of the horizon. (For a graphical reference, check Fig. 2).

Once these parameters are established, the user proceeds to draw line intersections and with this, a projection of the object of known height is obtained in the location of the object with unknown height.

Knowing all this, it was determined that, after uploading an image on the web page, the user would enter a "calibration" phase, where he would determine (in a graphical way) the parameters previously exposed so that later the calculation and projection of measurements would be performed (Fig. 3).

Fig. 2. Example of Single View Metrology application. Source: (Own elaboration)

Fig. 3. Example of the calibration phase of the tool. Source: (Own elaboration)

In the so-called "calibration phase", the user will be in charge of drawing lines on the image to define: parallel lines, horizon, known object (with its respective measurement) and unknown object, which will allow a correct calculation of measurements. It should be noted that, given the origin of the images captured with camera traps (static images), this calibration should only be performed once per scenario, since the tool allows storing the defined parameters of a previous image to be used in another one with the same background.

After having set all the necessary parameters, the user can continue to the "measurement phase", where all the previously drawn lines will be eliminated to give way to the "measurement lines", which, when drawn on the object to be measured, in addition to the line, the program will write the length of the line in centimeters. Finally, the program saves the image with the respective measurements, thus completing the process.

6   Results

After testing different types of images in different scenarios, the following results were obtained:

Regarding the measurement process an average response time of 0.49 s was obtained, time calculated from the moment the "calculate" button is clicked until the height result is displayed, it should be emphasized that this average does not include the time it takes the user to draw the lines on the screen in the "calibration" phase, something that was also calculated, obtaining an average of 32.95 s in a normal user. As for the error rate, a ground truth comparison of the generated measurements and the real ones of the analyzed objects was made, as follows: 2 of the tests performed (See Table 1).

Table 1. Comparison ground truth of two study objects (measured in centimeters). Source: (Own elaboration)

		Reality	Prediction
Dog	Rear legs	57	56.55
	Front legs	52	51.45
	Head to tail	71	70.7
Human	Height	178	178.95
	Shoulders	45	44.21
	Waist	39	39.83
	Ground at hand	72	72.34

In the table shown, it can be observed that the measurements have an average error rate of 0.55 cm, which also depends on the user's precision when placing the points on the image. It is worth mentioning that from this average, the tests performed in closed places or at short distances were omitted since, according to the purpose of this project (measuring animals in open areas), they were not relevant.

Regarding the percentage of success of the classification model based on YOLOv4, it was decided to use a confusion matrix to determine the F1 value of the model from the classification of 60 images divided among the 3 classes analyzed, giving us the following results (see Table 2).

Table 2. 3-class confusion matrix. Source: (Own elaboration)

		Reality		
	Classes	Human	Dog	Cat
Prediction	Human	21	0	1
	Dog	0	19	0
	Cat	0	3	21

After constructing the matrix, we proceeded to determine the percentages of accuracy, completeness and F1 for each class using the respective formulas (Table 3).

Table 3. Percentages of accuracy, completeness and F1. Source: (Own elaboration)

	Precision	Completeness	F1
Human	95,45%	100%	97,67%
Dog	100%	86,36%	92,68%
Cat	87,50%	95,45%	91,30%

With all this information analyzed, we finally determined the accuracy percentage of the trained model, giving us a total of 93.85% accuracy calculated from the sum of the true positives with the true negatives divided by the total number of objects analyzed.

7   Conclusions

This study shows that it is indeed possible to develop a web tool that allows a user to accurately classify and measure free-ranging animals photographed with camera traps. It is concluded that the previously proposed research gap was fully covered, since a measurement methodology capable of classifying and determining animal lengths by applying Single View Metrology algorithms and the YOLO model was implemented without the need to resort to methods that significantly modify the environment of the object of study.

The present research succeeds in proposing a new approach that seeks to contribute to the trend of not manipulating species in their natural habitat, since, by means of the proposed methodology, the researcher maintains minimal contact with the environment in which the objects of study develop. It is also concluded that the Single View Metrology algorithms work more efficiently in open spaces where there is a wider range of vision, and the horizon can be determined in a better way. It is recommended that future research should automate the drawing of parallel lines and the horizon, as well as the assignment of the reference points of the known object, so that the user is abstracted from these steps and concentrates only on the drawing of measurement lines, thus improving the user experience.

References

Baltsavias, E.P.: A comparison between photogrammetry and laser scanning (1999). www.els evier.com

Barrickman, N.L., Schreier, A.L., Glander, K.E.: Testing parallel laser image scaling for remotely measuring body dimensions on mantled howling monkeys (Alouatta palliata). Am. J. Primatol. (2015)

Berger, J.: Estimation of body-size traits by photogrammetry in large mammals to inform conservation. Conserv. Biol. (2012)

Bergeron, P.: Parallel Lasers for Remote Measurements of Morphological Traits (2007)

Best, P.B., Ruther, H.: Aerial photogrammetry of southern right whales, Eubalaena Australis. Mammal Research institute (1992)

Brager, S., Chong, A.: An application of close-range photogrammetry in dolphin studies. Photogram. Rec. (1999)

Bräger, S., Chong, A., Dawson, S., Slooten, E., Würsig, B.: A combined stereo-photogrammetry and underwater-video system to study group composition of dolphins. Helgol. Mar. Res. 53(2), 122–128 (1999). https://doi.org/10.1007/s101520050015

Crimsini, A., Reid, I., Zisserman, A.: Single View Metrology. Obtenido de Microsoft (2000). https://www.microsoft.com/en-us/research/wp-content/uploads/2000/11/Criminisi_ijcv2001. pdf

Cui, S., Chen, D., Sun, J., Chu, H., Li, C., Jiang, Z.: A simple use of camera traps for photogrammetric estimation of wild animal traits. J. Zool. (2020)

Durban, W.: Laser-metrics of free-ranging killer whales. Mar. Mammal Sci. (2006)

Pelletier, F., Hogg, J.T., Festa-Bianchet, M.: Effect of chemical inmovilization on social status of bighorn rams (2003). www.sciencedirect.com

Fernandes, A., Dórea, J., Fitzgerald, R., Herring, W., Rosa, G.: A novel automated system to acquire biometric and morphological measurements and predict body weight of pigs via 3D computer vision. Oxford J. Anim. Sci. (2018). https://academic.oup.com/jas/article-abstract/97/1/496/5146045

Hernández, R., Fernández, C., Baptista, P.: Metodología de la investigación. México D.F: Interamericana Editores (2010)

Horn, G.V., et al.: Building a bird recognition app and large scale dataset with citizen scientists: the fine print in fine-grained dataset collection (2015). https://ieeexplore.ieee.org/document/7298658

Mahendiran, M., Parthiban, M., Azeez, P.A.: In situ measurements of animal morphological features: a non-invasive. Obtenido de British ecological society (2017)

McDowall, P., Lynch, H.J.: Ultra-fine scale spatially-integrated mapping of habitat and occupancy using structure-from-motion. J. Plos (2017). https://journals.plos.org/plosone/article?id=10.1371/journal.pone.0166773

Tarugara, A., Clegg, B.W., Gandiwa, E., Muposhi, V.K., Wenham, C.M.: Measuring body dimensions of leopards (Panthera Pardus) from camera trap photographs. PeerJ (2019)

Tazdemir, S., Urkmez, A., Inal, S.: Determination of body measurements on the Holstein cows using digital image analysis and estimation of live weight with regression analysis (2011). www.elsevier.com

Willisch, C.S., Marreros, N., Neuhaus, P.: Long-distance photogrammetric trait estimation in free-ranging animals: a new approach (2013). www.elsevier.com

Rovero, F., Zimmermann, F., Berzi, D., Meek, P.: "Which camera trap type and how many do I need?" A review of camera features and study designs for a range of wildlife research applications. Obtenido de Hystrix, Italian J. Mammal. (2013). http://www.italian-journal-of-mammalogy.it/-Which-camera-trap-type-and-how-many-do-I-need-A-review-of-camera-features-and-study,77224,0,2.html

Côté, S.D., Festa-Bianchet, M., Fournier, F.: Life-historye ffectso f chemicalim mobilizatio and radiocollarso n mountaing oats. Obtenido de Wiley (1998). http://www.jstor.org/stable/3802351

Pezzuoloa, A., Guarinob, M., Sartoria, L., González, L.A., Marinello, F.: On-barn pig weight estimation based on body measurements by a Kinect v1 depth camera (2018). www.elsevier.com

Peixoto, H.M., Teles, R.S., Luiz, J.V.: Mice tracking using the YOLO algorithm (2019). https://www.researchgate.net/publication/334847999_Mice_tracking_using_the_YOLO_algorithm

Saxena, P.: TensorFlow-YOLOv4-TFLite (2020). https://github.com/pranjalAI/tensorflow-yolov4-tflite

Huang, R., Pedoeem, J., Chen, C.: YOLO-LITE: a real-time object detection algorithm optimized for non-GPU computers (2019). https://ieeexplore.ieee.org/abstract/document/8621865

Ravì, D., et al.: Deep learning for health informatics (2017). https://ieeexplore.ieee.org/abstract/document/7801947

Redmon, J., Divvala, S., Girshick, R., Farhadi, A.: You only look once (2016). https://arxiv.org/abs/1506.02640

Rovero, F., Tobler, M., Sanderson, J.: Camera trapping for inventorying terrestrial vertebrates (2009). https://www.researchgate.net/publication/229057405_Camera_trapping_for_inventorying_terrestrial_vertebrates

Zhu, R., et al.: Single view metrology in the wild (2020). https://arxiv.org/abs/2007.09529

Rose Plant Disease Detection Using Image Processing and Machine Learning

Anushka Sharma[1], Ghanshyam Prasad Dubey[1]([✉]), Ashish Singh[1], Ananya Likhar[1], Shailendra Mourya[1], Anupam Sharma[1], and Rajit Nair[2]

[1] Department of CSE, Amity School of Engineering and Technology, Amity University, Gwalior, Madhya Pradesh, India
ghanshyam_dubey2@yahoo.com, Anupam32@icloud.com
[2] VIT Bhopal University, Bhopal, India

Abstract. The first step in preventing reductions in agricultural product output and quantity is to identify plant diseases. The research on plant diseases refers to examinations of patterns on the plant that may be observed with the naked eye. A vital component of sustainable agriculture is the observation of plant health and the identification of disease. The manual monitoring of plant diseases is highly challenging. It necessitates a huge amount of work, knowledge of plant diseases, and lengthy processing times. So, by taking photos of the leaves and comparing them to data sets, image processing is utilized to find plant illnesses. It is incredibly challenging to physically screen plant sicknesses. It requires a colossal measure of work, information on plant illnesses, and extended handling times. In this research, the diagnosis of rose plant diseases is critical for preventing yield and quantity losses in agricultural products. Plant disease identification is crucial for long-lasting agriculture. It requires a significant amount of work, a specialist understanding of plant diseases, and more than enough processing time. As a result, digital image processing is utilized to detect rose plant illnesses. Image acquisition, image pre-processing, picture segmentation, feature extraction, and classification are phases of disease detection. This research will look into how to save the rose plant from various diseases.

Keywords: Plant illness · prevention and treatment · Image acquisition · Pre-processing · Feature extraction · Segmentation · classification · DCT · KNN · RBF · BPN · PNN · K-Means · SVM

1 Introduction

Around 70% of the populace in India is reliant upon farming. For forestalling crop misfortunes, it is critical to recognize plant infections [1]. The technique for finding disease used in plants (i.e., the ID of disease side effects) is completely found in the use of logical procedures. Infection discovery is simplified with the guide of farming researchers and given explicit illness side effects. The utilization of AI for sickness discovery and acknowledgment in plants is especially fruitful in distinguishing indications of recognizing contaminations as soon as conceivable [2, 3]. Plant infection discovery should

M. Botto-Tobar et al. (Eds.): ICAT 2023, CCIS 2050, pp. 69–85, 2024.
https://doi.org/10.1007/978-3-031-58953-9_6

be possible by utilizing picture handling and AI calculations. In this paper, they have portrayed a few strategies for distinguishing plant sicknesses utilizing pictures of the leaves. The subset of man-made brainpower called AI performs undertakings naturally or gives directions on the most proficient method to do them.

The plant species' technical and commercial significance lies in the classification and recognition of illnesses that affect rose plants. The rose is a popular ornamental plant for home gardening and commercial and residential planting. Roses are the **king of flowers.** Research on rose plants is focused on improving production quantity and quality at lower costs, with less waste, and with higher profits. Disease management is difficult. Numerous illnesses, including viruses, bacteria, and parasites, are seen on rose plant leaves [4]. Numerous diseases may be detected on rose leaves, and thanks to the internet and today's wired society, knowledge is readily available. Additionally, through picture processing on mobile devices, diseases will be detected. Pictures of some sick leaves are shown in Fig. 1.

(a)   (b)

Fig. 1. (a) Black spot on Rose plant leaves [5], (b) Powdery mildew in rose leaves [6]

In Fig. 1(a) Black spots of rose leaves are shown. Black spots can be easily identified by seeing the black or brownies dots on rose leaves. The rose black spot condition is caused by the fungus Diplocarpon rosea. However, badly afflicted plants will lack the circular patterning because they merge to form a huge, dark mass. The disease is commonly treated by removing the damaged leaves and spraying them with antifungal treatments [5].

In Fig. 1(b) Powdery mildew of rose leaves is shown. Powdery mildew can be identified by seeing the white powder on rose leaves. The fungus Sphaerotheca pannosa var. Rosea is responsible for the rose disease known as rose powdery mildew. It may also spread to the stems and young rose buds. It appears as a white powder on the surface of the rose leaves [6].

Black Spot
Diplocarpon rose, the fungus that generates black patches. The most common diseases affecting roses globally. Although sickness is unlikely to kill the plant, the loss of leaves over time may weaken it and make it more prone to other pressures, such as winter damage. These specks are frequently encircled by yellow halos. Infections cause yellowing of leaflets or the entire leaf. Yellowed leaves fall early, particularly on vulnerable cultivars [7].

Fig. 2. Black spot in rose plants [8].

Black spots in rose leaves are shown in Fig. 2. Black spots can be easily identified by seeing the black or brownies dots on rose leaves.

Powdery Mildew
Fine mold, brought about by Sphaerotheca pannosa var. Rosae is a typical rose infection that is particularly irksome for glasshouse roses. The white, fine development on leaves, shoots, and buds recognizes this sickness. Early signs of the illness incorporate chlorotic or ruddy spots or fixes on leaves, which later become white and fine [7].

Fig. 3. Rose leaves with powdery mildew [9].

In Fig. 3 Powdery mildew of rose leaves is shown. Powdery mildew can be identified by seeing the white powder on rose leaves.

Downy Mildew
Wool mold is an incredibly harmful rose infection delivered by the parasite-like life form Peronospora sparsa. Luckily, it happens just rarely in Connecticut. Cool, wet conditions favor illness improvement, which can happen in the scene and glasshouse roses. Side effects can show up on any of the plant's over-the-ground parts, including the stems, peduncles, leaves, etc. Leaf contaminations, then again, are the most continuous and are very direct to distinguish. Tainted leaves foster purple to red, rakish fixes or blotches on their upper surfaces. Yellowing, rot, and untimely leaf drop are much of the time related to these side effects [7].

Fig. 4. Rose leaves showing downy mildew [10].

In Fig. 4 Downy mildew of rose leaves are shown. Downy mildew can be identified by seeing the purple to red, angular patches or blotches on the upper surfaces of rose leaves.

Botrytis Blight

Botrytis curse is a typical rose sickness brought about by the organism Botrytis cinerea. This growth is generally conveyed and has a different scope of hosts. All elevated pieces of the plant, including blossoms, buds, and sticks and creating tips, show side effects. Chilly, desolate, and clammy weather conditions incline toward the advancement of the sickness. The improvement of dark brown, fluffy development on the surfaces of the impacted plant parts is the most unmistakable indication of Botrytis. Botrytis can contaminate the stumps of cuttings as well as any injuries brought about by cutting [7].

Fig. 5. Botrytis Blight of rose [11].

In Fig. 5 Botrytis blight of rose leaves is shown. Botrytis blight can be identified by seeing the grey-brown, fuzzy growth on the surfaces of rose leaves.

Rust

Many Phragmidium species cause rose rust, a fungal disease. Symptoms can appear on the plant's leaves and any other green sections. Rust symptoms might emerge on the entire plant in favorable conditions. In the early spring, little orange pustules appear on both leaf surfaces. On the abaxial (bottom) surface of the leaf, they gradually grow and become more prominent. On the adaxial (upper) surface of the leaf, Chlorate or mottled patches might form. Severe infections might cause premature defoliation [7].

Fig. 6. Rust on rose leaves [12].

In Fig. 6 Rust of rose leaves is shown. Rust can be identified by seeing the little orange pustules on rose leaves.

Crown Gall
The bacterium Agrobacterium tumefaciens causes crown gall. Common symptoms of this illness are swellings on the main stem at or slightly below the soil line. Galls can also occur on the plant's roots and, less frequently, on its aerial parts. Crown gall shapes are uneven, lack internal structure, and vary in size. Young galls are delicate and off-white or light green. Crown galls may be brown or black with age. Roses infected with crown gall exhibit a wide range of reactions and become hard and woody. Some plants appear stunted, while others have weak foliage and produce few or poor-quality blooms [7].

Fig. 7. Crown gall is showing on stem [13].

In Fig. 7 Crown Gall of rose leaves are shown. Crown gall can be identified by seeing the symptoms of galls or swellings on the main stem of rose leaves.

Mosaic
Rose mosaic is caused by a virus complex that includes the Prunus Necrotic Ring Spot Virus (PNRSV) and the Apple Mosaic Virus (AMV). The symptoms vary greatly depending on the climate conditions, species, cultivar, and the exact viruses infecting the plant. Typical symptoms include spiral or wave-like chlorate lines; however, symptoms can

also include ring spots and mottled patterns. Infection may also be indicated by yellow watermarks, vein clearing, or dull yellow patches. Some infected plants will appear stunted and feeble, while others will exhibit no symptoms at all [7].

Fig. 8. Mosaic on rose leaves [14].

In Fig. 8 Mosaic of rose leaves is shown. Mosaics can be identified by seeing the wavy or zigzag chlorate lines, ring spots mottled patterns, and yellow water-marks, vein clearing, or dull yellow patches on rose leaves (Table 1).

Table 1. Summary of diseases on rose leaves

S. No	Name of the disease	Causing Fungi	Fungicide Used
1	Black spot	Diplocarpon rosea	Chlorothalonil, copper sulfate, and myclobutanil [15]
2	Powdery Mildew	Sphaerotheca pannosa	Propiconazole
3	Downy mildew	Peronospora sparsa	Chlorothalonil and mancozeb
4	Botrytis blight	Botrytis cinerea	Fungicides containing thiophanate methyl, and chlorothalonil
5	Rust	Phragmidium species	Fungicides that contain the portions of myclobutanil, mancozeb or propiconazole
6	Crown gall	Agrobacterium tumefaciens	Disinfecting the plants in a solution of 0.5% sodium hypochlorite (NaClO) for several minutes

(continued)

Table 1. (*continued*)

S. No	Name of the disease	Causing Fungi	Fungicide Used
7	Mosaic	Prunus Necrotic	No particular fungi were used. Ringspot Virus (PNRSV) and the Apple Mosaic Virus (AMV)

2 Literature Review

S. Khirade et al. [1] utilized advanced picture handling procedures and back engendering brain organization (BPNN) to tackle the issue of plant illness distinguishing proof in 2015. The creators created different procedures for distinguishing plants disease utilizing photos of leaves. They utilized Otsu's thresholding, limit recognition, and spot discovery calculations to section the impacted area of the leaf. Following that, they removed boundaries like tone, surface, morphology, edges, etc. for plant infection order. BPNN is utilized for order, that is to say, to identify plant sickness. Shiroop Madiwalar and Medha Wyawahare explored different picture-handling calculations for plant sickness ID [16]. The creators took a gander at the variety and textural qualities of leaves to distinguish sickness. They tried their calculations on a dataset of 110 RGB photographs. The mean and standard deviation of the RGB and YCbCr channels, the dim level co-event network (GLCM) highlights and the mean and standard deviation of the picture convolved with the Gabor channel were recovered for characterization. For characterization, a help vector machine classifier was utilized. The creators reasoned that GCLM qualities can perceive typical leaves. Variety highlights and Gabor channel highlights, then again, are believed to be awesome for distinguishing anthracnose-contaminated leaves and leaf spots, separately. They achieved the most noteworthy precision of 83.34% while utilizing the extricated highlights in general.

Peyman Moghadam et al. demonstrated hyperphantom imaging's application in the undertaking of recognizing plant illnesses [17]. This study utilized the apparent and close infrared (VNIR) and short-wave infrared (SWIR) range. The creators utilized k-implies. For leaf division, a ghostly bunching method is utilized. They currently need to eliminate the lattice from hyper-otherworldly pictures, and an exceptional matrix evacuation calculation was proposed. The creators achieved an exactness of 83% involving vegetation records in the VNIR phantom reach. With full range, the reach is 93% and the precision is 93%. Despite the way that the suggested methodology was fruitful more noteworthy exactness, a hyper ghostly camera with 324 ghastly groups is required, so the arrangement turns out to be restrictively costly.

Garima Shrestha et al. used a convolutional neural network [18]. The authors categorized 12 plant diseases with an accuracy of 88.80%. Trial and error were done utilizing a dataset of 3000 high-goal RGB photos. This builds the organization's figuring cost. The model's F1 score is additionally 0.12, which is very low because of the expanded recurrence of wrong regrettable forecasts (Table 2).

Table 2. Literature Summary

Author	Title	Methods	Key points
Anand H. Kulkarni [19]	Detection of healthy regions of plant leaves using image processing and genetic algorithm	Artificial Neural Network (ANN) and Gabor filter are used	Accuracy of 91%
Rajneet Kaur, Manjeet Kaur [20]	A Brief Review on Plant Disease Detection using in Image Processing	Methods SVM and KNN are used	Support Vector Machine is very complex and the KNN classifier obtain the highest result as compared to SVM
Nitin Choubey, Prashant Udawant [21]	Study of Rose plant diseases and its identification with modern automation techniques	With the help of automatic disease identification	The latest research on the rose plant and helpful for disease identification
S. Arivazha Gan, R. Newlin Shebiah [22]	Detection of healthy regions of plant leaves and classification of plant leaf diseases using texture features	The co-occurrence matrix provides the basis for co-occurrence properties such as contrast energy, local homogeneity, shadow, and prominence	In this work, the author explains how texture analysis may be used to identify and categorize plant leaf diseases
Priyanka G. Shinde, Borate S. P. [23]	Plant Disease Detection using Raspberry PI by K-means Clustering Algorithm	For the image analysis k-means clustering algorithm is used	Through the GSM module, disease detection has been shown in the user's section
Aditya Parikh, Mehul S. Raval [24]	Disease Detection and Severity Estimation in cotton plant from Unconstrained Images	The proposed work utilizes two flowed classifiers and utilizing neighborhood factual elements infection is identified	The algorithm can be used for generalized disease detection if a proper set of training images is available

(*continued*)

Table 2. (*continued*)

Author	Title	Methods	Key points
M. Ravindra Naik, Chandra Mohan [25]	Plant Leaf and Disease Detection by Using HSV Features and SVM Classifier	In the classification process for recognition rate ANN, Bayes classifier, fuzzy logic, and hybrid algorithm can also be used	In this paper image segmentation technique is used for automatic detection as well as classification
Aniket Gharat, Krupa Bhatt, Bhavesh Kanase [26]	Leaf Disease Detection using Image Processing	The process of identifying an illness involves accepting the user's picture, using CNN, Hu's moment algorithm, and feature extraction	The obtained result shows a significant implementation with 79% accuracy
Hemanta Kalita, Shikhar Kr. Sarma, Ridip Choudhary [27]	Expert System for Diagnosis of Diseases of plants: Prototype Design and Implementation	Using information acquisition, knowledge base inference engines, and expert systems to provides accurate illness diagnosis	Authors can obtain findings by classifying and summarizing the expert system technique
S Khirade [1]	"Plant Disease Detection Using Image Processing,"	Digital image processing techniques and back propagation neural network (BPNN)	They extracted parameters such as color, texture, morphology, edges, and so on for plant disease categorization

(*continued*)

Table 2. (*continued*)

Author	Title	Methods	Key points
Shiroop Madiwala r, Medha Wyawaha re [16]	"Plant disease identification: A comparative study,"	They tested their algorithms on a dataset of 110 RGB photos. The mean and standard deviation of the RGB and YCbCr channels, the grey level co-occurrence matrix (GLCM) features, and the mean and standard deviation of the image convolved with the Gabor filter were retrieved for classification	GCLM qualities can perceive ordinary leaves. Variety highlights and Gabor channel highlights, then again, are believed to be awesome for distinguishing anthracnose-contaminated leaves and leaf spots, individually. They accomplished the most note-worthy exactness of 83.34% while utilizing the separated highlights in general
Peyman Moghadam et al. [17]	"Plant Disease Detection Using Hyperspectral Imaging"	Hyper otherworldly imaging's application and close infrared (VNIR) and short-wave infrared (SWIR) ranges. The creators utilized k-implies. For leaf division, a ghostly bunching method is utilized	The creators achieved an exactness of 83% involving vegetation records in the VNIR phantom reach. With full range, the reach is 93% and the precision is 93%
Garima Shrestha et al. [18]	"Plant Disease Detection Using CNN,"	Convolutional neural network	The creators ordered 12 plant sicknesses with a precision of 88.80%. Trial and error was done utilizing a dataset of 3000 high-goal RGB photos. The model's F1 score is additionally 0.12, which is very low because of the expanded recurrence of wrong regrettable forecasts

The table represents different Techniques of image processing that are used in different papers.

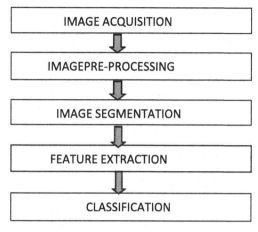

Fig. 9. Steps for Plant Disease Detection.

3 Steps to Detect Plant Disease

Image Acquisition: A digital camera is used to collect images of various leaves. Resized input image. The most crucial and initial step in automatically identifying diseases is this one. Hardware like a scanner or camera is used in this step. Hardware should be of very high quality to aid in future operations running smoothly [28] (Fig. 9).

Image Pre-processing: The input data for the clustering and classification process should be very clear. Clustering becomes challenging if the collected images are blurry. The technique of improving an input image by enhancing its attributes is known as image preprocessing. It includes color space conversion and image enhancement, which is the process of improving the quality of an image. With DCT, this is accomplished by scaling the transform coefficient [28].

Image Segmentation: There are numerous algorithms available for image segmentation. Almost all K-mean clustering techniques are commonly utilized for image segmentation. It aids in the classification of pixels depending on the parameters and features set. It simplifies picture representation by grouping images into distinct clusters. If a leaf carries multiple diseases, various clusters will appear [28].

Feature Extraction: The most common way of interpreting unrefined data into numerical components that may be taken care of while keeping the information in the first enlightening collection is alluded to as component extraction. It creates improved results than simply applying AI to crude information [28].

Classification: The exact matching of the processed picture disease must be compared based on the current dataset of rose plant diseases. It aids in the accurate diagnosis of illness. Various classification techniques are employed for this. K-nearest neighbor (KNN), Radial Basis Function (RBF), Probabilistic Neural Networks (PNN), Back Propagation Network (BPN), and Support Vector Machine (SVM) are the most often used classification approaches [28].

4 Techniques on Image Processing

DCT (Discrete Cosine Transform): The discrete cosine transform is utilized in lossy image compression due to its extremely strong energy compaction, which means that most of the information is stored in the signal's very low-frequency component while the remaining frequencies have very little information that can be stored using a very small number of bits (typically only 2 or 3 bits) [28]. To execute a discrete cosine transform (DCT) on an image, first get the image file information (pixel value expressed as an integer with a range of 0 to 255) and divide it into blocks of an 8×8 matrix. This technique is used in image pre-processing [29].

K-Mean Clustering Technique: K-means clustering is an unsupervised algorithm. K-means clustering is used to separate the interest area from the background. However, some stretching treatment is first given to the image to enhance its quality before the K-means algorithm is used [30]. This technique is used in image segmentation.

RBF (Radial Basis Function): Real-valued radial basis functions (RBFs) are supervised machine learning (supervised ML)-based non-linear classifiers. The distance between the input and a specific fixed point determines its value [31]. This technique is used in classification.

PNN (Probabilistic Neural Network): A feedforward neural network, or probabilistic neural network, is frequently employed in classification and pattern recognition issues. The PNN approach employs a Parzen window and a non-parametric function to approximate the parent probability distribution function of each class [32]. This technique is used in classification.

BPN (Back Propagation Network): An algorithm called backpropagation transfers faults from output nodes to input nodes. As a result, it is just known as the backward propagation of faults. It makes use of the numerous neural network applications in data mining, such as character recognition and signature verification, etc. [33]. This technique is used in classification.

SVM (Support Vector Machine): The approach employs numerous color representations at the moment of execution. An MLP neural network, which incorporates a color library created beforehand with suggestions of an unsupervised self-organizing map (SOM), is used to separate leaves from the background [34]. The way the colors on the leaves are then grouped resembles an uncontrolled, illogical self-organizing map. The number of clusters that should be used in each situation is decided using a genetic algorithmic program. Then, a Support Vector Machine (SVM) distinguishes between unhealthy and morbid regions [35]. This technique is used in classification.

Fuzzy Classifier: The approach attempts to detect four distinct organic process deficits in plants. The photos are segmented by the color similarities, but the authors do not explain how this was accomplished. If the segment portions, texture variation, and color features are extracted and presented to a fuzzy classifier, it will output the inadequacies themselves, revealing the amounts of fertilizers that should be used to repair those deficiencies [36].

Color Analysis: Victimization tests were carried out on various plants. Before color analysis, the photos are resized to the HSI and L* a * b * color regions. The color distinction between diseased and healthy leaves, as well as the leaves beneath, demonstrates the presence or distribution of deficiencies. The variances are quantified using geometer distances obtained in each color area [1, 37].

Feature-Based Rules: Three distinct forms of plant diseases must be identified and labeled. The healthy plant leaf segmentation and morbid regions are conducted in many various techniques, and on that basis, thresholding is implemented. The authors evaluated two types of thresholds, the first being native entropy, and the second being Otsu's technique, with the latter yielding good results. Following that, several color and form alternatives are retrieved. The premise for applying these alternatives is a set of rules that certify the ailment most closely matches the features of the specified place [38].

KNN (K-Nearest Neighbor): KNNs are a kind of supervised machine learning algorithm that can resolve both classification and regression issues. Its algorithm is straightforward and simple to apply, yet it requires labeled input for model training [39, 40]. K-Nearest Neighbour is one of the simple classifiers used in machine learning. Where category identification is accomplished by identifying the examples of a question that are closest to the category and using this information to determine the category of the query. The KNN classification to which the supplied purpose is assigned is based on the calculation of the minimal distance between the given purpose and various places. For the leaf of plant categorization, the distance between the look at coaching samples and samples is calculated [41]. When processing the method, it identifies comparable measures and, as a result, the category for sample collecting and analysis. This technique is used in classification.

5 Results and Discussion

To ensure effective and precise findings, the rose plant disease detection procedure is carried out progressively. The initial step i.e. image acquisition uses a high-quality digital camera, focusing on the need for precision technology. Subsequently, the image preprocessing process improves the quality of data by resolving issues caused by unclear photos using techniques such as color space conversion and DCT-based image augmentation. Image segmentation uses K-mean clustering to identify pixels and simplify image representation, particularly for leaves and roses with various illnesses. Feature extraction turns raw data into numerical components, which improves the result. The final classification stage compares the generated picture to a dataset of known rose plant illnesses, including techniques such as KNN, RBF, PNN, BPN, and SVM to ensure correct diagnosis. This complete process emphasizes the value of each stage in achieving a robust automated plant disease detection system (Table 3).

Table 3. Accuracy comparison

Author	Methods	Accuracy
Anand. H. Kulkarni [19]	Artificial Neural Network (ANN) and Gabor filter	91%
Priyanka G. Shinde, Borate S. P. [23]	K-means clustering algorithm and SVM classifier	86.54% and 95.71%
M. Ravindra Naik, Chandra Mohan [25]	SVM and hybrid algorithm(NN)	SVM:86.77% and NN: 95.74
Aniket Gharat, Krupa Bhatt, Bhavesh Kanase [26]	the user's picture, using CNN, Hu's moment algorithm, and feature extraction	79%
S. Khirade [1]	Digital image processing techniques and back propagation neural network (BPNN)	88.80%
Shiroop Madiwalar, Medha Wyawahare [16]	The mean and standard deviation of the RGB and YCbCr channels, the grey level co-occurrence matrix (GLCM) features, and the mean and standard deviation of the image convolved with the Gabor filter were retrieved for classification	83%
Peyman Moghadameal [17]	Hyper otherworldly imaging's application and close infrared (VNIR) and short-wave infrared (SWIR) ranges	The creators achieved an exactness of 83% involving vegetation records in the VNIR phantom reach. With full range, the reach is 93% and the precision is 93%
Garima Shrestha et al. [18]	Convolutional neural network	The creators ordered 12 plant sicknesses with a precision of 88.80%

Several authors have used several approaches for detecting plant diseases, each with different accuracies. Anand H. Kulkarni used Artificial Neural Network (ANN) and Gabor filter methods, getting a 91% accuracy. Priyanka G. Shinde and Borate S. P. used the k-means clustering technique and the SVM classifier, which produced accuracies of 86.54% and 95.71% respectively. M. Ravindra Naik and Chandra Mohan used SVM and a hybrid algorithm (NN), with accuracies of 86.77% and 95.74%, respectively. Aniket Gharat, Krupa Bhatt, and Bhavesh Kanase used CNN, Hu's moment algorithm, and feature extraction to achieve a detection accuracy of 79%. S. Khirade used digital image processing techniques and a back propagation neural network (BPNN) with an accuracy of 88.80%. Shiroop Madiwalar and Medha Wyawahare used a mixture of mean and standard deviation characteristics, together with the Gabor filter, to achieve an accuracy of 83%. Peyman Moghadam et al. utilized hyperspectral imaging in the VNIR and SWIR ranges, achieving accuracies of 83% and 93% in the VNIR and full spectrum, respectively. At last, Garima Shrestha et al. utilized a convolutional neural network and achieved an accuracy of 88.80% in classifying 12 plant diseases. These approaches underscore the effectiveness of different methodologies in achieving accurate plant disease detection.

6 Conclusion

A review of various rose plant diseases is provided here. In the different symptoms of a rose plant, illnesses are reviewed critically, as well as their preventative and cure strategies. It has been determined that early illness is beneficial to the growth of the rose plant. Plant identification is critical. Visual inspection is less important. However, accuracy and dependability are significantly superior in image processing used in automated approaches. It is critical to detect this at an early stage. Disease signs can be seen in various areas of a plant; nevertheless, plant leaves are the most usually observed part of the plant for detecting an infection. As a result, we attempted to automate the process of identifying plant diseases. The sooner the disease is diagnosed; the sooner measures can be implemented. Several works made extensive use of computer technologies and made significant contributions to this field. It offers a study on regularly investigated infections and research scenarios in various stages of a disease detection system. This research discusses how to utilize machine learning and image processing to determine whether or not leaves are diseased. This framework can be used as a starting point with a leaf image. To begin, the leaf photographs are cleaned up to remove any noise. The mean filter is used to get rid of noise. The act of dividing a single image into pieces or segments is known as segmentation. It can assist in determining the scope of the problem. The image is divided into pieces using the K-means method. To find features, principal component analysis is employed. Following that, photos are categorized based on their content using algorithms such as RBF-SVM, BPN, KNN, random forest, and so on.

References

1. Khirade, S.D., Patil, A.B.: Plant disease detection using image processing. In: 2015 International Conference on Computing Communication Control and Automation, pp. 768–771 (2015). https://doi.org/10.1109/ICCUBEA.2015.153
2. Hillnhuetter, C., Mahlein, A.-K.: Early detection and localization of sugar beet diseases: new approaches. Gesunde Pfianzen **60**(4), 143–149 (2008)
3. Rumpf, T., Mahlein, A.K., Steiner, U., Oerke, E.C., Dehne, H.W., Plümer, L.: Early detection and classification of plant diseases with support vector machines based on hyperspectral reflectance. Comput. Electron. Agric. **74**(1), 91–99 (2010). https://doi.org/10.1016/j.compag.2010.06.009. ISSN 0168-1699
4. Sawarkar, V., Kawathekar, S.: A review: rose plant disease detection using image processing. IOSR J. Comput. Eng. (IOSR-JCE) e-ISSN, 2278–0661 (2018)

5. Rose disease stocks. https://www.istockphoto.com/photos/rose-diseases. Accessed 15 Aug 2023
6. Powdery mildew. https://www.greenlife.co.ke/powdery-mildew-of-roses/. Accessed 15 Aug 2023
7. Common disease of Rose. https://portal.ct.gov/CAES/Fact-Sheets/Plant-Pathology/Common-Diseases-of-Rose. Accessed 16 Aug 2023
8. https://www.missouribotanicalgarden.org/gardens-gardening/your-garden/help-for-the-home-gardener/advice-tips-resources/pests-and-problems/diseases/fungal-spots/black-spot. Accessed 16 Aug 2023
9. https://pnwhandbooks.org/plantdisease/host-disease/rose-rosa-spp-hybrids-powdery-mildew. Accessed 16 Aug 2023
10. https://extension.umd.edu/resource/downy-mildew-flowers. Accessed 16 Aug 2023
11. https://www.sciencephoto.com/media/992559/view/botrytis-blight-on-rose. Accessed 16 Aug 2023
12. https://gardenerspath.com/plants/flowers/rose-rust/. Accessed 16 Aug 2023
13. https://extension.umd.edu/resource/bacterial-crown-gall-flowers. Accessed 17 Aug 2023
14. https://edis.ifas.ufl.edu/publication/PP338. Accessed 17 Aug 2023
15. Sinha, R.: Study on rose diseases: identification, detection, and cure (2017)
16. Madiwalar, S.C., Wyawahare, M.V.: Plant disease identification: a comparative study. In: 2017 International Conference on Data Management, Analytics and Innovation (ICDMAI), pp. 13–18 (2017). https://doi.org/10.1109/ICDMAI.2017.8073478
17. Moghadam, P., Ward, D., Goan, E., Jayawardena, S., Sikka, P., Hernandez, E.: Plant disease detection using hyperspectral imaging. In: 2017 International Conference on Digital Image Computing: Techniques and Applications (DICTA), pp. 1–8 (2017). https://doi.org/10.1109/DICTA.2017.8227476
18. Shrestha, G., Das, M., Dey, N.: Plant disease detection using CNN. In: 2020 IEEE Applied Signal Processing Conference (ASPCON), pp. 109–113 (2020). https://doi.org/10.1109/ASPCON49795.2020.9276722
19. Kulkarni, A.H., Patil, A.: Applying image processing technique to detect plant diseases. Int. J. Mod. Eng. Res. (IJMER) 2(5), 3661–3664 (2012). ISSN: 2249-6645
20. Kaur, R., Kaur, M.: A brief review on plant disease detection using in image processing. Int. J. Comput. Sci. Mob. Comput. 6(2), 101–106 (2017)
21. Choubey, N., Udawant, P.: Study of rose plant diseases and its identification with modern automation techniques (2017)
22. Arivazhagan, S., et al.: Detection of unhealthy region of plant leaves and classification of plant leaf diseases using texture features. Agric. Eng. Int. CIGR J. 15(1), 211–217 (2013)
23. Shinde, P.G., et al.: Plant disease detection using Raspberry Pi by K-means clustering algorithm. Int. J. Electr. Electron. Comput. Syst. 5(1), 92–95 (2017)
24. Parikh, A., Raval, M.S., Parmar, C., Chaudhary, S.: Disease detection and severity estimation in the cotton plant from unconstrained images. In: 2016 IEEE International Conference on Data Science and Advanced Analytics (DSAA), pp. 594–601. IEEE, October 2016
25. Naik, M.R., Sivappagari, C.M.R.: Plant leaf and disease detection by using HSV features and SVM classifier. Int. J. Eng. Sci. 3794(260), 372–379 (2016)
26. Gharat, A., et al.: Leaf disease detection using image processing. Imperial J. Interdisc. Res. 3 (2017)
27. Kalita, H., Sarma, S.K., Choudhury, R.D.: Expert system for diagnosis of diseases of rice plants: prototype design and implementation. In: 2016 International Conference on Automatic Control and Dynamic Optimization Techniques (ICACDOT). IEEE (2016)
28. Choubey, N., Udawant, P.: Study of rose plant diseases and its identification with modern automation techniques. Int. J. Current Res. 9(06), 53016–53021 (2017)

29. https://www.geeksforgeeks.org/discrete-cosine-transform-algorithm-program/. Accessed 16 Aug 2023
30. Khan, S.S., Ahmad, A.: Cluster centre initialization algorithm for K-means Cluster. Patt. Recogn. Lett., 1293–1302 (2004). Israil, S.: An overview of clustering methods. In: With Application to Bioinformatics
31. https://www.simplilearn.com/tutorials/machine-learning-tutorial/what-are-radial-basis-fun ctions-neuralnetworks#:~:text=Radial%20Basis%20Functions%20(RBF)%20are,and% 20a%20certain%20fixed%20point. Accessed 17 Aug 2023
32. https://en.wikipedia.org/wiki/Probabilistic_neural_network. Accessed 17 Aug 2023
33. https://www.geeksforgeeks.org/backpropagation-in-data-mining/. Accessed 17 Aug 2023
34. Savita, G., Parul, A.: Detection and classification of plant leaf diseases using image processing techniques: a review. Int. J. Recent Adv. Eng. Technol. 2, 2347–2812 (2014)
35. Arivazhagan, S., Newlin Sheiah, R., Ananthi, S.: Detection of the unhealthy region of plant leaves and classification of plant leaf diseases using texture features, vol. 15, pp. 211–217, March 2013
36. Phadikar, S., Sil, J.: Rice disease identification using pattern recognition techniques. In: Proceedings of 11th International Conference on Computer and Information Technology (ICCIT 2008), 25–27 December 2008, Khulna, Bangladesh, pp. 1–4244–2136–7 (2008)
37. Mitkal, P., Pawar, P., Nagane, M., Bhosale, P., Padwal, M., Nagane, P.: Leaf disease detection and prevention using image processing using Matlab. Int. J. Recent Trends Eng. Res. (IJRTER) 02(02) (2016). ISSN:2455-1457
38. Ghaiwat, S.N., Arora, P.: Detection and classification of plant leaf diseases using image processing techniques: a review. Int. J. Recent Adv. Eng. Technol. (IJRAET) 2(3), 2347–2812 (2014)
39. Liu, K., et al.: Coupling the K-nearest neighbor procedure with the Kalman filter for real-time updating of the hydraulic model in flood forecasting. Int. J. Sed. Res. 31(2), 149–158 (2016)
40. Liu, M., et al.: The applicability of LSTM-KNN model for real-time flood forecasting in different climate zones in China. Water 12(2), 440 (2020)
41. Kaur, R., Kang, S.S.: An enhancement in classifier support vector machine to Improve-Plant disease detection. In: IEEE 3rd International Conference on MOOCs, Innovation, and Technology in Education (MITE), pp. 135–140 (2015)

A Fine-Tuned Transfer Learning Approach for Parkinson's Disease Detection on New Hand PD Dataset

Sakalya Mitra⬤, Pranjal Mohan Pandey⬤, Vedant Pandey⬤, Trapti Sharma(✉)⬤, and Rajit Nair

VIT Bhopal University, Bhopal, Madhya Pradesh, India
{trapti.sharma,Rajit.nair}@vitbhopal.ac.in

Abstract. Parkinson's Disease (PD) is a neurological condition that affects large masses of individuals around the world, having a great impact on the quality of life and raising notable challenges to the existing healthcare systems. Detection of PD at an early stage in an individual is crucial for the on-time intervention, diagnosis and improved patient outcomes. In the current scenario, various Machine Learning (ML) techniques, specifically, transfer learning-based approaches have proved to show promising results in analysis of medical images for diagnosis of diseases. A lot of work has been done in this area of utilizing transfer learning-based models such as VGG-19, ResNet etc. for the early detection of PD. Although most of these approaches have proved to have high performance values up to 95% accuracy, but there seems to have a large scope to improve upon and achieve higher performance measures that minimizes the risk of error in PD detection. This study uses the New Hand PD Dataset to propose an improved transfer learning model using fine-tuning specifically intended for the diagnosis of Parkinson's disease. The proposed novel approach in this paper uses feature extraction from the images and feeding them to fine-tuned transfer learning model, ResNet-152 leading to an improved testing accuracy of 100% and loss of 0.0040 only. To illustrate the suggested model's detection capability, its performance is compared with current cutting-edge deep learning and transfer learning models.

Keywords: Parkinson's Disease · Deep Learning · Transfer Learning · Fine-tuning

1 Introduction

Parkinson's disease (PD) is a brain ailment which gradually develops neurological disorder that can affect a person's movement, causing stiffness, slowness, and imbalance as well as body shaking. Although the exact cause of Parkinson's disease is still unknown, a combination of genetic and environmental factors is thought to be involved, which slowly progresses with age. PD is one of the most common brain disorders and the percentage of PD found in men is significantly higher as compared to women. The symptoms of PD vary from person to person but with proper treatment, it can be controlled. In the

M. Botto-Tobar et al. (Eds.): ICAT 2023, CCIS 2050, pp. 86–98, 2024.
https://doi.org/10.1007/978-3-031-58953-9_7

case of patients suffering from chronic Parkinson's disease, with proper treatments and medicines, symptoms of PD can be reduced but cannot be cured properly. Various Deep Learning (DL) techniques are used to find whether a person is suffering from PD or not and checking how severe it is accordingly. The origins of Parkinson's disease (PD), which affects around 10 million people globally, is still a complex puzzle with variables like heredity, genetics and environmental factors being a potential of the disease. The dysfunction of primary motor functioning like tremors, stiffness, delayed motions and balance issues is caused by the decline of dopamine producing neurons in the substantia nigra, a region of the mid brain responsible for controlling movement. A common variation in pathophysiological processes is implied by the observation that PD patients' symptoms might vary greatly from one another and show high clinical diversity. DL algorithms uses the voice recordings, handwriting and gait dataset to analyze the PD of a patient. The feature extraction can be done using the KNN algorithm to generate high performance accuracies. Models like U-Net, Res-Net, VGG-16, VGG-19 are used to find the whether a person is suffering from PD or not and each model offers different accuracies for different datasets. Transfer Learning (TL) techniques are also used to find whether a person is suffering from PD or not by using some pretrained models to gather the features images or text or recordings from various data sources. Transfer Learning techniques proposes some advantages over other model like efficient extraction of features from the fathered datasets, reductions in the training data requirements, easy adaption of TL models to different data sources and ultimately the most important, improved accuracy when compared to other models.

The remaining paper is systematically arranged as follows: Section 2 provides an overview of the related work that has been done in the recent years on the Parkinson Detection domain, highlighting Transfer Learning applications. Section 3 provides the description of the dataset utilized and the various preprocessing steps followed to prepare the dataset. The next section, Sect. 4 focuses on the methodology where different memory optimization techniques, process of training and evaluation is outlined in detail. The experimental results and the related observations of the proposed fine-tuned model is presented in Sect. 5. The paper concludes with the recapitulation of the proposed work presented as conclusion in Sect. 6 with glimpses of the future scope in the domain.

2 Literature Review

Parkinson's Disease (PD) is an exponentially growing severe neurological disorder that directly affects the brain and eventually affects motor and non-motor movements like walking, thinking, logical reasoning, and shaking. The main cause of PD is due to loss of nerve cells in some components of the brain especially in the nigra region which in due course causes the reduction of dopamine production which is very crucial for controlling the movements. According to the data, men suffer more from PD as compared to women with various symptoms for easy identification like tremors, bradykinesia, rigidity, fatigue, depression, and anxiety. As of now, there are no such treatments to permanently cure PD but there are some medications that may stop the further spread of PD in the individual by increasing the dopamine levels and further research for eliminating this disease is still going on.

A wide range of Machine Learning (ML) models are used to predict the PD in an individual. These models are provided with datasets like clinical or neuroimaging data from which they extract the key attributes and analyze the subtle change that is visible in the patterns that will help in recognizing whether an individual is suffering from PD or not. In 2022, Makarious et al. [1], developed a GenoML model which is a type of an automated ML package, using which features are also extracted. The developed was tested on Parkinson's Disease Biomarker Program (PDBP) dataset, and gave 89.72% Area under curve (AUC) and when model is fine-tuned and tested on some other dataset, it yields 85.03% of AUC. In 2021, Nahar et al. [2], in his paper detected the PD using the feature extraction and selection techniques like Boruta, Recursive Feature Elimination (RFE) and Random Forest (RF) along with 4 classification algorithms, among which recursive feature elimination outshined the other models. In 2021, Krishna et al. [3], in his paper used ML induced Logistic Decision Regression (LDR) to detect the PD and found out that, as this technique focuses in ML with Big Data, it the best, accurate and the most reliable technique in the current scenario. Deep Learning (DL) unlike ML models deal with high dimensional data like MRI scans, speech and handwritings in order to predict PD in a person in an accurate manner. DL models are also capable to integrate data from multiple sources along with integration of multiple models. In 2020, Shahid et al. [4], in his paper firstly used Principal Component Analysis (PCA) in order to extract the features from the used dataset and then those features are fed into a fine-tuned DNN model to predict PD by predicting Motor and Total-UPDRS score. The MAE, RMSE, and R^2 values are 0.926, 1.422, and 0.970 respectively for motor-UPDRS and these values vary like 1.334, 2.221, and 0.956 respectively for Total-UPDRS. In 2021, Mozhdehfarahbakhsh et al. [5], in his paper applied Convolutional Neural Network (CNN) to differentiate between different stages of PD and found out that MRI based CNN is the best model, giving an accuracy of around 94%. In 2020, Wingate et al. [6], employed CNN and Recurrent Neural Network (RNN) on MRI and dopamine transporters scans to predict the Parkinson's Disease in a patient. The extracted information is comprised of internal representations of the trained DNNs. This knowledge is used through domain adaption and transfer learning to establish a unified framework for Parkinson's disease prediction in various medical settings.

Different techniques and algorithms are discovered to detect the Parkinson Disease in a patient. To predict the severity of PD in a patient by the model, the dataset must be fed. Spiral form of data is one of the most commonly used data. Digitised drawings of spirals created by individuals make up this kind of dataset. Tremors and poor fine motor control are common in people with Parkinson's disease (PD), which can cause distortions in spiral drawings as compared to those of healthy persons. Once the dataset is prepared, it is trained using different models and in current real-world scenario, Transfer Learning (TL) models are the best performing models. Transfer Learning is the process of using a model developed for one task as the basis for a new model developed for a different activity. It involves applying the knowledge gained from training a model for a certain task to improve performance on a related but unrelated task. In TL, there are two key steps: fine-tuning, where the pre-trained model is then modified and tailored to the intended task using the dataset that is being used in the current task, and pre-training, where the model is trained using the initial dataset. In 2021, Kamble et al. [7], used spiral drawing images of 25 patients and 15 healthy individual images as dataset and applied classification algorithms like KNN and Logistic Regression and achieved 91% accuracy. In 2021, Chandra et al. [8], in her paper used Random Forest Regressor in her research on spiral dataset to predict the severity of PD in the patients and the model gave 0.999 AUC on the dataset she tested. In 2021, Mital et al. [9] used 14 pretrained models on spiral dataset that were repeated under 4 distinct circumstances for their study. Following testing, he obtained the best accuracy of 93.94% for MobileNetV2, out of all the models, and the lowest accuracy of 27.27% for VGG-19.

Transfer Learning is considered as one the most accurate techniques to predict the PD in a patient and spiral dataset being the most used dataset around the globe for research provides abundant sample images as dataset for more accurate results. In 2021, Jahan et al. [10], applied CNN on the person's sketched images to distinguish between healthy and PD patient. Different CNN models with TL are applied on the spiral and wave dataset in which the best was ResNet50, giving an accuracy of around 96.67%. In 2023, Agrawal et al. [11], proposed a hybrid model which firstly perform feature extraction and data augmentation, followed by a pretrained CNN model for PD identification. A fined tuned VGG16 model was used along with SVM as classification technique, yielding an accuracy of 99.8%. In 2022, Varalakshmi et al. [12], in her paper used the hand drawing dataset, which contain 102 spiral images. After that, the images are augmented and the augmented photos are utilised to train multiple machine learning and deep learning models, as well as pre-trained networks like RESNET50, VGG16, AlexNet, and VGG19. Subsequently, a comparison is made between the performance measures of hybrid models combining machine learning and deep learning, as well as hybrid models combining deep learning for classification and feature extraction. With an accuracy score of 98.45%, sensitivity score of 0.99, and specificity score of 0.98, it was shown that the hybrid model of RESNET-50 and SVM outperformed other machine learning, deep learning, and hybrid models in terms of performance measures.

3 Dataset Description and Preprocessing

3.1 Dataset Description

This study utilizes the openlyaccessible NewHandPD [13] dataset, that is comprised of hand-drawn samples of patients who have good health and those who are suffering from Parkinson illness. The used dataset is an expansion of another dataset, which is the HandPD dataset [14], introduced by Pereira et al. [13]. The enhanced NewHandPD dataset is comprised of 310 images in total. The images are initially divided into 244 training images, among which 130 are of healthy patients and 114 are of patients with parkinson's disease. The test set consisted of 66 images, among which 39 are of healthy and 27 are of parkinson. As an example, in the case of an image named as 'sp1-H1.jpg' sp1 denotes the number of spiral image while H1 is an indication of a healthy individual. Similarly, an image named as 'sp1-P1.jpg' represents spiral image 1 but from the patient's group. Some images from spiral drawings collection from both healthy and patient groups are shown in Fig. 1.

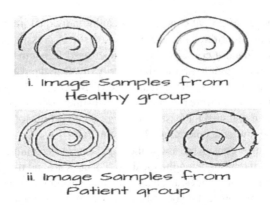

Fig. 1. Image samples from hand-drawn PD Dataset

3.2 Dataset Preprocessing

Image preprocessing involved using the ImageDataGenerator from Keras. For the images in the training directory, a horizontal_flip operation was applied that led to the increase in the number of training samples by randomly flipping the images. The images were scaled between 0 to 1 pixel by dividing them by 255.0, which is the highest pixel value for RGB images. The dataset consisted of 310 images, which was split into training, testing and validation sets. The dataset division can be observed in Table 1. The validation set was create from the test images, and 20% images were put into validation set. The input shape for all the generators were set to (224,224) as it is the default input size of the used model. keeping in mind of the dataset size, a batch_size of 32 was chosen.

Table 1. Dataset division for image distribution and model training

Division	Number of Images
Training	244
Testing	54
Validation	12

4 Methodology

4.1 Hardware and Memory Optimization

Memory Optimization. In the pursuit of optimizing deep learning model performance, memory management plays a pivotal role. The imperative strategy of enabling memory growth for each physical device within the TensorFlow framework mitigated potential memory overflow concerns. This adaptive allocation ensured that computational resources are efficiently utilized, as this work handles intricate and complex model architectures.

Utilizing Multiple GPUs. This study adopted the TensorFlow MultiWorkerMirrored-Strategy to harness the capabilities of multiple Graphics Processing Units (GPUs). The specific configuration indicated the utilization of two T4 GPUs, distributing the computational workload across these resources.

Mixed Precision Policy. The global adoption of a mixed precision policy, specifically the 'mixed_float16' policy, exemplified an approach that utilizes lower-precision data types for designated components of the neural network. This refinement contributed to the improved computational efficiency without compromising model accuracy.

4.2 Model Training and Evaluation

A largely emerging subfield of machine learning, called deep learning utilizes different algorithms that performs the simulation of the various intricate compositions and functions of the human brain. Among the various deep learning methods, image classification and the associated method that uses convolution process is widely leveraged, is CNN. A conventional CNN is composed of three different foundational layers: a fully-connected layer, a layer performing convolution operation, and a layer performing pooling operation.

Transfer learning is an emerging branch of deep learning that uses trained models on one task for another task. The learning of the model on one task is transferred for a completely different task. The pre-trained models are utilized, which are already trained on large image datasets such as ImageNet. This results in a great reduction on the need of large quantity of training data for a new job and makes complete use of the large-scale labelled datasets. These models are already occupied with the ability to generalize images from the test set even in the case where the number of training samples are smaller in quantity. Transfer Learning based image classification tasks are emerging advancements in CNN domain. The flexibility of these TL models allows various possible hyperparameters that can be tuned and performance can be highly optimized depending on the varied needs of the image classification task.

ResNet152. It is a deep convolutional neural network which is a layered expansion of the initial ResNet [15]. It has 152-layers. With the aim to reduce dimensionality prior to performing 3×3 convolution operations and maximize the computing performance, the ResNet-152 architecture inculcates a bottleneck design equipped with 1×1 convolutions. The input image dimensions for this model are $224 \times 224 \times 3$ (Fig. 2).

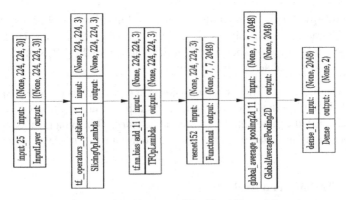

Fig. 2. Model architecture of ResNet-152 model used

Stepwise form of the proposed methodology is given in Fig. 3 and is described as follows:

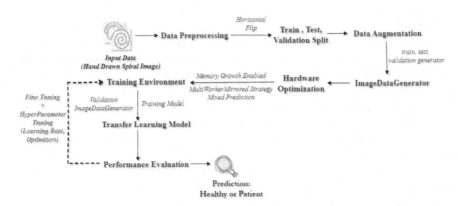

Fig. 3. Data Architecture Diagram

Step 1: This work utilizes a dataset of 310 images, that are diversified with healthy and patiend spiral hand-drawn images. This dataset is split into training, testing and validation.

Step 2: The ImageDataGenerator is used to augment and load the images from the respective directories.

Step 3: Loaded the pretrained transfer learning model of ResNet-152.

Step 4: Perform feature extraction from Images.

Step 5: Compile and train the model on the dataset without fine-tuning and freezing all the trainable layers and applying callback as EarlyStopping.

Step 6: Perform fine-tuning and hyperparameter tuning of the transfer learning model.

Step 7: Compiling and training the fine-tuned model on the dataset.

Step 8: Tested the performance of trained model in both cases using confusion Matrix and other classification metrics: accuracy, precision, recall, F1-score and AUC.

5 Results and Discussion

The classification model was developed using a Python library widely used for modelling Transfer Learning models in a user-friendly way, TensorFlow. The model training was carried out in Kaggle Kernel. Kaggle kernel was chosen as it provides free T4 GPUs for a limited worktime and allows work distribution using different distribution strategies of TensorFlow. The image classification task involves and requires lot of memory and hardware resources in order to model the high-resolution images. So, various hardware optimizations were performed to significantly accelerate the training process. Memory growth was enabled for all the physical devices and the mixed precision of mixed_float16 was used.

Utilization of accelerated hardware environment led to significant reduction in overall training time. Without the memory and hardware optimization techniques, the code utilized Kaggle CPU at 100% potential and the avaialble GPUs were not utilised. This resulted in slow training of transfer learning models and execution of the entire task in around 2 h timeframe. Whereas the hardware optimization step, led to the utilization of 2T4 GPUs along with the CPU resulting in accelerated training. The entire training with and without fine-tuning was completed within a very short time span of 8 to 10 min. The Speedup calculation is shown in Eq. 1.

$$Speedup = \frac{Time_{CPU}}{Time_{GPU}} = \frac{120}{10} = 12 \tag{1}$$

The model training involved two different scenarios. The initial model training was performed on the dataset without any fine-tuning and using the pre-trained ResNet-152 TL model for 500 epochs along with callback paramater as EarlyStopping to monitor val_loss for a patience of 10 steps. The model was trained for 40 epochs and then it sopped due to callback and no significant change in val_loss. The accuracy and loss can be observed in Fig. 4. Although this scenario demonstrated high training accuracy of 93.30%, validation accuracy of 94.44% and test accuracy of 96.67%, the associated test loss was relatively higher having a value of 21.9, indicating a probable case of overfitting.

Based on the performance of the model and a high loss, a fine-tuning based approach was devised and the model underwent fine-tuning. Among all the 515 trainable layers in the model, the top 18 layers were frozen and allowed fine-tuning for the rest layers after the 18th layer. This was done by setting all these layers' trainable value to True. In this scenario as well, callback was applied and EarlyStopping was used to save computation units and ensure efficient memory utilization. The Adaptive Moment Estimation (ADAM) optimizer was used along with a learning rate of 0.0001. All the parameters were set and experimented to observe and obtain the best results. Hyperparameter tuning of trainable layers, optimization function etc. was done to finally reach the above mentioned values. This approach led to a significant improvement in the performance of the

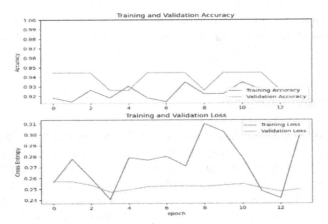

Fig. 4. Accuracy and Loss curve of ResNet-152 without fine-tuning

transfer-learning model. The training accuracy was observed to be 97.95%. The testing accuracy observed was 100% with a testing loss of 0.0040 approximately. The fine-tuned model's performance was also evaluated based on other performance metrics such as Accuracy, Precision, F1-Score, Recall, Area Under the Curve (AUC). The accuracy and loss curves for this scenario can be observed in Fig. 5.

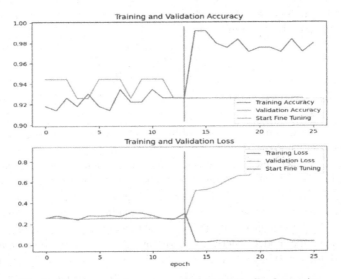

Fig. 5. Accuracy and Loss curve of ResNet-152 after fine-tuning

From the figure it can be clearly observed, that there is a gradual increase in performance right after the fine-tuning was done. The accuracy increase steadily and the loss decrease steadily. The exceptional performance of the fine-tuned transfer learning model can also be captured from the confusion matrix and the ROC curve in Fig. 6.

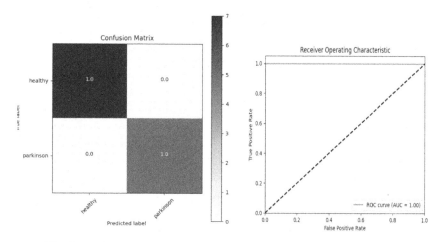

Fig. 6. Confusion Matrix and ROC Curve for Fine-tuned ResNet-152 model

The various performance metrics for the fine-tuned as well as the initial model is presented in Table 2.

Table 2. Effect of fine-tuning on the performance of Transfer Learning model, ResNet-152

Model Type	Performance Metrics							
			Healthy			Parkinson		
	Accuracy (Testing)	AUC	Precision	Recall	F1-Score	Precision	Recall	F1-Score
Without fine-tuning	96.67%	0.9242	1.00	0.85	0.92	0.80	1.00	0.89
With fine-tuning	**100%**	**1.0000**	1.00	1.00	1.00	1.00	1.00	1.00

As per the previous works that have been carried out, that utilizes different strategies for PD classification, the proposed fine-tuned approach outperformed all of them. The performance comparison of the benchmarked models along with the proposed model is presented in Table 3 and visually represented in the form of barplot representing the varying accuracies in Fig. 7.

Table 3. Comparison of performance of difference benchmarked models

Model	Accuracy	Recall	Precision	Loss	AUC
Improved KNN [16]	93.88	0.97	–	–	–
Multi Fine-tuned CNN [17]	92.7	–	–	–	–
CNN Multistage Classifier [18]	93.3	0.94	0.935	–	–
Deep Learning with Genetic Algorithm for Feature Selection [19]	95.29	0.86	0.98	0.12	0.90
Proposed Model	100	1.00	1.00	0.0040	1.00

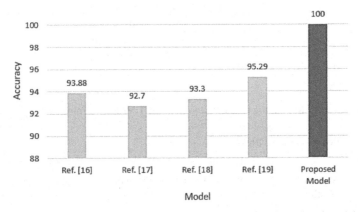

Fig. 7. Comparison of accuracies of proposed model and other related models.

One can clearly observe and infer that the performance of the proposed model is superior to the benchmarked models and work carried out in this direction. Further improvement can be done to reduce loss and most importantly generalize the fine-tuned model on varied dataset, to create a robust and powerful model.

6 Conclusion

Machine Learning as well as Deep Learning models have become an integral part in the healthcare domain and is a core component of the advance research techniques that are being employed to better understand and diagnose Parkinson's Disease (PD). Transfer Learning methodologies have seen a growth in their popularity and usage due to their easy implementation and better performance on smaller medical image datasets. Applying a transfer learning model with and without fine-tuning brings in major differences. When trained on custom spiral hand-drawing new hand PD dataset, ResNet-152 performed fairly with a testing accuracy of 96.67% but a huge loss of 21.9 indicating overfitting scenario and hence poor performance and generalization on unseen data. On the other hand, whenthe same model is fine-tuned and udergoes rigorous hyperparameter tuning proceedings, it performs exceptionally well and understand and captures patterns from training data. The fine-tuned ResNet-152 model outclassed the non-fine tuned version by achieving the training accuracy of 100% and a test loss of 0.0040. Although the performance is significantly well for this dataset, larger datasets can be involved with the same model to better understand how it performs on completely new data outside dataset. It will be proven beneficial for further studying and understanding how fine-tuning transfer learning model can have impact on the model's performance. It will also open scope for studying and better understanding the internal working of different fine-tuning approaches and their corresponding impacts. There exists a future scope to further investigate and obtain the performance of fine-tuned TL models on large datasets and analyzing if the benchmarked performance is sustained or not.

References

1. Makarious, M.B., et al.: Multi-modality machine learning predicting Parkinson's disease. npj Parkinson's Disease **8**(1), 35 (2022)
2. Nahar, N., Ara, F., Neloy, Md.A.I., Biswas, A., Hossain, M.S., Andersson, K.: Feature selection based machine learning to improve prediction of Parkinson disease. In: Mahmud, M., Kaiser, M.S., Vassanelli, S., Dai, Q., Zhong, N. (eds.) BI 2021. LNCS (LNAI), vol. 12960, pp. 496–508. Springer, Cham (2021). https://doi.org/10.1007/978-3-030-86993-9_44
3. Krishna, P.G., StalinDavid, D.: An effective Parkinson's disease prediction using logistic decision regression and machine learning with big data. Turk. J. Physiother. Rehabil. **32**(3), 778–786 (2021)
4. Shahid, A.H., Singh, M.P.: A deep learning approach for prediction of Parkinson's disease progression. Biomed. Eng. Lett. **10**, 227–239 (2020)
5. Mozhdehfarahbakhsh, A., Chitsazian, S., Chakrabarti, P., Chakrabarti, T., Kateb, B., Nami, M.: An MRI-based deep learning model to predict Parkinson's disease stages. medRxiv, pp. 2021-02 (2021)
6. Wingate, J., Kollia, I., Bidaut, L., Kollias, S.: Unified deep learning approach for prediction of Parkinson's disease. IET Image Proc. **14**(10), 1980–1989 (2020)
7. Kamble, M., Shrivastava, P., Jain, M.: Digitized spiral drawing classification for Parkinson's disease diagnosis. Meas. Sens. **16**, 100047 (2021)
8. Chandra, J., et al.: Screening of Parkinson's disease using geometric features extracted from spiral drawings. Brain Sci. **11**(10), 1297 (2021)
9. Mital, M.E.: Detection of Parkinson's disease through static and dynamic spiral test drawings: a transfer learning approach. In: 2021 13th International Conference on Information & Communication Technology and System (ICTS), pp. 247–251. IEEE (2021)
10. Jahan, N., Nesa, A., Layek, M.A.: Parkinson's disease detection using resnet50 with transfer learning. Int. J. Comput. Vis. Signal Process. **11**(1), 17–23 (2021)
11. Agrawal, S., Sahu, S.P.: Image-based Parkinson disease detection using deep transfer learning and optimization algorithm. Int. J. Inf. Technol. **16**, 1–9 (2023)
12. Varalakshmi, P., Priya, B.T., Rithiga, B.A., Bhuvaneaswari, R., Sundar, R.S.J.: Diagnosis of Parkinson's disease from hand drawing utilizing hybrid models. Parkinsonism Relat. Disord. **105**, 24–31 (2022)
13. Pereira, C.R., Weber, S.A.T., Hook, C., Rosa, G.H., Papa, J.P.: Deep learning-aided Parkinson's disease diagnosis from handwritten dynamics. In: Proceedings - 2016 29th SIBGRAPI

Conference on Graphics, Patterns and Images, SIBGRAPI 2016, pp. 340–346 (2017). https://doi.org/10.1109/SIBGRAPI.2016.054

14. Pereira, C.R., et al.: A new computer vision-based approach to aid the diagnosis of Parkinson's disease. Comput. Methods Programs Biomed. **136**, 79–88 (2016)

15. He, K., Zhang, X., Ren, S., Sun, J.: Deep residual learning for image recognition. In: Proceedings of the IEEE Conference on Computer Vision and Pattern Recognition, pp. 770–778 (2016)

16. Fang, Z.: Improved KNN algorithm with information entropy for the diagnosis of Parkinson's disease. In: Proceedings of the International Conference on Machine Learning and Knowledge Engineering (MLKE), February 2022, pp. 98–101 (2022)

17. Gazda, M., Hires, M., Drotar, P.: Ensemble of convolutional neural networks for Parkinson's disease diagnosis from offline handwriting, Dept. Comput. Inform., Intell. Inf. Syst. Lab, Tech. Univ. Kosice, Košice, Slovakia, Technical report 9 (2022)

18. Chakraborty, S., Aich, S., Seong-Sim, J., Han, E., Park, J., Kim, H.-C.: Parkinson's disease detection from spiral and wave drawings using convolutional neural networks: a multistage classifier approach. In: Proceedings of 22nd International Conference on Advanced Communication Technology (ICACT), February 2020, pp. 298–303 (2020)

19. Abdullah, S.M., et al.: Deep transfer learning based Parkinson's disease detection using optimized feature selection. IEEE Access **11**, 3511–3524 (2023)

Smart Guide for Pedestrian Traffic Light Status Identification

Byron Lechón⬤, Johanna Celi⬤, and William Montalvo^(✉)⬤

Universidad Politécnica Salesiana, UPS, 170146 Quito, Ecuador
blechona@est.ups.edu.ec, {cceli,wmontalvo}@ups.edu.ec

Abstract. This paper develops a low-cost electronic visual assistant for visually impaired people, which determines the status of pedestrian traffic lights using artificial intelligence. By means of audio notifications, it describes the status of traffic lights, assisting blind people when moving around the streets. The computer vision and artificial intelligence software runs locally, avoiding the problem of latency in connectivity and is hosted on a Raspberry pi 4 development board. The transfer learning technique is used to obtain a reliable and adaptable convolutional neural network model for the problem of image identification. Employing conducting field tests on all the components of the prototype and its computer vision system, its effectiveness is verified. Through statistical analysis, detection results of 83.3% were obtained for red pedestrian traffic lights and an average of 77.7% in three out of the four categories for green traffic light detection. Additionally, a 100% error-free classification rate was determined, demonstrating its effectiveness and reliability.

Keywords: artificial vision · visually impaired · pedestrian traffic lights · artificial intelligence · convolutional network · MobileNetV2

1 Introduction

The advancement of technology has allowed the development of new and modern solutions to satisfy human needs and solve problems in different areas [1]. For example, help is provided to people who have lost a limb by implementing robotic prostheses that adequately fit the needs required by the person with physical disabilities [2]. Similarly, exoskeletons have been developed to facilitate the rehabilitation of the body movements of a person who has lost mobility [3].

Machine Learning applications are generally linked to web pages and mobile applications that are processed in the cloud. However, personal needs require that these algorithms be incorporated into mobile devices, for which algorithms optimized for portable processing capabilities are required [4].

Later works have developed vision systems using traditional image processing applying color histograms. The main issue here is the variation in lighting that occurs during the day, causing color to alter their hue, saturation, and other properties. This, in turn, reduces the effectiveness of object detection. More modern systems propose the development of systems that run on mobile phones, which means the intelligent vision system

© The Author(s), under exclusive license to Springer Nature Switzerland AG 2024
M. Botto-Tobar et al. (Eds.): ICAT 2023, CCIS 2050, pp. 99–112, 2024.
https://doi.org/10.1007/978-3-031-58953-9_8

runs in the cloud. This generates a delay depending on the cloud connection, in addition to the privacy risks involved. However, there is still a significant problem: these models must be robust in detecting traffic lights in varying lighting conditions [5, 6].

The reference [7] proposed a system consisting of two stages, based on HSV colour segmentation for the detection of possible pedestrian traffic lights within an environment and the next stage of image classification based on CNN convolutional neural networks, however. in this system the first stage allows to entry of more information on objects that emit colours similar to those emitted by traffic lights where red light can be confused with other objects, in addition, this system based on regional Mask-CNN requires more computational resources making real-time detection impossible on mobile devices that consist only of CPUs.

This study is focused on the development of a low-cost in real-time assistance system for blind people through the implementation of a tiny Machine Learning model, which has created a system that provides voice notifications by recognizing the light color of pedestrian traffic lights. The prototype is integrated with sensors, electronic cards, software, and other electronic components where its vision algorithm is executed internally in the embedded device, to provide a solution for their mobility, provide alternatives for pedestrian traffic avoiding the dependence on human companions, Furthermore, it boasts a 100% reliability, making it suitable and dependable for daytime use.

2   Methodology

2.1   3D Modeling of Protective Structure

The design starts from all the components necessary for the operation and the dimensions that each of these elements has, placing them in such a way that they occupy an optimal space and fulfill their function.

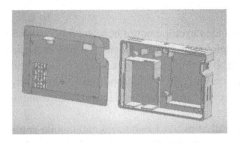

Fig. 1. a. 3D modeling of structure b. Assembled structure

The modeling of the structure shown in Fig. 1a, allows understanding of the finally assembled structure with the components inside shown in Fig. 1b, which has a size of 17.8 cm long, 13.8 cm high, 3.61 cm thick with a total weight of 625.95 g.

2.2 Operation of the Artificial Vision Algorithm Model

This paper proposes a two-stage algorithm, that implements the MobileNetV2 convolutional neural network architecture. The first stage consists of an object detector where the image is previously processed and normalized to a size of 320 × 320 pixels and enters the CNN that locates and determines the coordinates of the traffic light that is in the environment of the image; From these coordinates that determine the position, the new image is extracted, which is resized to the size of 160 × 160 pixels to fit the size that allows the CNN to enter, this image enters the classification stage where the next neural model performs the extraction of characteristics and classification through the corresponding label according to the classification group to which it belongs as shown in Fig. 2.

Fig. 2. Proposed model of image detection and classification

2.3 Development of the Dataset or Database

Deep Learning systems require a large database for feature extraction and prior training [7]. For the collection of the dataset used for training, several crosswalks were walked at different times of day and images of traffic lights were captured at different distances and positions, to obtain a robust database. A total of 1000 photographs were collected of pedestrian traffic lights in the red state and 1000 in the green state. Additionally, 875 images of traffic lights were captured, which were duplicated and cropped, leaving only the outline of the traffic lights visible, as shown in Fig. 3. The uncropped images are used in the detection model training, while the cropped images are used in the classification model training.

2.4 Training of the Artificial Neural Network

Training of the artificial neural network is done in the online platform Edge Impulse is used, which is dedicated to the development of intelligent models with easy implementation in embedded devices and provides an intuitive environment for the creation of advanced neural network models [8, 9].

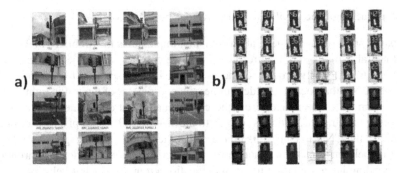

Fig. 3. a) Images of pedestrian traffic lights for training detection model, b) Cropped images of pedestrian traffic lights for classification model

The platform creates object detection and image classification models based on convolutional neural networks, using the transfer learning technique and the MobileNetV2 architecture, Architecture that is characterized by optimizing latency because it factors the standard convolution reducing the number of parameters and the operational calculation. [10, 11].

Edge Impulse allows for adjusting hyperparameters for the training of the last layer of the MobileNetV2 architecture while keeping the values of the hidden layers of the CNN model intact, which have been set for the image classification or detection task that this architecture specializes in.

2.5 Object Detection Model

In the Edge Impulse platform, for the object detection model, a total of 1415 images of pedestrian traffic lights in both red and green states are loaded. This amount has an equal percentage of these two classes of pedestrian traffic lights. This dataset is divided by the platform into 78% for training and 22% for testing.

Fig. 4. Labeling of traffic lights using the Edge Impulse platform.

Subsequently, the platform moves on to the labelling phase where green and red pedestrian traffic lights are labelled as "traffic lights." as shown in Fig. 4.

The MobileNetV2 architecture for object detection models works with an image size of 320 × 320 pixels for the input layer. Therefore, labeled images are normalized to this size, and their features are extracted as shown in Fig. 5.

The detection model is trained using these extracted features.

Fig. 5. Extracted feature map

2.5.1 Object Detection Training

In the training phase, the hyperparameters are adjusted to the values shown in Table 1.

Table 1. Hyperparameters detection model.

Number of cycles	Learning rate	Validation set size
21	0.005	30%

With these hyperparameters, it is possible to obtain an accuracy of 80.5% in the model, in addition to an inference time of 291 ms, these performance values are shown in Fig. 6.

Fig. 6. Precision value and performance parameters of the trained detection model.

2.6 Image Classification Model

For the image classification model, 3 groups are used: pedestrian traffic lights in green, red and traffic lights, captured in different positions to improve the classification system.

A total of 963 images of green and red pedestrian traffic lights and 876 images of traffic lights are used, labeled as "green", "red" and the third category of traffic lights which are called "NO"; this last category has the function of a filter in case the detection model identifies another traffic light that is not a pedestrian traffic light. The Edge Impulse platform is parameterized with training and test data, using 81% for training and 19% for testing.

Unlike the detection model for the classification model, the MobileNetV2 architecture allows an image size in its input layer of 160 × 160 pixels, so the whole set of images is adjusted to this size and proceeds with the feature extraction of the 3 classes of traffic lights established.

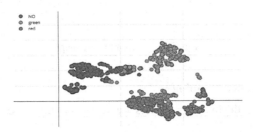

Fig. 7. Feature map extracted from the 3 traffic light classifications

Through the feature map in Fig. 7, a clear separation can be observed among the 3 classes of traffic lights identified by colours, indicating that there are differences in the features of each category. This will enable training the model very effectively.

2.6.1 Image Classification Training

In the training phase of the classification model, the hyperparameters are set to the values of Table 2.

Table 2. Hyperparameters.

Number of cycles	Learning rate	Validation set size	Dropout
15	0.015	20%	0.1

The last layer is configured with 2 neurons, activating the "data augmentation" to have a more robust and varied set for training, avoiding overfitting. With the aforementioned parameterization, a classification model accuracy of 100% is shown by the confusion matrix in Fig. 8.

Fig. 8. Accuracy value and confusion matrix of classification model.

In addition, model performance parameters such as inference time and memory usage are analyzed, as shown in Fig. 9.

Fig. 9. Performance values of the classification model on a Raspberry Pi.

The neural network models created on the platform, for both the detection and classification models, are downloaded directly to the Raspberry pi electronics board.

Figure 10 shows the download message of the models whose extension is ".eim" of the platform.

Fig. 10. Downloading neural network models on raspberry.

2.6.2 Creation of Audios for Voice Notification

The audios used for the voice notification are created in the online page called oddcast, which converts text to voice in mp3 format.

The generated audios are 4, which by voice give the following alerts:

- Traffic light green, you may cross.
- Traffic light on red, stop
- Device on
- Device turning off

2.7 Voice Notifications

For the programming of voice notifications and manipulation of the created neural network models, the Python programming language is used. The variables used for the activations of the audio notifications are the labels named "green" and "red", these variables activate the respective notifications through conditions that must be met, including the accuracy value and the number of times that the system manages to detect between one label and the other by making the following inferences.

- If the tag is "green" with an accuracy greater than or equal to 80% and performs minimum of 4 detections, then it sends the corresponding green traffic light alert indicating "green traffic light, may cross"
- If the label is "red" with an accuracy greater than or equal to 55% and detects 3 continuous detections, then it sends the corresponding red traffic light voice notification indicating "red traffic light, stop".

2.8 General Architecture of the Prototype

Figure 11 shows the block operation of each stage of the prototype, where in stage 1 is the acquisition of information through the video captured by the camera, in stage 2 the artificial vision algorithm implemented inside the Raspberry Pi is executed and in stage 3 the voice notification is performed, which can be through the connection of a headset or speaker.

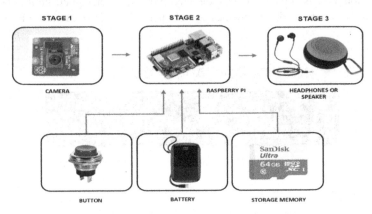

Fig. 11. General scheme in prototype blocks

3 Results

The tests are performed by evaluating the distance per number of lanes and in meters, as well as the detection time. In addition, the test is performed for 4 types of pedestrian traffic lights.

It is worth mentioning that, as for the pedestrian red traffic light, in all kinds of traffic lights, the pedestrian figure is static, that is to say, it has no movement.

In addition, the tests are performed at traffic lights where the luminosity of the signals is clearly and intensely visible.

In the red state of category "a" in Fig. 11, 30 tests are performed with following a good detection with a maximum distance of 10.1 m up to test number 26.

The percentage mean of Table 3 is 86.6%, obtained by Eq. (1).

$$x = 26 * \frac{100}{30} = 86.6\% \tag{1}$$

In the green state of category "a" in Fig. 12, 30 tests are performed, achieving a good detection with a maximum distance of 8.6 m until test number 23.

The percentage mean of Table 4 is 76.6% obtained by Eq. (2).

$$x = 23 * \frac{100}{30} = 76.6\% \tag{2}$$

Fig. 12. a) traffic light visible with movement, b) traffic lights with visible movement c) traffic light without movement d) traffic lights not visible to the camera. (Color figure online)

Table 3. Traffic light visible with movement red state

Test	Lanes	Time of day	Distance (m)	Time (s)	Detection
1	1	08:30	5.5	3.74	YES
2	1	09:30	5.6	3.52	YES
--	--	--	--	--	--
24	2	16:00	9.8	10.98	YES
26	2	17:30	10.1	13.15	YES

Table 4. Traffic light visible with movement green status.

Test	Lanes	Time of day	Distance (m)	Time (s)	Detection
1	1	08:00	5.5	3.74	YES
2	1	09:30	6	3.53	YES
--	--	--	--	--	--
22	2	15:00	8.4	11.43	YES
23	2	15:30	8.6	14.51	YES

In the red state of category "b" in Fig. 12, 30 tests were performed, achieving a good detection with a maximum distance of 8.8 m up to test number 23. The results are presented in Table 5.

The percentage mean of Table 5 is 80% obtained by Eq. (3)

$$x = 24 * \frac{100}{30} = 80\% \tag{3}$$

In the green state of category "b" in Fig. 12, 30 tests were performed, achieving a good detection with a maximum distance of 8.8 m until test number 24. The results are presented in Table 6.

Table 5. Traffic light with visible movement red status

Test	Lanes	Time of day	Distance (m)	Time (s)	Detection
1	1	08:00	5.6	4.71	YES
2	1	09:30	5.7	4.15	YES
--	--	--	--	--	--
22	2	15:00	8.6	9.82	YES
23	2	16:00	9	13.46	YES

Table 6. Traffic light with visible movement green status.

Test	Lanes	Time of day	Distance (m)	Time (s)	Detection
1	1	08:00	5.5	4.58	YES
2	1	09:30	5.6	5.59	YES
--	--	--	--	--	--
23	2	15:30	8.6	10.57	YES
24	2	16:00	8.8	13.87	YES

The percentage mean of Table 6 is 80% obtained by Eq. (4)

$$x = 24 * \frac{100}{30} = 80\% \tag{4}$$

In the red state of category "c" in Fig. 12, 30 tests were performed, achieving a good detection with a maximum distance of 9 m up to test number 24. The results are presented in Table 7.

Table 7. Non-moving traffic light red status.

Test	Lanes	Time of day	Distance (m)	Time (s)	Detection
1	1	08:30	5.6	3.71	YES
2	1	09:30	5.7	4.15	YES
23	2	15:30	8.5	10.68	YES
24	2	16:00	9	13.87	YES

The percentage mean of Table 7 is 80% obtained by Eq. (5).

$$x = 24 * \frac{100}{30} = 80\% \tag{5}$$

In the green state of category "c" in Fig. 12, 30 tests were performed, achieving a good detection with a maximum distance of 8.8 m until test number 23. The results are presented in Table 8.

Table 8. Traffic light no movement green status.

Test	Lanes	Time of day	Distance (m)	Time (s)	Detection
1	1	08:30	5.5	4.28	YES
2	1	09:30	5.6	4.59	YES
--	--	--	--	--	--
22	2	14:30	8.4	8.5	YES
23	2	15:30	8.8	11.54	YES

The percentage mean of Table 8 is 76.6% obtained by Eq. (6).

$$x = 23 * \frac{100}{30} = 76.6\% \tag{6}$$

In the red state of category "d" in Fig. 12, 30 tests were performed, achieving a good detection with a maximum distance of 10 m up to test number 26. The results are presented in Table 9.

Table 9. Traffic lights not visible to the camera red state.

Test	Lanes	Time of day	Distance (m)	Time (s)	Detection
1	1	08:30	5.6	3.91	YES
2	1	09:30	5.7	4.15	YES
--	--	--	--	--	--
25	2	16:00	9.8	10.54	YES
26	2	17:30	10	11.35	YES

The percentage mean of Table 9 is 86.6% obtained by Eq. (7).

$$x = 26 * \frac{100}{30} = 86.6\% \tag{7}$$

In the green state of category "d" in Fig. 12, 30 tests were performed, reaching 8 detections in the green state as shown in Table 10, the deficiency in this state is due to the lack of illumination by the traffic lights of this category.

The percentage mean of Table 10 is 26.6% obtained by Eq. (8).

$$x = 8 * \frac{100}{30} = 26.6\% \tag{8}$$

Table 10. Traffic lights not visible to the camera green state

Test	Lanes	Time of day	Distance (m)	Time (s)	Detection
1	1	08:00	5.5	---	NO
2	1	09:30	5.6	15.54	YES
–	–	–	–	–	–
9	1	14:30	6.3	---	NO
10	1	15:00	6.4	20.72	YES

With the tests performed, it can be seen that in the "red" state, detection is achieved at a greater distance since in that state the pedestrian figures are static, making their accuracy remains constant, contrary to the "green" state, since the movement of the figure generates variation in accuracy, so the detection time is slightly longer; also in the fourth category of traffic lights analyzed the "green" state is deficient because the cameras fail to capture the movement of the pedestrian, being unpredictable to understand what state this is in.

Table 11. Algorithm accuracy

Color	successful classification	Average precision
Red	150/150	100%
Grenn	120/120	100%

The matter of accuracy, which determines reliability, is presented in Table 11. With all tests conducted, there has been no confusion in the classification, resulting in an overall classification accuracy of 100% for both red and green pedestrian traffic lights, based on the 4 types of traffic lights tested. These results can also be observed in the confusion matrix in Fig. 8. As a result, a 100% reliable algorithm has been obtained to assist blind individuals.

4 Discussion

In [6], a traffic light recognition system implemented in a mobile device is established, which is executed through a server in the cloud, making it dependent on a cell phone and its operation will depend on the quality of the camera that this device has; likewise, the study developed by [5]. An AdaBoost algorithm based on multilayer characteristics is proposed, however only the algorithm has been generated and it is proposed to implement it in a DSP or FPGA chip, taking into account that these devices have a considerable size for their transport and mobility, which would not be considered comfortable for a blind person. The present study uses a multi-stage model consisting of an object detector and an image classifier that together determine the state of a pedestrian traffic light, in addition to creating a portable and friendly model that runs locally on an embedded device in real-time with very low latency. This system is characterized by its ability to detect in environments with varying lighting conditions, where other proposed models have encountered difficulties due to their processing methods. Furthermore, this system has proven to be highly reliable with no confusion, achieving a reliable device that is easy and intuitive to use and transport.

5 Conclusion

The transfer learning technique used in this research allows the creation of an advanced convolutional neural network model, by performing its training starting with previous knowledge taken from another model that has been trained with thousands and millions of parameters, so its learning did not start from scratch since it was feasible to use relatively small data for its training, which leads to decrease the training time and its computational cost, obtaining a model with favorable results in the detection of pedestrian traffic lights that determines the red or green state in which it is located.

The tiny models of Machine learning (TinyML) have appropriate architectures such as MobileNetV2, which is characterized by optimizing its computational calculation as its memory size, which allows the creation of a portable intelligent algorithm that facilitates the execution locally within a microprocessor such as the Raspberry Pi card that has reduced computational resources, thus avoiding processing in the cloud, thus reducing the inference time involved in a network connection and also provides greater security in their privacy.

The artificial vision algorithm obtained favorable results in the detection of pedestrian red traffic lights resulting in effectiveness of over 80% in the 4 categories of pedestrian traffic lights based on Tables 3, 5, 7, 9 and an effectiveness of 77% in 3 categories based in Tables 4, 6, and 8, furthermore, the classification system achieved a precision rate of 100% reliability, as demonstrated in Table 11. Consequently, it can be determined that the system provides favorable results in conditions of visible light from traffic lights at various times of the day and is reliable, given that it has not produced erroneous results. It was established that the best detections in a limited timeframe are achieved with traffic lights displaying a static pedestrian figure.

References

1. Lengua, I., Dunai, L., Peris Fajarnés, G., Defez, B.: Navigation device for blind people based on Time-of-Flight technology. DYNA **80**(179), 33–41 (2013)
2. Espinoza Moncayo, D.A., Peña Mendoza, C.D.: Diseño e Implementación de un Prototipo de Gafas Electrónicas con Comunicación Bluetooth a un Celular para la Detección de Objetos Circundantes que Servirá como Ayuda en Personas no Videntes, p. 112 (2015)
3. Yanchatuña Aguayo, L.Á.: VISIÓN ARTIFICIAL POR ALERTAS DE VOZ Y MOVIMIENTO PARA PERSONAS CON DISCAPACIDAD VISUAL EN LA BIBLIOTECA DE NO VIDENTES DE LA UNIVERSIDAD TÉCNICA DE AMBATO (2016)
4. Arias Zuluaga, A.: Etapas, Requerimientos y Recomendaciones para Implementacion de Modelos de Machine Learning en Sistemas Embebidos (2022)

5. Wu, X.H., Hu, R., Bao, Y.Q.: Fast vision-based pedestrian traffic light detection. In: Proceedings - IEEE 1st Conference on Multimedia Information Processing Retrieval, MIPR 2018, pp. 214–215, June 2018. https://doi.org/10.1109/MIPR.2018.00050

6. Ash, R., Ofri, D., Brokman, J., Friedman, I., Moshe, Y.: Real-time pedestrian traffic light detection. In: 2018 IEEE International Conference on the Science of Electrical Engineering in Israel, ICSEE 2018, February 2019. https://doi.org/10.1109/ICSEE.2018.8646287

7. Hassan, N., Ming, K.W., Wah, C.K.: A comparative study on HSV-based and deep learning-based object detection algorithms for pedestrian traffic light signal recognition. In: 2020 3rd International Conference on Intelligent Autonomous Systems, ICoIAS 2020, pp. 71–76 (2020). https://doi.org/10.1109/ICoIAS49312.2020.9081854

8. Ruiz Herrero, J.D.: SISTEMA DE MONITORIZACIÓN DEL TRANSPORTE DE VACUNAS MEDIANTE EL USO DE TECNOLOGÍA IOT Y MACHINE LEARNING (2021)

9. Cuerva Gutiérres, J.M.: Desarrollo de aplicaciones basadas en aprendizaje automático en sistemas empotrados STM32. Trab. Fin Grado en Ing. Electrónica, Robótica y Mecatrónica (2020)

10. Sandler, M., Howard, A., Zhu, M., Zhmoginov, A., Chen, L.-C.: Inverted Residuals and Linear Bottlenecks (2019)

11. Torra Villarejo, M.: USO DE TINYML PARA LA DETECCIÓN DE ROTURA DE CRISTALES, p. 6 (2021)

Conversion of MRI into CT Images Using Novel Dual Generative Adversarial Model

Mohammed Ahmed Mustafa[1(✉)], Zainab Failh Allami[2], Mohammed Yousif Arabi[3], Maki Mahdi Abdulhasan[4], Ghadir Kamil Ghadir[5], and Hayder Musaad Al-Tmimi[6]

[1] Department of Medical Laboratory Technology, University of Imam Jaafar AL-Sadiq, Tehran, Iran
Mohammed.ahmed.mustafa@sadiq.edu.iq
[2] Al-Manara College for Medical Sciences, Maysan, Iraq
[3] College of Computer, National University of Science and Technology, Dhi Qar, Iraq
[4] Department of Medical Laboratories Technology, AL-Nisour University College, Baghdad, Iraq
[5] College of Pharmacy, Al-Farahidi University, Baghdad, Iraq
[6] Hayder Musaad Al-Tmimi, College of Health Medical Techniques, Al-Bayan University, Baghdad, Iraq

Abstract. When many medical images are obtained to complete a diagnostic test on a sample patient and the amount of radiation to which the human body is subjected. As a result, understanding how medical images are created is critical in the clinical setting. This region currently offers a wide range of options, which is convenient. For example, due to the unique clustering concept used by the fuzzy C-means (FCM) clustering methodology, the images produced by this method do not clearly indicate the attribution of specific firms. As a result, the image's finer details will become obscured, and the overall quality of the image will suffer. As a direct result of the GAN model's development, a plethora of novel techniques built on top of the deep generative adversarial network (GAN) model has emerged. Pix2Pix is based on the UNet model. This method employs two distinct medical photo types, as well as the calibration of a deep neural network, to generate high-quality photographs. There are strict data criteria, and the two sorts of medical pictures must be tailored to each individual patient. Transfer learning is used throughout the development of DualGAN models. The 3D image is divided into slices, and then simulations are run on each individual slice. The results of these simulations are then combined to produce the result. The disadvantage is that whenever a new image is created, "shadows" in the shape of bars present in the three-dimensional image will appear. Method or material. This study proposes a transfer learning based Dual3D & PatchGAN model as a solution to the problems described above and as a means of ensuring high-quality image production. Unlike traditional machine learning, which needs one-to-one matching of data sets, Dual3D and PatchGAN are based on transfer learning. As a result, just two distinct types of medical imaging data sets are required. This has a significant impact on the practical application of applications. By utilizing the images generated by DualGAN, this model can remove the bar-shaped "shadows" and transform the two different types of images in a different manner. Results: According to many evaluation indicators, Dual3D & PatchGAN are superior to

M. Botto-Tobar et al. (Eds.): ICAT 2023, CCIS 2050, pp. 113–125, 2024.
https://doi.org/10.1007/978-3-031-58953-9_9

other models in terms of their suitability for the development of medical images as well as their generation effect.

Keywords: Artificial Intelligence · Convolutional Neural Networks · Data Augmentation · Deep Learning · Generative Adversarial Networks · Medical Imaging · Transfer Learning · Variational Autoencoders

1 Introduction

Through its integration into a wide range of domains, artificial intelligence has brought significant convenience to humans. Text data analysis using used by medical practitioners to aid in the diagnosis and prevention of sickness in a more successful and efficient manner. The proposed technique's implementation will have no effect on data sets utilized in medical imaging, such as MRI scans. Deep learning algorithms were employed to analyse the medical imaging data [1–3]. Hundreds of distinct digital images are used to train the deep learning neural network. Once trained, the network can analyze images and make judgments about them. This network is capable of continually abstracting and revealing new degrees of quality. When applied to the processing of medical image data sets, this method can produce very precise results. Traditional machine learning algorithms, as well as deep learning algorithms developed in recent years, all require a significant amount of data, which has been incorrectly labeled as a prerequisite, and they all require enough data to ensure that the algorithm's findings are accurate [4–6]. Due to the scarcity of uncommon diseases and the need to maintain the confidentiality of those who have submitted medical information, obtaining information about medical picture samples may be difficult. Due to this factor, it is impossible to guarantee that the medical image data sets contain a diverse range of samples. We are all aware that a large amount of data pertaining to medical images is required to train an effective machine learning algorithm. As a result, imbalanced categorization and a lack of sample diversity will be the root causes of poor classification performance. Techniques such as Variational Adversarial Environments (VAEs) and Generative Adversarial Networks [7] can be used to enhance photographs that are difficult to access. When a high number of picture samples are created, overfitting is more likely to occur. The VAE method, which is based on a single photo, can be used to solve the overfitting problem. The VAE pictures, on the other hand, are exceedingly blurry, rendering them unsuitable for use in future medical imaging research. VAE can utilize a photograph as a reference to measure the quality and accuracy of an image formed from it. GANs employ continuous adversarial learning in conjunction with the generator and discriminator to create medical pictures that are both understandable and valuable. This allows for a more accurate diagnosis.

Traditional image data improvement methods, on the other hand, not only provide highly relevant image training data, but may also help lessen the difficulty of a limited number of medical samples. A single image can be used to alleviate the overfitting problem; however, the VAE approach produces indistinct pictures, lowering the utility of medical imaging. It is critical that a solution to the lack of medical image data be identified as soon as feasible, preferably one that broadens the breadth of the medical image data pool. It is critical that this be completed as quickly as possible. Traditional methods for enhancing image data, such as rotating or inverting photographs, are ineffective since there is nowhere for extra information to be transferred [8]. This is since there is nowhere to enhance the data, which is why it is in such a bad form. The scope of coverage includes tactics like these as well as others like them. The fact that these methods have been used far less frequently in recent years than in the past may be contributing to their waning popularity. The image samples utilised in the evaluation of algorithmic approaches for medical imaging have a shocking lack of diversity. Even if data augmentation methods could be employed to enhance the number of picture samples, this would not overcome the shortage problem. There are just not enough image examples. If the same picture data augmentation procedures are used on a constant basis, the system has a chance of overfitting. This might have unfavourable consequences. This might result in unanticipated consequences.

The following is an illustration of an adversarial network model, to do this, it employs a neural network generator that is entirely convolutional in nature. MRI and CT images of brain tumours were changed to achieve the study's objectives. A DCGAN is used to do this. Several research [9] advocate that generative confrontation networks be used as a data storing mechanism for medical visual information. Despite privacy concerns, the information generated by this technology will remain accessible to the public. References [10] discuss the evolution of stain generative adversarial networks, which are built on generative adversarial networks. (GANs). Our model is successful at visually resembling the target domain without the need for images as a point of reference for the target domain's look. The Stain image-to-image translation approach necessitates the use of single photographs rather than pairs. Its design is inspired by the Cycle GAN. When compared to more traditional classification methodologies, the breast cancer classification reveals that the model can generate a greater image conversion. This was identified using the breast cancer categorization.

Even though GAN research is still in its early stages, these models have already achieved previously unthinkable levels of complexity [11] and several other academic researchers 2019 proved that a conditional generative confrontation network may be utilized to generate multi-contrast pictures. Because GANs are continually taught during the process, the output they create has a contrast level consistent with what was first gathered. The use of GANs in clinical practice for multi-contrast synthesis offers a great lot of potential and promise. The most typical use for a GAN is to allow a system to learn on its own without the intervention of a person while increasing the number of small samples utilised. This is the most popular application of a GAN. To manage sparse medical imaging data, a growing number of generative adversarial networks, or GANs, are being built. In other cases, GANs are simply referred to as GANs. Due to GAN restrictions, convolutional networks are unable to create a wide range of image types in a timely and efficient manner [12]. Discriminators cannot be trained to function as intended during the training process due to the restricted data sets at their disposal. To overcome the restrictions described before, this study employs not one, but two unique transfer learning algorithms, namely Dual3D and Patch GAN. The following are only a few of the distinguishing characteristics of this strategy:

2 Background

The overall philosophy to which it adheres distinguishes it from the other members of the organisation. Transfer learning is not necessary for GAN's conflict generating and fuzzy clustering capabilities. The phrase "Point-to-Point" refers to the type of algorithm that is most used in modern computers. It is true that the capabilities of these programmes are limited, which significantly limits the way they may be employed. The one-of-a-kind network model is ranked second on the list. Two-dimensional models are commonly utilised to generate visuals for medical purposes [13]. It is feasible to construct two-dimensional representations of pictures by slicing a picture into several separate portions. To slice a two-dimensional image into three dimensions, the two-dimensional slices must be integrated into a three-dimensional image. The Dual3D and Patch GAN paradigms will never generate two-dimensional blocks because of the creation process. Three-dimensional blocks are always the unavoidable result. In many circumstances, three-dimensional block output is more accurate than two-dimensional block output. This is since three dimensions allow for the storing of more data. As a result of this, a wide range of possible implementation options have become accessible. In the great majority of situations, the module in charge of network construction is also in charge of creating the SoftMax algorithm parameter. This approach considers the SoftMax value for each domain to arrive at an accurate assessment of the average value. As a result, the original image has been divided into many more manageable fragments.

Each component of the collection has its own personality features as well as quirks and eccentricities. Traditional GAN model training examples frequently consist of medical pictures taken at the same time and from the same location [14]. You will need two images taken at the same time to fully grasp this strategy. The data gathering strategy used in this inquiry was governed by a very particular set of criteria. They are both appropriate for use in clinical settings since they both require two unique types of medical images to work successfully. The conversion process's success rate can vary. The transformation of CT scans to MR images performed by traditional GAN models is a one-way process. Picture conversion can only occur in one direction when the model is trained from scratch each time. It is possible to convert between two domains in either direction using the Dual3D and Patch GAN paradigms. This is true in both directions. The Dual3D and Patch GAN models are employed to convert the data more effectively. In 2014, Goodfellow presented his GAN approach at Backgrounds. The two pieces of the network that may be separated are discriminant model D and generating model G. Figure 1 depicts the network topology.

The structure of the building comprises both a generator and a discriminator in this precise combination. The submitted picture serves as the foundation to produce discriminator samples. For you to stand out from the crowd, your adversary must be able to offer samples and validate their credibility. The discriminator returns probability values ranging from 0 to 1. The probability value indicates how likely it is that a discriminator input sample is genuine [15, 16]. Losses in the discriminator and generator are represented by symbols. The generator and discriminator must minimize their losses during the GAN's learning phase. During training, the generator learns how to build images and attempts to persuade the discriminator that its own image is a valid sample. It is difficult to develop a binary classifier that can distinguish between legitimate and fraudulent data.

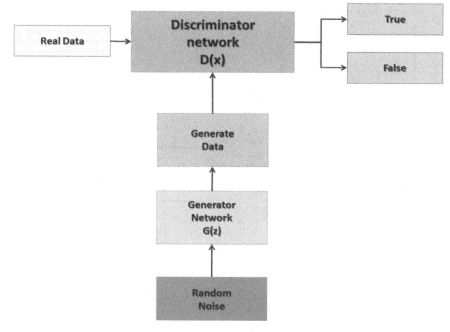

Fig. 1. GANs Network Structure Diagram

Our top aim is to get to a point where the percentage of genuine data to created data is about equal. To distinguish between real and bogus samples, the output of each input sample must be set to 1/2. Training is finished when the network model converges.

3 Proposed Model

Learning-based transfer to generate images, Dual GAN does not require matching data sets. Simulated medical images are far superior to what was previously available [17–19]. It is simple to create horizontal stripes throughout the image using this method. This was previously only feasible. In addition to Patch GAN, it is important to improve the discriminating network. The Dual3D and Patch GAN models were also considered feasible alternatives in this inquiry. The fundamental components of this network architecture are 3DGANs and transfer learning. Figure 2 depicts the model's overall organisational structure, which may be seen in its full for reference. One network oversees creating new data, while the other oversees categorising the freshly created data (D). People's access to certain services is being restricted because of the "growing" network's fake data, which is being used to deceive those customers. This is happening because of those customers being duped (G). It is feasible to change images concurrently if two distinct sets of generating and discriminating networks are used. As shown in Fig. 2, using a 3D generation network will allow you to modify images in both directions at the same time if Dual3D and Patch GAN are used (G) shown in Fig. 3. To limit the simulation's possibilities, the network model will incorporate a variety of various loss factors.

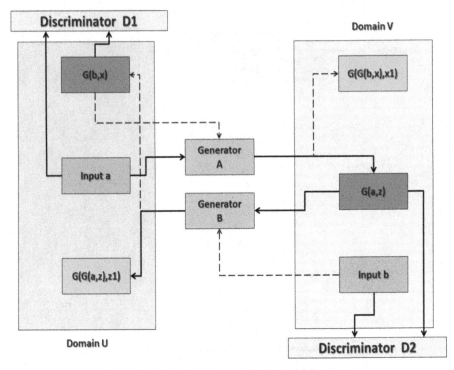

Fig. 2. The Dual3D and Patch GAN Model Structures

Table 1 gives a full description of the generating network's parameters while focusing on the model's most critical components (G). The generative network includes a synthesis path, designated by G, and an analysis path, marked by AH (SH).

Photographic image alteration and retouching It is suggested that you start by comparing the medical images collected from both places. It is critical to employ CT and MR images to conduct this study appropriately. The next stage is to assemble a collection of images related to the issue at hand. Keep an eye out for high-quality photos with precise elements and proportions that are constant throughout. Putting in some practise time in this manner will not jeopardise your safety in any way. Furthermore, you must make the test images available as soon as possible [20–22]. The data set comprises a total of nine samples, eight of which are meant to be used as training sets and the ninth as a test set. Students are subjected to eight distinct tests after only one hour of instruction. Next, create a dataset. You can remove blurry, artifact-filled, or unclear photos by re-filtering the images from the two domains. For model training, two collections of medical photos are separated into two folders and given domain names. The text has replaced the image, save the image as a.png before converting it to a.gif. Before using Dual3D and Patch GAN, convolve the 3-D space.

Data enhancements Rotation and reflex may add to the basic data set. The model can generalize better if as much data as possible is collected. In-depth modelling instruction Photos from both domains are used in 800 rounds of model training. This enables

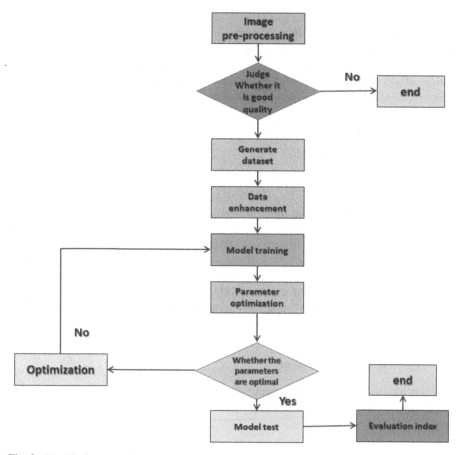

Fig. 3. Model of a generative network (G) constructed with Dual3D&PatchGAN and PatchGAN

Table 1. Setting the parameters of a Dual3D and Patch GAN generator (G)

AH	Value	SH	Value
Convolution Block	3 × 3 × 3	Convolution Block	33 × 3 × 3
Downnsampling	2 × 2 × 2	Downnsampling	2 × 2 × 2
Step Size	2	Step Size	2
Activation Function	SoftMax	Activation Function	Relu

modelling. Tensor board in TensorFlow can be used to track model training and identify model parameters as it progresses. A modification to the grid so that it may be tailored to the needs Because network deviations change as new data is acquired, it is critical that the grid be built as efficiently as possible. Its principal duty is to assist the network in determining the appropriate data parameters [23, 24]. Use the best possible range of values for the network parameter to gradually zero in on the best possible model parameter value. The best model training parameters are determined by grid optimization. Examine the network model's training data in the Tensor board to see if it is optimal. As needed, change the model parameters. Data examination of the trained model is tested in front of a live audience to determine how well it performs. Ten indicators are used in the evaluation. The evaluation index formula can compute multiple indices at the same time.

4 Experimental Result

4.1 PSNR and SSIM Index

PSNR and SSIM are used to investigate the model effects of the experiment. Before delving into the PSNR formula, familiarize yourself with the MSE function. Both PSNR and MSE have several definitions in common. PSNR is measured in decibels. This equation value represents the image's highest-value pixel. SSIM assesses the dependability of image data (Brightness, contrast, and structure are all measured.) The correlation between and is the variance of the data. SSIM connects the three measures using a unique coupling method at 0.01, with 0.03 as the default, calculations are simplified by resetting the beginning formula to 1.

4.2 Experimental Environment

Experiments require an appropriate environment to yield accurate results. Experiments can be carried out in a variety of settings. Table 2 contains the necessary information.

Table 2. Software's Required for Implementation

Development environment	Matlab2018b, PyCharm
Development language	Python, Matlab
Compilation framework	Tensorflow, Keras

4.3 Results

In experiments, four well-known models were pitted against Dual3D and Patch GAN. The FCM-based, WGAN-based, Cycle GAN transfer learning and Dual2DGAN model-based comparison algorithms are among the most important. For this experiment, researchers obtained brain images from the brain web. For this study, nine sets of brain CT and MR images were obtained from databases. An evaluation index is created from each model's expected outcomes to provide a fair and reliable assessment of the chosen model's performance. Determine how well each model creates a picture using assessment indicators. The initial step is to clean the data by eliminating any photographic artifacts, haze, or other potential flaws. Then, high-quality photographs should be chosen. Many photos must be chosen. Sort images into CT and MR domains. Due to the small sample size, CT and MR images are augmented. The goal of data augmentation is to make any amount of data more useful. The basic data needed to be improved as much as possible by flipping, rotating, cropping, deforming, and zooming. The model can be trained after the data has been processed. The data sets do not need to be connected because Dual3D and Patch GAN use transfer learning. A data set can be created by using only high-quality photos from two domains. The model must be trained before it can be used. When training, it's a good idea to keep an eye on the model's parameters and make changes as needed. During this procedure, using a Tensor board in conjunction with an output console gives various advantages. Following training sessions, a stable, functional network model is constructed. The training set includes CT and MR images from eight samples, with the remaining photos used to generate simulation images during each training session. Save and categorize the results of each test. The network model can be adjusted in real time, and the best parameter configuration can be discovered by comparing test images. MR scans are one type of medical image that is commonly used in practice. This necessitates new lesion imaging. The use of computerized photo analogy conversion shortens detection time and reduces radiation exposure. The PSNR for each of the models is shown in Table 3 where models are cycle GAN(A), GAN(B) and Dual2DGAN (C) and Fig. 5, respectively. The SSIM results for each model are mirrored in Table 4 and Fig. 4, as shown below.

Table 3. PSNR indicators of each model

Sample	FCM	A	B	C	Proposed Model
Type 1	23.5820	35.5622	29.9945	39.4427	39.8952
Type 2	9.8647	38.7939	29.6749	36.5639	39.6974
Type 3	24.6523	38.4839	32.6977	37.4997	42.8254
Type 4	25.7929	36.5520	33.5647	34.6352	43.5297
Type 5	23.3476	33.4697	38.6793	38.4462	38.6766
Type 6	25.7623	39.6262	33.6620	39.7748	39.6233
Type 7	28.8825	39.6985	33.6909	34.5620	44.5354
Type 8	25.3398	35.3697	34.5925	38.6979	39.6499
Type 9	26.7743	39.7735	32.2950	39.6239	40.0029
Means	24.9998	37.4823	33.4425	37.9085	40.3953
Variance	6.2998	6.4393	6.5899	6.3996	4.5873

The two assessment indicators established here show that the FCM paradigm fails to produce visuals. The evidence supports this conclusion. This post employs a network model that outperforms previous models in terms of generation performance. The Dual3D and Patch GAN models are more stable than other models. The model was created to work with 3D models, resulting in more accurate results. The transfer notion of

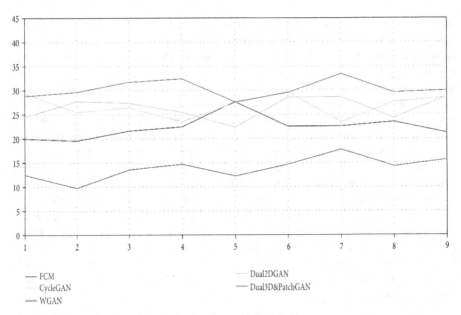

Fig. 4. Comparison of PSNR Indicators

Table 4. The Comparative Analysis of the SSIM value of the Proposed Model with Traditional Models

Sample	Fuzzy C Means	A	B	C	Proposed Model
Type 1	0.6499	0.7202	0.7806	0.7406	0.9363
Type 2	0.5986	0.8943	0.8843	0.8032	0.8996
Type 3	0.6645	0.8306	0.7360	0.7663	0.9203
Type 4	0.6902	0.8033	0.8643	0.8407	0.9632
Type 5	0.6004	0.7463	0.7709	0.9062	0.9023
Type 6	0.6909	0.7020	0.7930	0.8445	0.8976
Type 7	0.5542	0.7906	0.7789	0.7999	0.8959
Type 8	0.5907	0.6506	0.8002	0.8006	0.9603
Type 9	0.6005	0.7709	0.8304	0.7978	0.9207
Means	0.6308	0.7727	0.7969	0.8069	0.9249
Variance	0.0035	0.0067	0.0033	0.0036	0.0007

the model makes efficient use of source domain data knowledge, increasing generating efficiency. Dual2DGAN was the foundation for Dual3D and Patch GAN. Previously, the Dual3D and Patch GAN models could only produce a 2-D image, but they can now produce a 3-D image as well. It previously only produced 2D images. Because Patch GAN is now included in this model, computing SoftMax no longer necessitates the full

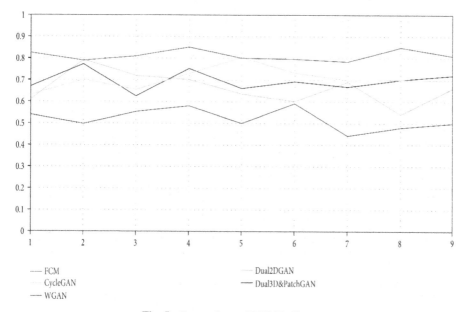

Fig. 5. Comparison of SSIM Indicators

image. The image is divided up before it is computed. Because of the model's module. Each block is calculated first, and then the results are summed up and averaged. Random cropping and training sequence disruption both disrupt the training sequence of the model. At the beginning of their development, network models will be trained at a rate of 2E−4, which will be utilized as a baseline. Because the Tender board fluctuates throughout the evaluation process, it is difficult to minimize a model's loss function only by looking at it. Developing a solid training model is becoming increasingly challenging. In experiments, DualGAN3D and Patch GAN images performed best.

5 Conclusion

This paper relies heavily on transfer learning to generate medical images. Many techniques and ideas are debated during this time. The Dual3D and Patch GAN models, which are based on 3D convolution and fuzzy C-means, are more profitable and require fewer data sets than the traditional GAN model. This approach does not need a precise match between medical imaging and a patient's condition. This is the result of the GAN model's popularity. The idea is to portray a sense of optimism and hopefulness while doing so. During the investigation, an underlying model is continually improved using transfer learning, 3D convolution, and Patch GAN. It is vital to discuss the potential of turning low-information medical pictures into high-information images, and we anxiously await more discoveries in this field. Improved network performance is required to generate medical images from a variety of fields.

Dataset. The dataset will be provided on request.

Conflicts of Interest. There is no potential conflict of interest.

Funding Statement. No funding was received for this study.

References

1. Dehghan-Dehnavi, S., Fotuhi-Firuzabad, M., Moeini-Aghtaie, M., Dehghanian, P., Wang, F.: Decision-making tree analysis for industrial load classification in demand response programs. IEEE Trans. Ind. Appl. **57**(1), 26–35 (2020)
2. Shaheen, M., Zafar, T., Sajid, A.K.: Decision tree classification: ranking journals using IGIDI. J. Inf. Sci. **46**(3), 325–339 (2020)
3. Nair, R., Bhagat, A.: An introduction to clustering algorithms in big data. In: Encyclopedia of Information Science and Technology, 5th edn., pp. 559–576 (2021). https://doi.org/10.4018/978-1-7998-3479-3.ch040
4. Shi, J., Yang, L.: A climate classification of China through k-nearest-neighbor and sparse subspace representation. J. Clim. **33**(1), 243–262 (2020)
5. Nair, R., et al.: Blockchain-based decentralized cloud solutions for data transfer. Comput. Intell. Neurosci. **2022**, 1–12 (2022). https://doi.org/10.1155/2022/8209854
6. Pareek, P.K., et al.: IntOPMICM: intelligent medical image size reduction model. J. Healthc. Eng. **2022** (2022). https://doi.org/10.1155/2022/5171016. Article ID 5171016, 11 pages
7. Kashyap, R.: Big data and high-performance analyses and processes. In: Research Anthology on Big Data Analytics, Architectures, and Applications, pp. 262–293 (2022). https://doi.org/10.4018/978-1-6684-3662-2.ch013
8. Tseng, B.W., Wu, P.Y.: Compressive privacy generative adversarial network. IEEE Trans. Inf. Forensics Secur. **15**, 2499–2513 (2020)
9. Kashyap, R.: Dilated residual grooming kernel model for breast cancer detection. Pattern Recogn. Lett. **159**, 157–164 (2022). https://doi.org/10.1016/j.patrec.2022.04.037
10. Phan, H., McLoughlin, I.V., Pham, L., et al.: Improving GANs for speech enhancement. IEEE Signal Process. Lett. **27**, 1700–1704 (2020)
11. Peng, W., Dai, Y.-H., Zhang, H., Cheng, L.: Training GANs with centripetal acceleration. Optim. Methods Softw. **35**(5), 955–973 (2020)
12. Kashyap, R.: Machine learning for internet of things. In: Research Anthology on Artificial Intelligence Applications in Security, pp. 976–1002 (2021). https://doi.org/10.4018/978-1-7998-7705-9.ch046
13. Mustafa, M.A., Khaleel, Z.I., Saab, N.G., Meri, M.A.: The role of microbial pathogens in infection of lung organs and spleen of laboratory albino rats. AIP Conf. Proc. **5**, 0182764 (2023). https://doi.org/10.1063/5.0182764
14. Mustafa, M.A., Taha, W.A., Shakir, O.M., Meri, M.A.: Study of some biochemical indicators levels in the people infected by Toxoplasma gondii. AIP Conf. Proc. **5**, 0182763 (2023). https://doi.org/10.1063/5.0182763
15. Mustafa, M.A., Govindarajan, S., Kiyosov, S., Duong, N.D., Raju, M.N., Gola, K.K.: RETRACTED: an optimization based feature extraction and machine learning techniques for named entity identification. Optik, 170348 (2023). https://doi.org/10.1016/j.ijleo.2022.170348
16. Zhang, L., Zhao, J., Ye, X., Chen, Y.: Cooperation: a new force for boosting generative adversarial nets with dual-network structure. IET Image Proc. **14**(6), 1073–1080 (2020)
17. Nair, R., Gupta, S., Soni, M., Kumar Shukla, P., Dhiman, G.: An approach to minimize the energy consumption during blockchain transaction. Mater. Today Proc. (2020). https://doi.org/10.1016/j.matpr.2020.10.361

18. Teng, L., Fu, Z., Yao, Y.: Interactive translation in echocardiography training system with enhanced cycle-GAN. IEEE Access **8**, 106147–106156 (2020)

19. Nair, R., Bhagat, A.: An application of big data analytics in road transportation. In: Advances in Systems Analysis, Software Engineering, and High-Performance Computing, pp. 39–54 (2018). https://doi.org/10.4018/978-1-5225-3870-7.ch003

20. Amirjavid, F., Barak, S., Nemati, H.: A fuzzy paradigmatic clustering algorithm. IFAC-PapersOnLine **52**(13), 2360–2365 (2019)

21. Bui, Q.T., Vo, B., Snasel, V., et al.: SFCM: a fuzzy clustering algorithm of extracting the shape information of data. IEEE Trans. Fuzzy Syst. **29**(1), 75–89 (2021)

22. Heidari, S., Abutalib, M.M., Alkhambashi, M., Farouk, A., Naseri, M.: A new general model for quantum image histogram (QIH). Quantum Inf. Process. **18**(6), 1–20 (2019)

23. Krishnamoorthi, R., et al.: A novel diabetes healthcare disease prediction framework using machine learning techniques. J. Healthc. Eng. **2022**, 1–10 (2022)

24. Ahmad, I., Serbaya, S.H., Rizwan, A., Mehmood, M.S.: Spectroscopic analysis for harnessing the quality and potential of gemstones for small and medium-sized enterprises (SMEs). J. Spectrosc. **2021**, 1–12 (2021)

Accurate and Fast Segmentation of MRI Images Using Multibranch Residual Fusion Network

Mohammed Ahmed Mustafa[1]([✉]), Abual-hassan Adel[2], Maki Mahdi Abdulhasan[3], Zainab Alassedi[4], Ghadir Kamil Ghadir[5], and Hayder Musaad Al-Tmimi[6]

[1] Department of Medical Laboratory Technology, University of Imam Jaafar AL-Sadiq, Baghdad, Iraq
Mohammed.ahmed.mustafa@sadiq.edu.iq
[2] Al-Manara College for Medical Sciences, Maysan, Amarah, Iraq
[3] Department of Medical Laboratories Technology, AL-Nisour University College, Baghdad, Iraq
[4] College of Computer, National University of Science and Technology, Dhi Qar, Nasiriyah, Iraq
[5] College of Pharmacy, Al-Farahidi University, Baghdad, Iraq
[6] Hayder Musaad Al-Tmimi, College of Health Medical Techniques, Al-Bayan University, Baghdad, Iraq

Abstract. Before moving on with the structural parts of the research magnetic resonance imaging (MRI) scan is required because of its ability to highlight morphological changes in the brain over time, it has given researchers a unique viewpoint on the dynamic process by which the mind grows and adapts over one's lifespan. As a result, they might have a more in-depth understanding of mental processes. The knowledge gathered in this manner has a monetary value that cannot be precisely represented. Because of the complexity of the data, the bulk of neuroimaging analytical pipelines rely on registration methods, which need labor- and time-intensive optimization processes. This is since mapping one image to another necessitates the use of registration procedures. The significance of registration in neuroimaging stems from the fact that this is the circumstance, which is why it exists. Recent deep learning algorithms have demonstrated the ability to accelerate the segmentation process. As an illustration, this is a risk because it raises the possibility of missing opportunities to precisely establish the boundaries of regions with uncertain borders. This is justified by the fact that giving up now would mean forfeiting the opportunity to accomplish anticipated future successes. This is especially crucial to remember when considering the challenge of multi-grained whole-brain segmentation, in which the size and structure of various parts of the brain might be highly diverse. We were able to make a deep learning network and use the information from this study to map the whole brain and figure out what its different parts are, this network can do so because it successfully partitions the brain. Given that its network can disassemble the brain into its constituent parts, this is a possibility. Our Multi-branch Residual Fusion Network (MRFNet) can quickly and precisely partition the whole brain into 136 subregions, making it far more efficient than the networks currently regarded to be the best in this field. The multi-branch cross-attention module (MCAM) allows for control over the organization's more granular levels. As a result, the following actions were taken: Even if they know the full name, most individuals just use its

M. Botto-Tobar et al. (Eds.): ICAT 2023, CCIS 2050, pp. 126–140, 2024.
https://doi.org/10.1007/978-3-031-58953-9_10

abbreviation while discussing it. It has chosen that one of its primary goals will be to organize and synthesize the large amounts of granular context data that it will receive, and it has set a timeframe for achieving this goal. Another proposal is to use something called a residual error fusion module (REFM). We chose two separate datasets to demonstrate the validity and usefulness of the approach we developed for dissecting the whole brain. This will be done by comparing the results of the two datasets. The results show that the Proposed method is a reliable and effective way to find important parts of neuroimages before they are studied.

Keywords: Image Segmentation · Deep Learning · Magnetic Resonance Imaging · Residual Dense Blocks · Multi-Branch Residual Fusion Network

1 Introduction

Neuroanatomical segmentation techniques must be employed to understand more about the causes of neurodegenerative illnesses and how an infant's brain grows over the course of their lifetime. The process of determining the size of the human brain and generating a precise picture of its anatomy is known as segmentation. The notion of "brain mapping" is also known as "segmentation". At this point, the scenario has been in place for quite some time. This is true in most situations. This has been the case for a very long time. You may access both programs through the internet if you like. This obligation will be fulfilled when the brain creates an updated, hand-drawn atlas [1]. Smoothing, nonlinear registration, careful parameter change, and image processing are all part of the process of numerical optimization. "Image processing" refers to the process of reviewing digital photos and improving their quality. Non-linear registration generally fails to deliver correct registration results because of the costly computation and extended execution time required. This problem is exacerbated by the fact that proper evaluation of the three-dimensional deformation field is a critical component of effective registration [2]. The estimate was written in such a way that this outcome was guaranteed. This is since producing an estimate requires a significant amount of time and effort on the part of the individual. Due to its limited effectiveness, the data segmentation approach in question is unsuitable for analyzing very large datasets. This is owing to the time necessary to process such a study. There is now a high need for brain segmentation algorithms that are both fast and precise [3]. This enables medical research to be conducted utilizing incredibly fine-grained divisions of the brain's architecture. The development of accurate and time-efficient whole-brain segmentation algorithms involves substantial challenges due to a variety of diverse factors. Among the difficulties are the brain's complicated three-dimensional design; the high dimensionality of neuroimaging data; the spatial interdependence between the numerous brain slices; and the unequal label distribution.

Deep learning algorithms have seen an increase in use in recent years, particularly for semantic segmentation of medical pictures. It is expected that things will continue in the same manner. This aim can be accomplished by using computer programs. This concept, for example, may be used in the process of localizing brain lesions. Convolutional neural network (CNNs) based approaches provide insight into how to explore the brain in its entirety, from the earliest stages to the most advanced [4]. This study may be used at any stage of brain development. The brain may be dissected into microscopic parts, and the findings obtained using this method are more dependable than atlas-based procedures. Our technique, which employs a deep fully convolutional neural network, is capable of swiftly and accurately analyzing 3D MRI T1 brain data. This might result in both the completion of larger-scale segmentation projects and an improvement to the segmentation process. FastSurfer [5] improves on previous efforts to construct accurate spatial representations. This is made possible using a competition block and the addition of a more detailed background inside each slice. The researchers who conducted the study are mentioned in the preceding phrase. This measure was taken to ensure that the events at hand were appropriately depicted. This precaution was taken to ensure that the However, there are several gaps in this study, such as how difficult border scenarios and items with odd forms were handled. These are only two examples.

MRF-Net is an innovative method for constructing networks that can dissect things into their essential pieces with this approach, it may just take a few seconds to entirely remove the parenchyma from a person's whole brain. To increase the quality of our network, we will most likely need to update the multi-grained representations, notably the fuzzy borders. There is no need to repeat what was stated in the paragraph preceding this one on the approaches that are presently being used [6]. One of the greatest ways to express what we've given is as follows: To address the issue of geographical places whose physical characteristics greatly depart from the norm; We designed a multi-tiered technique for splitting our focus across many areas. This is done to improve the accuracy of the marginal representations. These enhancements were made possible using residual errors. The diligent work of the REFM can be directly attributed to this result. We were able to attain our objectives because we decided to ignore some shortcomings [7]. As noted in the paragraph preceding this one, the efficacy of this module is backed by tests and assessments performed on two independent datasets. The outcomes of the dataset analysis lend support to this theory. These outcomes may be observed by comparing the two sets of data. Because of this, we can say with certainty that the strategy works better than what we are doing now.

2 Background

Traditional Brain Partitioning Methods Some specialized tools for whole-brain segmentation support the MRI processing pipeline. The designers of the program do routine maintenance. These pipelines are known by several names, including FreeSurfer, FSL, BrainSuite, and ANTs, among others [8]. These pipelines identify distinct sections of the brain using atlas-based models and registration approaches, which increases the amount of processing necessary to accomplish different graphical modifications. Compilations for atlas-based models are often time-consuming. Inference, text analysis, and image recognition have all grown significantly in recent years, deep learning may be applied to improve comprehension of lesions, chaotic patterns, and morphological evaluations, to mention a few [9]. These are only a few of the numerous deep learning applications currently available. Medical imaging is one application area where deep learning has been effectively used. When it comes to extracting data from medical images, the UNet system performs admirably. The primary focus of future research has turned to network performance optimization over a wide range of diverse configurations to achieve the ultimate objective of outperforming UNet. This was done to provide clients access to more functionality than UNet provided. The research described in this paper inspired the development of various new networks, including "UNet++," and "UNet3+,". To accept and maintain semantic data, networks such as UNet use the skip connection technique at both the upper and lower levels of the network [10]. This activity is carried out by both the top and bottom levels of the network. This strategy is used not only in strategic but also in operational planning. You will be able to accomplish the project efficiently if you follow this strategy, which allows you to manage both the basic and difficult components of the assignment. Getting rid of unnecessary structures quickly raises the accuracy of the learning model while lowering the parameters. It directly makes learned representations more accurate, which is why it does this. There had to be 3D segmentation networks because most medical shots are taken in 3D [11] say that 3D-UNet and V-Net-like networks have been made by other academics. These networks have moved forward thanks to their better three-dimensional design. They have become so popular that they have sometimes replaced two-dimensional methods. 3D feature maps are hard to compute, which means they can't be used in many common situations. This impediment inhibits the widespread application of 3D technology. This is especially important to keep in mind while engaging in activities that rely heavily on the extensive circulation of visual material [12] created 2.5D segmentation methods that make use of several 2D slices as input. The major purpose of doing so was to shorten the time required for processing. This is done to shorten the total time necessary to complete the activity as much as feasible. These segmentation algorithms need little processing resources, yet they may maintain the accuracy of the local geographic environment [13]. Because of the circumstances, we took special care to conduct our research in such a way that the conclusions would be not only more accurate but also immediately applicable to the world as it is.

Several deep learning networks have recently been constructed, each with the goal of building a map of the whole human brain. This map will be used to better understand human behavior. This map will be utilized during clinical studies. This has been the primary goal of artificial intelligence research. They designed these systems and oversaw their construction. A 3D network-based segmentation strategy is not possible for any photos that are not among the most challenging images due to the quantity of processing required [14]. Prior work must be completed before the algorithm may be utilized to analyze anything that happens in the real world. Because these preprocessing procedures generate errors that inhibit their use, they are difficult to apply in computer systems that use massively parallel computation. It was long thought that physically segmenting a convolutional network from start to finish would be impossible. This notion persisted for a long time. Despite this, SD-Net was the first technology to achieve this goal. Even though the human brain may be divided into 27 categories, this approach is rarely employed because it was the first of its kind developed the QuickNAT technique, which is a method for anatomically segmenting the whole brain. Combining these three distinct SD-Net-based viewpoints can considerably increase forecast accuracy. FastSurfer is without a doubt the most sophisticated CNN for whole-brain segmentation currently available. When compared to QuickNAT's performance, as seen above, it obviously shows an advantage. It is strongly encouraged to use competitive dense blocks rather than the more typical common dense blocks (CDB). Furthermore, instead of attempting to exceed the competition by avoiding it, you should focus on determining how to gain from it. The ability of FastSurfer to separate human cognition into 95 distinct subfields opens the door to a wide range of possible medical applications. The partition of the brain into several subregions, each of which oversees a separate function, is an example of this type of application.

3 Proposed Method

Evaluate the system components in charge of its functioning as well as how those components communicate with one another. During our investigation, we collected two distinct sets of data to share our findings with others, determine their feasibility, and assess how well they worked. You should be aware that possible group members' attributes such as age and gender will be considered during the selection process. Each dataset is initially divided into three distinct subsets, making the analysis process more efficient. The training phase accounts for 70% of the total, while the validation phase accounts for 15% and the testing phase accounts for 15%. The type of scanner, the intensity of the magnetic field, and the acquisition settings are strongly linked to the number of healthy controls in each group. JHU is a collection of 136 T1 brain MRIs from people aged 22 to 90, and it is part of the Johns Hopkins University Brain Atlas. After MRICloud cut the pictures into 136 pieces, radiologists carefully fixed each one. Researchers at Johns Hopkins University used 3T Philips cameras and MPRAGE to gather information. It is possible to get a one-millimeter isotropic precision with these measures [15]. Alzheimer's is a disease The American Neuroimaging Initiative (ADNI), which is the main group in this area, uses imaging to help us learn more about the sickness. We can better understand Alzheimer's now. The ADNI collection was put together using a reliable method from previous study. It has 5074 T1 MRI pictures of the whole brain divided into 138 brain areas. The ADNI dataset was used to investigate how the brain changes as people get older. ADNI was used to study TBI-AD at least two packets were lost or could not be found in every set of data.

Figure 1 shows the links between nodes in a multi-node residual fusion network. It shows that MRFs and Nets are made up of encoder-decoder pairs. For 2.5D image segmentation, you need an axial or coronal slice of the source picture that has seven slices. These cuts help show areas of the image that need to be separated. Any method will work. This method is now the only way to send input. You can make a world that helps you focus on problems with meditation slices.

On the right, you can see the whole color scheme that was used to display the various tactics, and by clicking on any of them, you can learn more about that specific approach.

3.1 Residual Matter Dense Particles

These residual dense blocks are constructed using three convolution layers and 64 channels. It is reasonable to state that residual dense blocks play a vital role in the design of encoders and decoders. Both the encoder and the decoder use many data shards in their

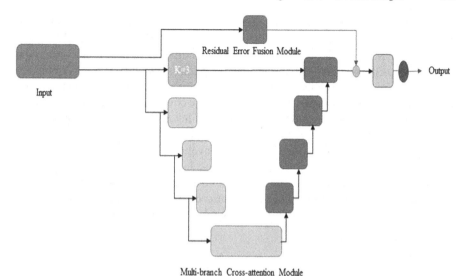

Fig. 1. The connections between the many nodes that comprise a multi-node residual fusion network.

production. Fastsurfer CNN enhances the dense block residual using a convolutional dense block (CDB), sometimes known as a CDB [16]. The remaining dense blocks given by a convolution layer are what result in the short-distance residual connections. According to reports, the CDB's densely populated heart will be relocated to this cluster of blocks. There is no upper limit to the amount of data that may be kept on a CDB at any given moment. CDB's prior pattern of behavior, which entailed achieving its maximum, has been replaced by this new pattern of activity. In the first situation, it would have behaved similarly to peaking. Before proceeding, ensure that the convolution kernel size is always set to 3. A grey strip separates the N-1 and 2–3 forking possibilities in the bottom feature.

3.2   Residual Error Fusion Module

It is believed that representations of the properties of the boundaries of each brain area would be enhanced. Data collecting on the local geographic constraints of each brain area is one of the approaches we are using to create a more precise picture of the defining elements of the borders of each brain area. This is something we're thinking about as a possible strategy. In the seven-slice image processing pipeline, the fourth slice enters the branch that comes before the branch that comes just after the last one. Therefore, the encoding step, which occurs in the branch immediately following the last one, can profit from the fourth slice. Once the outputs of the previous slices have cancelled each other out, the fourth slice's output is added to the outputs of the three slices that came before it. The many tree branches are made with the help of two stages of convolutional processing and a scSE attention module. The scSE component's two subcomponents, channel attention and spatial attention, can then be split further. Resolving Differences in a Complex Organization (with a dilation of two and a group size of seven, respectively) reassembling previously separated components to form new wholes (with a group size of seven and a dilation of four) The convolution demonstrates both a four-stage dilation and a seven-step cascade. Concatenating a seven-degree dilation with a group convolution yields a group convolution [17–19]. Grouping and convolution are coupled (group size = 7, dilation size = 4). In addition, we use a convolutional group approach (with a group size of seven and a dilation size of four) To finish the concatenation, group convolution with a group size of seven di was utilized. The classifier obtains feature mappings from each of the five subtrees using a process known as cascading. To enhance the network's receptive area, dilated convolution and group convolution can be utilized. You will be able to do so without increasing the quantity of data lost due to ambiguity. One solution to this problem is to enlarge the network's coverage area. This component provides users with access to the border detail's characteristics and data at various sizes. Figure 2, which is now displayed, provides a more detailed picture of the Residual Error Fusion Module's architecture.

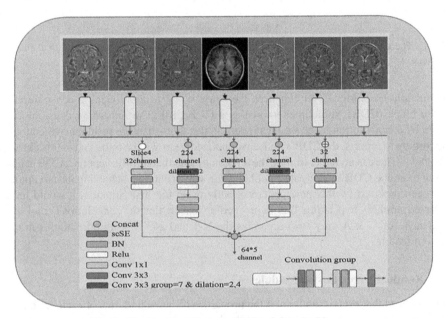

Fig. 2. The Residual Error Fusion Module's Architecture

3.3   An Attention Multiplier Dispersed Throughout the Brain

The MCAM may have up to three branch decoders, each with a different kernel size that provides more precise information about the environment. All this structural connectivity is enabled by a cross-attention module that supports the blending and synthesis of information on several levels. This module is also responsible for all the structural connectivity. It should be mentioned for clarity that the decoder (a) is used to evaluate the system's efficacy [20, 21]. The ensemble is made up of a single limb that revolves around a triangle convolution kernel of any size. The kernel size of these blocks' ranges from 2 to 4, with the largest having a kernel size of 5. Furthermore, each of the branches continues to encounter significant challenges. At the conclusion of the day, two feature maps will be created, one from each fork, because of the process of combining the encoder's output features with those of the encoder itself. These maps will then be merged. When the cross-attention module has finished processing these feature maps, the next convolution group will process them further. The kernel sizes of the dense blocks can be 3, 5, or 7 depending on which of the decoder's three (c) branches is used. These are the unsold construction supplies in the warehouse. These maps will incorporate both an up sample and multiscale data. This will be done to ensure that the knowledge is completely digested. These feature maps will then be transmitted to the convolutional processing layer that follows. The decoder can attain the maximum level of segmentation accuracy theoretically attainable.

4 Results

We compared our recently created MRF-Net to cutting-edge FastSurferCNN, UNet++ and UNet 3+. Table 1 depicts the standard Hausdorff distance between dice pairs from the validation set, whereas Table 2 depicts the same distance between dice pairs from the test set. Both tables provide the same information. Positive findings were highlighted and placed in a separate section to emphasize their potential relevance. This was done to illustrate their potential. When we tested our proposed MRF-Net with the decoder, we discovered that it had the best accuracy (86.00%) and dice score (81.70%) on the JHU/ADNI dataset. The outcomes of our assessments were considered, and it was concluded that this was the best course of action to adopt. The techniques' success in segmenting the brain is provided as evidence of this. Deep learning algorithms that have recently been developed have the potential to improve the speed and accuracy of neuroimaging processing systems by adding novel ideas. New data is being added to aid in the achievement of this goal.

Table 1. The Dice scores Comparison of the traditional methods and Proposed method on JHU and ADNI

Dice	JHU		ADNI	
	Validation	Test	Validation	Test
Fast Surfer	80.94 + −4.19	81.30 + −5.33	85.75 + −5.61	85.83 + −2.81
Unet++	81.19 + −4.21	81.23 + −6.79	86.37 + −5.85	86.81 + −3.18
Unet+++	81.68 + −4.12	82.50 + −4.22	86.92 + −4.98	86.46 + −3.31
MRF NET + decoder(b)(ours)	82.21 + −3.00	82.47 + −3.06	87.46 + −4.87	86.95 + −2.55
MRF NET + decoder(c)(ours)	82.47 + −4.10	82.81 + −2.68	87.56 + −5.45	87.11 + −0.94

Table 1 gives an overview of the four comparison networks' average Dice scores and a summary of what was found about axial segmentation. We also investigated the many ways in which the ablative treatment altered the disease. Remember that there are no other planes, so the 2.5D segmentation algorithms can only be used on the sagittal plane. Convolutions are unable to discriminate between spatial information stored in the left and right hemispheres of the brain due to this direct cause-and-effect relationship. This criterion cannot be applied to it since the coronal plane consistently outperforms the axial plane on these datasets. Examining the MRF-Net results on the JHU datasets will show this. The three tables show that these results are consistent with one another. These rises have been seen in both the coronal and axial planes. The approach proposed may successfully segment the biplane brain in an efficient manner. Table 2 and 3 shows the results of the axial and coronal segmentations.

Table 2. Summarizes the axial segmentation, coronal segmentation, and average dice score results.

Hausdorff	JHU		ADNI	
	Axial	Coronal	Axial	Coronal
Fast Surfer	79.83 + −3.08	80.04 + −3.09	84.64 + −4.50	85.40 + −2.87
Unet++	80.08 + −3.10	80.28 + −3.11	85.26 + −4.74	86.15 + −1.94
Unet+++	80.57 + −3.10	80.76 + −3.04	85.81 + −3.87	86.26 + −3.67
MRF NET + decoder(b)(ours)	81.10 + −2.99	81.20 + −3.01	86.35 + −3.76	86.46 + −2.02
MRF NET + decoder(c)(ours)	81.36 + −3.09	81.26 + −3.04	86.45 + −4.34	86.68 + −1.92

Table 3. The average Hausdorff gap between the coronal and axial segmentation findings was observed.

Hausdorff	JHU		ADNI	
	Axial	Coronal	Axial	Coronal
Fast Surfer	0.299 + −0.046	0.287 + −0.048	0.266 + −0.239	0.219 + −0.053
Unet++	0.292 + −0.053	0.274 + −0.052	0.427 + −0.422	0.200 + −0.051
Unet+++	0.269 + −0.051	0.257 + −0.049	0.399 + −0.315	0.197 + −0.061
MRF NET + decoder(b)(ours)	0.272 + −0.045	0.259 + −0.047	0.203 + −0.102	0.189 + −0.043
MRF NET + decoder(c)(ours)	0.261 + −0.045	0.255 + −0.050	0.201 + −0.170	0.183 + −0.040

4.1 Ablation Study

The outcomes of our ablation research indicate that residual dense blocks, REFM, and MCAM might all be useful techniques. To begin with, we conducted an experiment to discover if any exceptionally large chunks remained approachable. The experiment's findings, which demonstrated how good the backbone was at whole-brain segmentation, are displayed alongside the data from the other four networks that were evaluated. Figure 1 depicts Resnet50 network examples, these two networks' decoders begin with the letter "an". The Resnet50 plus decoder(a) is specifically connected to the network using the following connection method: The resnet50 decoder (a) does not merge the first, second-, and third layers output feature maps until after the first and second upsampling, which reset the size to its beginning dimensions. This stage is completed before executing the upsampling procedure. In the vgg16 + decoder(a) architecture, the decoder (a) performs the linking function by concatenating the feature maps created at each layer of the vgg16 network. Table 4 illustrates that there is no relationship between performance increases and backbone complexity. However, the performance of our MRF-Net + decoder (a) is comparable to or better than that of FastsurferCNN. According to our findings, preserving information that is both complicated and semantically high-level does not increase whole-brain segmentation accuracy much. Because of our research, we have come to this conclusion. So, the next phase of testing will focus mostly on the decoding process and the low-level semantic data it creates.

Table 4. Comparative Dice Values of the traditional versus the Proposed Network

Dice	JHU	ADNI
Resnet 50 + decoder(a)	80.77 + −4.19	84.16 + −5.67
VGG16 + decoder(a)	80.54 + −3.05	83.56 + −5.05
FastsurferCNN	80.94 + −4.19	85.75 + −5.61
MRF-Net + decoder (a) (w/o REFM)	81.43 + −4.31	86.40 + −5.28

Table 4 shows the results of performing the Dice test on each of the four unique networks.

In the second trial, we concentrated on ablative therapies such as REFM and MCAM. The Dice scores of the seven networks in relation to the two datasets are shown in Fig. 3. Figure 3 depicts the encoder and decoder models, as well as additional information on the context of each of the seven networks. When paired with supplementary input boundary information and employed in this context, REFM can be beneficial for segmenting fuzzily defined borders between distinct parts of the brain. Networks A and B are excellent instances of this phenomenon. One approach is to aid in the segmentation of brain areas with uncertain borders. In terms of whole-brain segmentation, network C surpasses network B, which only has one branch. The existence of numerous branches affects Network C's performance. This is due to network C's having several subnets. The cross-attention module can aid in the shift from network C to network E, which performs better and so contributes to improved performance. By sliding your mouse over the network diagram, you can see that network D is connected to network E in a way that clearly shows an increasing trend. There is an obvious distinction between Network E and Network F, and their dice scores are comparable. This is true even if there is a distinct rising pattern connecting networks D and E. When the intermediate layer kernels of two branches differ, multi-grained contextual information may be able to improve segmentation performance while utilizing fewer parameters. This is the case when there is an intermediate branch. This is because in this scenario, fewer factors must be considered.

If a decoder does not explicitly state that it is "(without REFM)," it does not have a residual error fusion module pre-installed. The initial encoder is followed by a series of distinct decoders. A table at the very bottom of the image has a detailed correspondence chart for the letters and the networks that connect them. This table may be seen at the bottom of the picture. These letters serve as a visual depiction of the links between the image's many aspects. The decoder in this example lacks a cross-attention module, as denoted by the notation (w/o), and the intermediate layer's convolution kernel sizes are $(3, 3)$ and $(k = 5, 5)$, indicating that the decoder's two branches were trained separately. According to the notation (w/o), the intermediate layer convolution kernel sizes for the decoder are $(3, 3)$ and $(k = 5, 5)$. The decoder makes use of these two integers throughout its investigation. $(5, 5)$. There are two distinct notations for this on the list, and you may encounter each of them at different times. An Investigation into the Meaning of Dependability using the ICC technique, we were able to compare the two test groups side by side (intraclass correlation).

Figure 3 depicts the intraclass correlation coefficient for a collection of ten unique structures obtained using each of the four separate techniques like MRF-Net, Fastsurfer, Unet++, and Unet+++ (Huang et al., 2020). When a significance level of 0.05 is used as the criterion, the upper and lower limits are shown in a tone like dark gray. Performance levels closer to one are desirable, and the ICC score shows how confident one is in the processes used. The findings obtained using both datasets suggest that the MRF-Net we developed beats the three previously used approaches based on these structures. Both the left and right inferior lateral ventricles' inter-correlation coefficient (ICC) values are found to be within acceptable limits (ICC values greater than 0.975). The inferior lateral portions of each ventricle may be affected. However, the consistent improvements show that the proposed strategy outperforms earlier techniques that were thought to be state-of-the-art. This is true even though the information in the two databases is of variable quality. The most significant thing to take away from these enhancements is that they illustrate why the proposed solution is superior to alternative options. The fact that the MRF-ability Net produces smaller confidence intervals than competing techniques supports the claim that it can deliver more trustworthy segmentations. These results demonstrate unequivocally that the MRF-ability Net outperforms the current approaches.

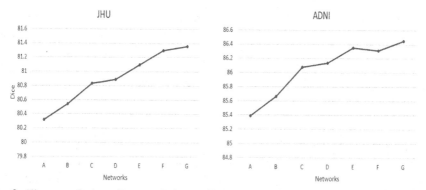

Fig. 3. Illustrates the intraclass correlation coefficient for each of the four methodologies used to examine the segmented structural volume of 10 distinct types of structures.

When computing the intercorrelation coefficient (ICC) with a significance threshold of 0.05, the error bars show the most likely and least likely values that might have been achieved. The inferior temporal gyrus (ITG), hippocampal formation (HCF), inferior lateral ventricle (ILV), left hemisphere (LH), and right hemisphere (RH) each have their own separate acronym (RH). For example, ITG stands for "inferior temporal gyrus" (RH). Furthermore, the Pearson correlation coefficient (PCC) and intraclass correlation coefficient (ICC) values of distinct people and groups are compared (PCC). The findings of the comparisons are supplied in the form of an even more complete study in Table 5 which are displayed below.

Table 5. Individual and group-level volume estimates using the intraclass correlation coefficient

Methods	JHU		ADNI	
	PCC	P-value	Individual PCC	p-value
Fast Surfer	0.9789 + −0.0587	–	0.9864 + −0.0054	–
Unet++	0.8742 + −0.0355	0.223	0.8864 + −0.0049	0.2481
Unet+++	0.9776 + −0.976	<0.002	0.8849 + −0.0040	0.0592
The Proposed Method	0.9712 + −0.0198	0.359	0.8866 + −0.0058	0.034

The segmentation volume scores and ground truth scores for each picture are compared to provide tailored comparisons. The average test score and standard deviation from the mean for each participant are then computed. To complete the group level comparison, measurements were obtained throughout the whole data set for each different brain area. A previous study by Henschel and colleagues reveals that the values offered represent the global average for cognitive ability (2020). Furthermore, statistical scores are employed to demonstrate that the new way outperforms the FastSurfer methodology, demonstrating that the updated strategy is ultimately more trustworthy. Pairwise tests are used to determine if the improvements are statistically significant. The ADNI dataset has a considerable impact on both the individual nodes that comprise our proposed MRF-Net and the network. The FastSurfer result of 0.0223 is a significant improvement above the 0.9977 ICC score recorded for each image. Furthermore, MRF-Net has the highest PCC ratings of the four processes, indicating that its results are more accurate than the other three techniques combined. These findings were obtained by combining the previous three procedures. Both sets of data reveal that there has been a consistent and noticeable growth (the JHU dataset shows a p value of 0.001 while the ADNI dataset shows a value of 0.033). Both the JHU dataset and the ADNI dataset yielded statistically significant results (p 0.001 and p 0.033, respectively). The intraclass correlation coefficient (ICC), which was used on both individuals and groups, was used to estimate the volumes in Table 6. Extensive testing revealed that the MRF-Net, the network we developed for brain segmentation, beat any CNN-based solution in terms of both accuracy and processing speed. These trials demonstrate that MRF-Net has great overall performance and can accurately segment a T1 brain MRI into 136 separate areas. Our neural network can finish the segmentation in less than a minute (on the GPU), and the following preprocessing is kept to a bare minimum. Traditional photo segmentation algorithms may take a long time to complete. For segmentation FreeSurfer and FSL need more complicated registration procedures. This has a direct impact on the amount of time necessary for photo editing. Defining the settings for these procedures is a critical stage in the photo registration process. The utility of these technologies is further limited by the fact that this stage demands a substantial number of picture iterations. Researchers must have a deep grasp of both the user interface of the program or instrument as well as all the precise parameter settings. This may take some time to complete. Deep learning, a recently proposed approach, has immense potential in this situation. It offers a wide range of applications and does not need complex parameter sets or long inference procedures.

5 Conclusion

According to the results of the ablation experiment, there is no evidence that the strengthened backbone network increased the model's accuracy. This is because the specifics are more likely to come under the category of "low-level semantics" than any of the high-level semantic knowledge categories. This is because the specifics are more likely to come under the category of "low-level semantics." We may say this to delve deeper into the situation. The findings of an ablation investigation demonstrate that the ResNet and VGG networks lacked deep convolutional layers when they were initially constructed. At this point of learning, the ResNet network utilizes just one convolutional layer with max pooling, whereas the VGG network uses two convolutional layers at initialization. In contrast to the initial VGG network iteration, which only employed two of these types of layers, this network features three convolutional layers in total. After examining these two approaches, validating the data, and concluding our work, we disclosed the ICC and PCC values discovered because of our research. These two metrics demonstrate that the MRF-segmentation net yields more accurate results than the other approaches. A tabular examination of the ICC values gathered from various brain regions during various activities is also shown. Nobody should be shocked that the performance of our solutions outperforms that of FastSurfer. This is only a guess, but it is likely that the reason has something to do with the fact that both MCAM and REFM have optimized a wide variety of structures and fuzzy boundaries. However, this is only a concept. Regardless, there is a very good likelihood that this is merely a coincidence. Our self-learning MRF-Net might one day be used in cutting-edge brain mapping. Scientists can even develop their own segmentation models if they like. We can confidently assume that our discoveries will have a significant influence on the field of neurology. The drug's therapeutic efficacy will be evaluated in a larger patient sample, which will include people with advanced Alzheimer's disease whose bodies have lost structural integrity because of the disease's progression.

Data Availability. Weichonghit. (n.d.). Weichonghit/BRAIN_SEG: Whole-brain segmentation code for eval. GitHub. Retrieved October 5, 2022, from https://github.com/weichonghit/brain_seg.git.

References

1. Agrawal, M., Kumar Shukla, P., Nair, R., Nayyar, A., Masud, M.: Stock prediction based on technical indicators using deep learning model. Comput. Mater. Continua **70**(1), 287–304 (2022). https://doi.org/10.32604/cmc.2022.014637
2. Avants, B.B., Tustison, N., Song, G.: Advanced normalization tools (ants). Insight J. **2**, 1–35 (2009). https://doi.org/10.54294/uvnhin
3. Çiçek, Ö., Abdulkadir, A., Lienkamp, S.S., Brox, T., Ronneberger, O.: 3D u-net: learning dense volumetric segmentation from sparse annotation. In: Ourselin, S., Joskowicz, L., Sabuncu, M.R., Unal, G., Wells, W. (eds.) Medical Image Computing and Computer-Assisted Intervention – MICCAI 2016: 19th International Conference, Athens, Greece, October 17-21, 2016, Proceedings, Part II, pp. 424–432. Springer International Publishing, Cham (2016). https://doi.org/10.1007/978-3-319-46723-8_49
4. Dou, H., Karimi, D., Rollins, C.K., Ortinau, C.M., Gholipour, A.: A deep attentive convolutional neural network for automatic cortical plate segmentation in fetal MRI. arXiv:2004.12847 (2020). https://doi.org/10.1109/TMI.2020.3046579
5. Fischl, B., et al.: Whole brain segmentation: automated labeling of neuroanatomical structures in the human brain. Neuron **33**, 341–355 (2002). https://doi.org/10.1016/S0896-6273(02)00569-X
6. He, K., Zhang, X., Ren, S., Sun, J.: Deep residual learning for image recognition. In: Proceedings of the IEEE Conference on Computer Vision and Pattern Recognition (Las Vegas, NV: IEEE), pp. 770–778 (2016)
7. Mustafa, M.A., et al.: Adsorption behavior of Rh-doped graphdiyne monolayer towards various gases: a quantum mechanical analysis. Inorg. Chem. Commun. **160**, 111928 (2024). https://doi.org/10.1016/j.inoche.2023.111928
8. Mustafa, M.A., et al.: The potential of 2D carbon nitride monolayer as an efficient adsorbent for capturing mercury: a DFT study. Diamond Relat. Mater. **141**, 110566 (2024). https://doi.org/10.1016/j.diamond.2023.110566
9. Mustafa, M.A., Alabbasy, R.H., Azeez, A.K., Meri, M.A.: Histological study of the effect of some oncology drugs on heart muscle. AIP Conf. Proc. **2977**, 040024 (2023). https://doi.org/10.1063/5.0182762
10. Isensee, F., et al.: nnu-net: self-adapting framework for u-net-based medical image segmentation. arXiv preprint arXiv:1809.10486 (2018). https://doi.org/10.1007/978-3-658-25326-4_7

11. Kashyap, R.: Object boundary detection through robust active contour based method with global information. Int. J. Image Min. **3**(1), 22 (2018). https://doi.org/10.1504/ijim.2018.100 14063

12. Kashyap, R.: Big data analytics challenges and solutions. In: Big Data Analytics for Intelligent Healthcare Management, pp. 19–41 (2019).https://doi.org/10.1016/b978-0-12-818146-1.000 02-7

13. Kashyap, R.: Machine learning for internet of things. In: Comşa, I.S., Trestian, R. (eds.) Next-Generation Wireless Networks Meet Advanced Machine Learning Applications, pp. 57–83. IGI Global (2019). https://doi.org/10.4018/978-1-5225-7458-3.ch003

14. Ledig, C., Schuh, A., Guerrero, R., Heckemann, R.A., Rueckert, D.: Dataset-structural brain imaging in alzheimer's disease and mild cognitive impairment: biomarker analysis and shared morphometry database. Sci. Rep. **8**, 11258 (2018). https://doi.org/10.1038/s41598-018-292 95-9

15. Mueller, S.G., et al.: Ways toward an early diagnosis in alzheimer's disease: the alzheimer's disease neuroimaging initiative (ADNI). Alzheimers Dement. **1**, 55–66 (2005). https://doi. org/10.1016/j.jalz.2005.06.003

16. Nair, R., Bhagat, A.: An introduction to clustering algorithms in big data. Encycl. Inf. Sci. Technol. Fifth Ed. 559–576 (2021). https://doi.org/10.4018/978-1-7998-3479-3.ch040

17. Nair, R., Sharma, P., Sharma, T.: Optimizing the performance of IOT using FPGA as compared to GPU. Int. J. Grid High Perform. Comput. **14**(1), 1–15 (2022). https://doi.org/10.4018/ijg hpc.301580

18. Ronneberger, O., Fischer, P., Brox, T.: U-net: convolutional networks for biomedical image segmentation. In: Navab, N., Hornegger, J., Wells, W.M., Frangi, A.F. (eds.) Medical Image Computing and Computer-Assisted Intervention – MICCAI 2015: 18th International Conference, Munich, Germany, October 5-9, 2015, Proceedings, Part III, pp. 234–241. Springer International Publishing, Cham (2015). https://doi.org/10.1007/978-3-319-24574-4_28

19. Roy, A.G., Conjeti, S., Navab, N., Wachinger, C., Initiative, A.D.N., et al.: Quicknat: a fully convolutional network for quick and accurate segmentation of neuroanatomy. Neuroimage **186**, 713–727 (2019). https://doi.org/10.1016/j.neuroimage.2018.11.042

20. Sakalle, A., et al.: Genetic programming-based feature selection for emotion classification using EEG Signal. J. Healthc. Eng. **2022**, 1–6 (2022). https://doi.org/10.1155/2022/8362091

21. Tiwari, S., Gupta, R.K., Kashyap, R.: To enhance web response time using agglomerative clustering technique for web navigation recommendation. In: Behera, H.S., Nayak, J., Naik, B., Abraham, A. (eds.) Computational Intelligence in Data Mining. AISC, vol. 711, pp. 659–672. Springer, Singapore (2019). https://doi.org/10.1007/978-981-10-8055-5_59

Voice Pathology Detection Demonstrates the Integration of AI and IoT in Smart Healthcare

Mohammed Ahmed Mustafa[1], Abual-hassan Adel[2], Maki Mahdi Abdulhasan[3], Zainab Alassedi[4], Ghadir Kamil Ghadir[5]([✉]), and Hayder Musaad Al-Tmimi[6]

[1] Department of Medical Laboratory Technology, University of Imam Jaafar AL-Sadiq, Baghdad, Iraq

[2] Al-Manara College for Medical Sciences, Maysan, Amarah, Iraq

[3] Department of Medical Laboratories Technology, AL-Nisour University College, Baghdad, Iraq

[4] College of Computer, National University of Science and Technology, Dhi Qar, Nasiriyah, Iraq

[5] College of Pharmacy, Al-Farahidi University, Baghdad, Iraq
zaidkhalid92@yahoo.com

[6] College of Health Medical Techniques, Al-Bayan University, Baghdad, Iraq

Abstract. An artificial intelligence discipline has lately made considerable strides toward fully autonomous systems for classification and detection. Furthermore, with the aid of 5G networking and other next-generation wireless communications, the speed at which users may transport data while being undetectable to end users will increase. Because of a confluence of variables, the intelligent healthcare business is booming. There has never been a greater need for medical personnel to focus on the needs of their patients than today, in the aftermath of the COVID-19 epidemic. The pre-outbreak condition has changed dramatically. Vocal pathology accounts for a significant share of the population's communication issues. If detected early enough, this illness is treatable and curable. This paper proposes a strategy for recognizing speech difficulties in the context of a hypothetical intelligent healthcare network. Devices used to capture speech activity, such as microphones and electroglottography (EGG) sensors, can be used to collect input for the Internet of Things (IoT). Before putting the input into a previously trained convolutional neural network, the signals are converted to spectrograms. The efficacy of the presented technique was proved by comparing the results to the publicly available Saarbrucken voice database. According to the experimental data, a bimodal input outperforms a single input in almost every regard. The recommended strategy has a 95.65% success rate, according to research.

Keywords: Convolution Neural Network · Deep Learning · Electroglottography · Internet of Things · Smart Healthcare · Vocal Pathology Detection

© The Author(s), under exclusive license to Springer Nature Switzerland AG 2024
M. Botto-Tobar et al. (Eds.): ICAT 2023, CCIS 2050, pp. 141–155, 2024.
https://doi.org/10.1007/978-3-031-58953-9_11

1 Introduction

Many people suffer from vocal problems because of the widespread use of people's voices in today's culture. Educators, students, musicians, and legal professionals are among those who are routinely presented with these difficulties [1]. People's voices hold a multitude of information, and as a result, they reveal a lot about their mental and physical health. Several abnormal growths in the vocal folds, such as polyps, nodules, cysts, and sulci, can cause voice abnormalities [2]. Some of the most common signs of speech pathology are a hoarse voice that doesn't go away, a scratchy throat, speaking too loudly, and a decreased ability to speak clearly. Analytical or empirical approaches might be used to analyse concerns with one's speech or voice. The GRBAS (grade, roughness, breathiness, asthenia, strain) scale measures roughness, breathiness, tiredness, and other characteristics in speech. However, because these techniques of assessment are extensively utilised in clinical practice, there are certain constraints put on the analytical test. Because the auditory exam didn't work, doctors and researchers came up with the speech recognition meter, which is a better way to measure how much dysphonia a patient has [3].

An acoustic exam can give you numbers about how bad the problem is and a treatment plan, which you can then share with other people who need to know. The continuous vowel does not have this impact. It is crucial to acquire the capacity to detect specific defects to successfully diagnose and resolve problems with vocal pathology detection (VPD) technologies. The VPD technique is only effective with sustained vowels, which are vowels that remain in the speech stream for six to nine seconds. Individuals should employ continuous expression rather than extensive speech while chatting about everyday concerns. Voice impairments can be caused by a variety of situations and circumstances, including mental health issues, traumatic events, physical disorders, and diseases [4]. Speech disorders, in general, do not endanger one's life and are not difficult to treat. One of the most common causes of speech impairment is the employment of incorrect vocal practices. Stuttering and lisping are two more reasons for speech difficulty. Following on from the preceding discussion, we may conclude that it is necessary to analyse vocal pathology as soon as it reveals itself. Within the scope of this study, we build a VPD system within the context of intelligent healthcare. The technology makes use of EGG signals as well as spoken signals. A model combining long short-term memory (LSTM) is used to integrate the properties. To evaluate and rank individual voices fairly, there must be trustworthy techniques for gauging voice quality. Auditory-perceptual exams of voice problems may be valuable diagnostic tools. Laryngoscopes should not be used as the primary diagnostic tool when screening people with laryngopharyngeal symptoms. Limiting the natural vibrating of the larynx might be one of the various ways to change your voice. Voice changes can also occur because; There may be no warning signs or symptoms at all, or there may be more than one, depending on the origin of the vocal issue. Researchers studied 99 people who had polyps, cysts, or nodules on their vocal folds. Biomechanical data was extracted from a sound sample to enable noninvasive prediction of vocal fold displacement. The incorporation of acoustic and auditory perception data resulted in a remarkable boost in classification accuracy. Dysphonia is also known as disorganized speech. Dysphonia can be fully diagnosed by using an endoscope to look at the larynx and vocal folds. Acoustic evaluation of a patient's voice, which is now available to scientists and clinicians, can aid in the diagnosis. Jitter accounted for more than half of overall pathology diagnostic accuracy (54.8%). Researchers uncovered MFCC traits that gave insight into the distinctions between dysphonic and normal voices.

Researchers studied 99 people who had polyps, cysts, or nodules on their vocal folds. Biomechanical data was extracted from a sound sample to enable noninvasive prediction of vocal fold displacement. The incorporation of acoustic and auditory perception data resulted in a remarkable boost in classification accuracy. Dysphonia is also known as disorganized speech. Dysphonia can be fully diagnosed by using an endoscope to look at the larynx and vocal folds. Acoustic evaluation of a patient's voice, which is now available to scientists and clinicians, can aid in the diagnosis. Jitter accounted for more than half of overall pathology diagnostic accuracy (54.8%). Researchers uncovered MFCC traits that gave insight into the distinctions between dysphonic and normal voices. The use of publicly available speech corpora has enabled significant advances in the testing and improvement of voice recognition systems [5]. Dysarthria is one of the most challenging speech disorders to diagnose. Vocal cord lesions can cause a variety of symptoms, including hoarseness and a reduction in the normal vibrating of the vocal cords. Research on transferable learning processes is now being done as a possible answer. The following is a list of the most significant contributions made by this research: Scientists are now working on a multi-modal VPD system that uses both speech and EGG data to enhance dysarthria diagnosis. If you follow these steps, you'll have a good idea of how to spot pathological voice problems in the future. The use of this technology makes it easier to combine the two methods and gives more confidence in the results. The VPD system might be developed on top of a variety of pre-trained CNN models. Among the different available models are XceptionNet, MobileNet v2, and ResNet50. This is an attempt to reduce training time while enhancing accuracy. The VPD system may recreate spectra from an input signal. These spectrograms can then be used as inputs for convolutional neural network models. A large increase in the overall amount of a certain type of input may significantly improve performance. Deep learning also has a way to pay attention, which can be used to make the system work better. LSTM networks were employed to improve classification accuracy. We were able to do this by removing extraneous information and adding subtlety to the acoustic characteristics utilized for categorization.

2 Background

There are several distinct categories of vocal problems. Several voice disorders can be caused by the wrong development of one or both vocal folds. Figure 1 depicts a recently developed technique for categorizing various forms of human speech.

Depending on the context, someone's voice may be perceived as "normal" or "disturbed" by others (pathological). One of the most common causes of sickness is inflammation. Other possible causes include an abnormal structure or neuromuscular design, as well as an imbalance in muscle tension. Sulcus vocalis, cysts, polyps, and nodules are a few of the disorders that can cause structural abnormalities in the vocal folds [5]. Sulcus vocalis and paralysis are two further possibilities. The structural pathology of the voice will be the primary focus of this study (Fig. 2).

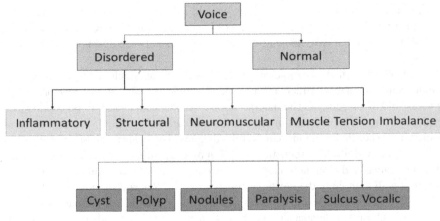

Fig. 1. Voice Pathology Classification

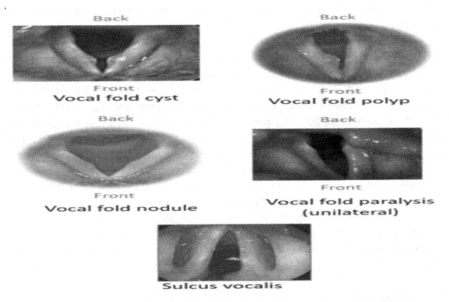

Fig. 2. Vocal fold with issues like cyst, polyp, nodule, paralysis, and vocalis

2.1 Cyst

The mucosa of the vocal folds is frequently so thin that an abnormal growth known as a cyst may be seen through it. A cyst is a benign development that is deemed abnormal. Cysts are well known for causing several unpleasant side effects, including pain and discomfort. When there is less airflow, the vocal folds are unable to vibrate as efficiently, resulting in worsening sound quality. When the mucosal thickness increases, the normal vibrating of the vocal folds is restricted, making it more difficult to speak. If a person has a cyst, the cyst may affect the volume and maturity of their voice. Single cysts on the vocal folds are relatively rare, although they are difficult to locate. There are different sounds that can be made with the voice, such as natural, breathy, harsh, and scratchy. Many of these patients have cysts, and they complain of exhaustion after a long chat.

2.2 A Benign Growth on the Vocal Folds

Polyps and cysts are commonly seen in the mucosa that surrounds the vocal folds. Several of them have lately been constructed here. If they are compacted together or combined with liquids, they can grow to enormous sizes. The strength of the vibrations depends on how big the vocal folds are and where they are. The voice might range from scarcely audible to severely dysphonic (extremely poor voice quality). Cysts are often linked to tiredness after a long talk and throat inflammation that is too painful to bear.

2.3 Nodules

Vocal nodules are more frequent among younger people, both men and women, who work in professions that require them to speak in public, such as teaching, law, and the performing arts. Because of the existence of nodules on the vocal folds, a person's voice may sound unaltered, breathy, or raspy. Individuals with significant hearing loss may have difficulty producing or understanding quiet speech or soothing tones. Practice is required to get a higher and softer voice without the sound progressively fading in. The activity abruptly resumes after a brief pause in which no sound can be heard. Most of them have cysts, and it hurts them to talk for lengthy periods of time.

2.4 Paralysis

When the vocal folds become rigid, this is the most prevalent cause of voice inactivity. Because the vocal folds are immovable in their current form, they have a large space between them. This opens a breach through which air may hypothetically escape, but it also inhibits air from freely travelling. Furthermore, this illness may cause the vocal folds to deteriorate or become paralysed. The Greek word paresis, which translates as "weakness," is a broad term that may be used to describe a variety of medical disorders. Most of them have cysts, which are known to sap energy and make it difficult for patients to appropriately project their voices. Patients frequently have many of them.

2.5 Sulcus

This crater-like feature is referred to as a sulcus, the depth of the sulcus fluctuates slightly, and its two sides are not exact clones of one another. This condition can range from moderate to highly severe. In the following paragraphs, we'll go over a couple of the concepts we've covered thus far in greater depth. To evaluate and rank individual voices fairly, there must be trustworthy techniques for gauging voice quality. Auditory-perceptual exams of voice problems may be valuable diagnostic tools due to their inexpensive cost, short length, and flexible scheduling possibilities [6]. We may also measure speech quality and voice strength through auditory-perceptual evaluation by evaluating separate auditory aspects of sound. This is accomplished using spectrum analysis. To achieve this goal, multiple recordings of the same person speaking might be compared. There are a few difficulties that prevent it from being completely objective: Because there is no quantitative measurement and no widely acknowledged procedure for analyzing subjective experiences. Some hypotheses on why sensory scales could impact error and variation are as follows:

Scales should not be used as the primary diagnostic tool when screening people with laryngopharyngeal symptoms [7]. Although scales are often used in clinical and scientific settings, they are not always the most accurate instrument for evaluating a person's overall voice quality. Several studies [8] have revealed that instrumental testing (machine assessments of speech quality) and perceptual evaluations (the listener's perception of voice quality) only have a moderate correlation. In contrast to objective evaluations, perceptual evaluations are based on the listener's ideas and feelings. Judges may utilize vocal clues such as the length of a speaker's vowels and their natural tempo of speaking to assess the quality of performance. Others say that using continuous vowels instead of flowing speech is a more realistic and understandable way to show speech [9]. Permanent voice handicaps can be caused by either loss of vocal function or biological damage to the larynx. Chemical exposure, inadequate hygiene practices in high-stress vocal-use occupations, stress, and other factors can all increase the likelihood of getting one of these illnesses. Limiting the natural vibrating of the larynx might be one of the various ways to change your voice. There are various approaches that may be taken to achieve this purpose. Voice changes can also occur because: There may be no warning signs or symptoms at all, or there may be more than one, depending on the origin of the vocal issue. There is no universal rule; it is dependent on the circumstances. Many laboratories across the world are currently working on diagnostic assistance systems that employ acoustic speech analysis to better diagnose health issues [10–12]. A probability distribution map, which uses probability density functions as input vectors to discriminate between healthy and sick states, lies at the heart of their approach. To do this, a formula that depends on individual comparisons rather than just comparing a threshold with a distance or similarity measure was developed. Their discoveries enhanced the precision with which people might be categorised and set in motion a screening scheme for laryngeal diseases. According to the findings of this study, this method might be employed before and during therapeutic voice treatment sessions to regain original formant AM (amplitude modulation) features. The study's authors say that the extracted function could help us figure out what's normal and what's wrong with how the vocal folds vibrate. New pathological evaluation approaches have been created to improve the capacity to identify healthy and unwell people [13–15]. In reference number 25, the removal of features is detailed in-depth, and its evolution is examined considering cutting-edge concepts and dynamic networks. This approach gives a visual aid that may be utilized to distinguish between a healthy and obese person quickly and simply. Researchers concluded that 96.1% accuracy was achievable after studying extended vowel articulation. In research with 99 people who had polyps, cysts, or nodules on their vocal folds, researchers tested numerous pitch identification systems.

3 Proposed VPD System

Our findings imply that until a VPD system is integrated into a bigger and more complex healthcare network, it cannot successfully fulfill its intended function. The intelligent healthcare architecture incorporates deep learning, edge computing, cloud storage, and 5G networks to increase the quality of care provided to patients. The use of IoT-related software and hardware extends considerably farther.

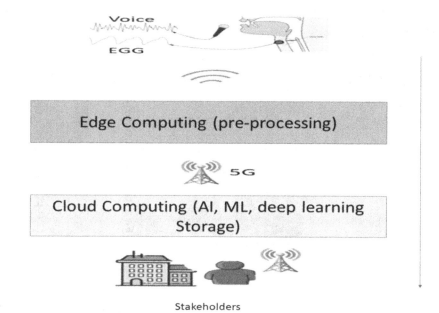

Fig. 3. The VPD system is built around a smart healthcare foundation

Figure 3 depicts an intelligent healthcare architecture like that employed by the VPD. To record the expected signals flowing from the user, the system employs internet-connected microphones and EGG devices. The distributed computing infrastructure nodes placed at the network's periphery conduct the first processing of these signals. This includes the procedure of obtaining the spectrogram. After that, the spectrograms are transferred to a cloud computing provider to be stored and processed in accordance with the demands of AI, ML, and DL. Then, via 5G technology, notifications are delivered to all purchasers and participants. The voice and EGG signals employed in the proposed VPD system are shown in Fig. 4. In this case, these two forms of functioning are merged into a single seamless whole. Using this procedure, different signals are analysed individually and then combined. An EGG device, like a microphone, may pick up the user's voice signal and vice versa for the EGG signal [16–18]. The user will be unable to make any vocal noises while using the EGG since the vocal folds will be immobilized within the device. As a result, the term "gadget" is commonly used to designate the topic of this discussion. A spectrogram can be used to examine the frequency spectrum of a signal as it changes over time. A Mel-spectrogram, which is formed by band-pass filtering scaled to Mel intervals, is also used in the research. Preprocessing the voice sample before employing the STFT is particularly advantageous since it reduces the amount of obvious high-order harmonic distortion in the spectrogram. At sample rates of 16 kHz and above, the amount of data that must be collected for training is greatly decreased. Because this is the case, we will only need a small amount of data to perform the feature mapping quickly. Pre-emphasis is a method that is regularly used to improve the high-frequency clarity of a picture before it is taken.

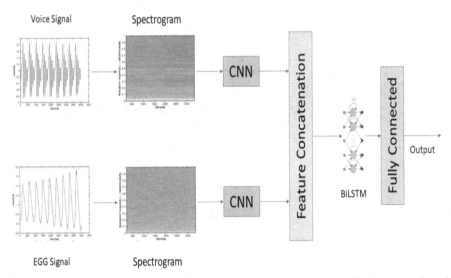

Fig. 4. A schematic of the suggested microphone and environment categorization system based on audio, as well as a deep neural network architecture that employs CNN

The spectrograms are then analysed using a previously trained convolutional neural network model. During the testing, three distinct networks were used: ResNet 50, Xception, and MobileNet. Due to a lack of available data, we have no alternative but to use previously trained models. In the table below, you can see what the three different CNN models have in common. MobileNet is a great alternative for use in real-time applications since it has a substantially smaller total number of parameters than ResNet50 and ResNet50. However, in the not-too-distant future, when processing speeds are expected to be substantially faster, a CNN with many parameters may be practical for rapid data processing [19–22]. Although ResNet50 and MobileNet can only handle inputs of size 50, Xception can handle inputs of sizes 399 and 299. When the scale of the spectrogram or Mel-spectrogram is changed, the input levels are taken into account and adjusted as needed.

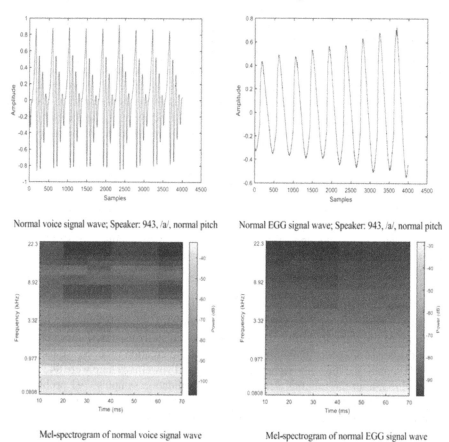

Normal voice signal wave; Speaker: 943, /a/, normal pitch   Normal EGG signal wave; Speaker: 943, /a/, normal pitch

Mel-spectrogram of normal voice signal wave   Mel-spectrogram of normal EGG signal wave

Fig. 5. Here are several examples of spectrograms, Mel-spectrograms, and spectrograms of speech and EGG signals

The top row of Fig. 5 depicts a healthy person's speech and EGG signals, while the middle and bottom rows depict the equivalent spectrograms and Mel-spectrograms. These LSTM construction parts are used to build both new and old LSTM components [23–25]. The input gate, storage gate, and output gate are the three gates in charge of running the LSTM unit. Each gate requires a certain procedure that must be followed. Long-term short-term memory gates, also known as LSTM gates, will soon oversee the processing of both current temporal input and previously categorised data. The values utilised by each of the three gates are determined using a connected, three-level sigmoid function. There is a connection between the previous and subsequent levels in the game. By stacking multiple LSTM cells on top of one another, an LSTM layer may be created. LSTMs may be built in either a unidirectional or bidirectional manner with the help of these layers. A BiLSTM, also known as a bidirectional long short-term memory, is made up of two layers, each of which can process time in either the forward or backward direction independently. These increasing phases make it easier to learn about time-dependent interactions. Each BiLSTM layer is composed of 256 LSTM blocks stacked on top of one another in increasing order. SoftMax is the method of choice for categorising the embedded patterns in the BiLSTM model's final layer. After the CNN model has been trained to recognise features and then frozen to retain the knowledge it has learned, these characteristics are utilised to teach the BiLSTM model to recognise temporal aspects. The CNN model then passes on its understanding of temporal features to the BiLSTM model. The CNN model only gathers information that is always kept secret [26–28]. The recommended strategy asks for a fifty-percent dropout before applying the completely connected layer. The loss function is mathematically represented by cross-entropy.

4 Results

After several tests, it was determined that the VPD system could meet the requirements. The suggested system was contrasted with other comparable systems that were previously available in the literature. When figuring out which techniques worked the best, the F1 score, accuracy, recall, and precision were all considered.

4.1 Database

The SVD database contains around 2000 voice recordings of people with each of the 71 categories of voice abnormalities. This database is frequently used in studies pertaining to the diagnosis of speech pathology. Throughout the creation process, we used both the EGG signals and the voice signal for the sustained vowel/a/. There were 842 groups in total throughout the training, verification, and validation samples: 791 problematic groups across all three datasets, accounting for 60% of the entire sample; and 281 healthy groups across all three datasets, accounting for 20% of the total sample. During the trials, we used voice samples from people as young as 15 and as old as 60. One definition of accuracy is the proportion of potential samples that are suitable for inclusion in the set. Each of the 200 courses had a maximum of 32 students enrolled. There were two hundred and zero training iterations in all. The Adam optimizer was used in our optimization strategy, with the following parameters: set learning rate = 104, batch size = 32, and several training epochs = 100. Figures 6 and 7 depict the proposed system's accuracy and loss curves, respectively. Figure 6 depicts the amount of precision that may be reached by using our language. An "Xception" is a one-time usage of a CNN model in extremely rare circumstances.

Figure 8 depicts the ROC curve of the proposed system. The value of the area under the curve was calculated to be 0.998% as a percentage. The credibility interval varied from 0.987 to 0.998, encompassing both standard and unusual data formats. This range contains 95% of the information.

The accuracy of a speech-only examination was compared to that of an EGG-only examination and a bimodal test in this study (the proposed system). The comparative advantages and drawbacks of the systems are depicted in a chart, revealing that the proposed technique is preferable to using only one means of communication. The addition of both speech and EGG signals into the VPD system's design improved the system's overall performance. The utility of its suggested system is shown as a percentage is shown in Table 1.

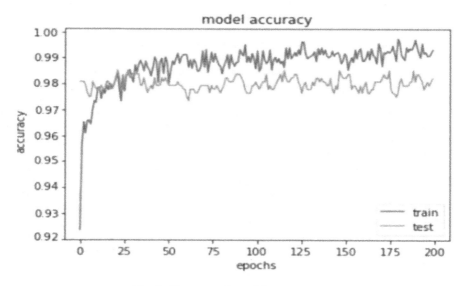

Fig. 6. New system's model accuracy curve

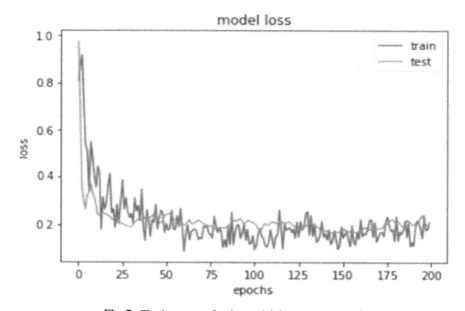

Fig. 7. The loss curve for the model that was suggested

We developed our strategy by comparing the results of three different pre-trained CNN models. Figure 9 shows the results of various CNN models to demonstrate the system's credibility. When all the facts are considered, it is evident that Xception is the best alternative. It's impressive that MobileNet beat the other two techniques despite having fewer optimization possibilities.

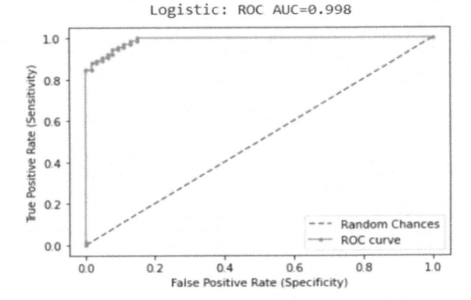

Fig. 8. The Receiver Operating Characteristic Curve of the Proposed System

Table 1. The utility of its suggested system the data is shown as a percentage

Method	Accuracy	Recall	F1-Score	Precision
Entropy Features	94.69	93.92	92.87	94.19
Electroencephalogram Based Method	94.82	95.88	95.36	95.97
Proposed Method	96.77	96.89	95.98	96.46

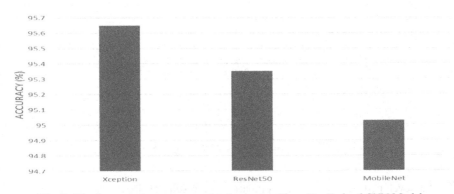

Fig. 9. The System's Accuracy was Attained using Three Pre-Trained CNN Models

Table 2. The levels of accuracy (in percent) obtained by various methodologies are compared

Correlation Functions	Entropy Features	Deep Learning	Bimodal	Proposed Method
91	92.8	93.9	94.2	95.6

Data was set to compare the suggested system against several others, and it was discovered that it performed admirably. Prior research seldom combined speech and EGG data for analysis. Table 2 of the results clearly demonstrate that the proposed method outperformed the other choices. A VPD system might be installed in a cutting-edge lecture hall to assist professors in providing their students with the knowledge they can use for the rest of their lives. This is because vocal pathology has a big impact on people who work in the field of education.

5 Conclusion

This study used two forms of data to create a system for detecting erroneous speech. This technique can accept a variety of data types, including audio, video, and even EGG signals. For example, the VPD system may recreate spectra from an input signal. These spectrograms can then be used as inputs for convolutional neural network models. The BiLSTM model is then fed a consolidated set of features generated from both inputs. These characteristics are put into the model for use in simulation. The results of the testing revealed that the proposed method was very effective, with success rates in accuracy, precision, and recall all above 95%. Its performance also outperformed that of other computers with comparable designs. A large increase in the overall amount of a certain type of input may significantly improve performance. One of our long-term goals is to explore what happens to the VPD's configuration as signals travel through a network. Deep learning also has a way to pay attention, which can be used to make the system work better.

Conflict of Interest. There is no conflict of interest.

References

1. Mohammed, M.A., et al.: Voice pathology detection and classification using convolutional neural network model. Appl. Sci. **10**(11), 3723 (2020)
2. Muhammad, G., Alhussein, M.: Convergence of artificial intelligence and internet of things in smart healthcare: a case study of voice pathology detection. IEEE Access **9**, 89198–89209 (2021). https://doi.org/10.1109/ACCESS.2021.3090317
3. Kempster, G.B., Gerratt, B.R., Verdolini Abbott, K., Barkmeier-Kraemer, J., Hillman, R.E.: Consensus auditory-perceptual evaluation of voice: development of a standardized clinical protocol. Amer. J. Speech-Lang. Pathol. **18**(2), 124–132 (2009)
4. Muhammad, G., Rahman, S.M.M., Alelaiwi, A., Alamri, A.: Smart health solution integrating IOT and cloud: a case study of voice pathology monitoring. IEEE Commun. Mag. **55**(1), 69–73 (2017)

5. Mustafa, M.A., et al.: The potential of 2D carbon nitride monolayer as an efficient adsorbent for capturing mercury: a DFT study. Diamond Relat. Mater. **141**, 110566 (2024). https://doi.org/10.1016/j.diamond.2023.110566

6. Mustafa, M.A., Alabbasy, R.H., Azeez, A.K., Meri, M.A.: Histological study of the effect of some oncology drugs on heart muscle. AIP Conf. Proc. **2977**, 040024 (2023). https://doi.org/10.1063/5.0182762

7. Mustafa, M.A., Khaleel, Z.I., Saab, N.G., Meri, M.A.: The role of microbial pathogens in infection of lung organs and spleen of laboratory albino rats. AIP Conf. Proc. **2977**, 040070 (2023). https://doi.org/10.1063/5.0182764.. Study of running speech versus sustained vowels," J. Acoust. Soc. Amer., vol. 87, no. 5, pp. 2218–2224, May 1990

8. Muhammad, G., Hossain, M.S., Kumar, N.: EEG-based pathology detection for home health monitoring. IEEE J. Sel. Areas Commun. **39**(2), 603–610 (2021)

9. Amin, S.U., Hossain, M.S., Muhammad, G., Alhussein, M., Rahman, M.A.: Cognitive smart healthcare for pathology detection and monitoring. IEEE Access **7**, 10745–10753 (2019)

10. Hossain, M.S., Muhammad, G., Song, B., Hassan, M.M., Alelaiwi, A., Alamri, A.: Audio–visual emotion-aware cloud gaming framework. IEEE Trans. Circuits Syst. Video Technol. **25**(12), 2105–2118 (2015)

11. Hossain, M.S., Muhammad, G.: Emotion-aware connected healthcare big data towards 5G. IEEE Internet Things J. **5**(4), 2399–2406 (2018)

12. Saarbruecken Voice Database. http://www.stimmdatenbank.coli.uni-saarland.de/help_en.php4. Accessed 20 Apr 2021

13. Navadia, N.R., et al.: Applications of cloud-based internet of things. In: Integration and Implementation of the Internet of Things Through Cloud Computing, pp. 65–84. IGI Global (2021). https://doi.org/10.4018/978-1-7998-6981-8.ch004

14. Bhardwaj, H., Tomar, P., Sakalle, A., Acharya, D., Badal, T., Bhardwaj, A.: A DeepLSTM model for personality traits classification using EEG signals. IETE J. Res. **69**, 7272–7280 (2021)

15. Sakalle, A., Tomar, P., Bhardwaj, H., Alim, M.: A modified LSTM framework for analyzing COVID-19 effect on emotion and mental health during pandemic using the EEG signals. J. Healthc. Eng. **2022**, 1–8 (2022).https://doi.org/10.1155/2022/8412430

16. Sakalle, A., et al.: Genetic programming-based feature selection for emotion classification using EEG signal. J. Healthc. Eng. **2022**, 1–6 (2022). https://doi.org/10.1155/2022/8362091

17. Alnuaim, A.A., et al.: Human-Computer interaction for recognizing speech emotions using multilayer perceptron classifier. J. Healthc. Eng. **2022**, 1–12 (2022). https://doi.org/10.1155/2022/6005446

18. Hammarberg, B.: Voice research and clinical needs. Folia Phoniatr. Logop. **52**(1–3), 93–102 (2000)

19. Ali, Z., Muhammad, G., Alhamid, M.F.: An automatic health monitoring system for patients suffering from voice complications in smart cities. IEEE Access **5**, 3900–3908 (2017)

20. Hossen, M.N., Panneerselvam, V., Koundal, D., Ahmed, K., Bui, F.M., Ibrahim, S.M.: Federated machine learning for detection of skin diseases and enhancement of internet of medical things (IoMT) security. IEEE J. Biomed. Health Inform. **27**(2), 835–841 (2022)

21. Shuaib, M., et al.: Identity model for Blockchain-based land registry system: a comparison. Wirel. Commun. Mobile Comput. **2022**, 1–17 (2022). https://doi.org/10.1155/2022/5670714

22. Aggarwal, S., Gupta, S., Alhudhaif, A., Koundal, D., Gupta, R., Polat, K.: Automated COVID-19 detection in chest X-ray images using fine-tuned deep learning architectures. Expert Syst. **39**(3), e12749 (2022). Yar, H., Hussain, T., Khan, Z. A., Koundal, D., Lee, M. Y., & Baik, S. W. (2021). Vision sensor-based real-time fire detection in resource-constrained IoT environments. Computational intelligence and neuroscience, 2021.

23. Kashyap, R.: Big data analytics challenges and solutions. In: Big Data Analytics for Intelligent Healthcare Management, pp. 19–41. Elsevier (2019). https://doi.org/10.1016/B978-0-12-818 146-1.00002-7
24. Chen, M., Yang, J., Hu, L., Hossain, M.S., Muhammad, G.: Urban healthcare big data system based on crowdsourced and cloud-based air quality indicators. IEEE Commun. Mag. **56**(11), 14–20 (2018)
25. Ahmed, N., Amin, R., Aldabbas, H., Koundal, D., Alouffi, B., Shah, T.: Machine learning techniques for spam detection in email and IoT platforms: analysis and research challenges. Secure. Commun. Netw. **2022**, 1–19 (2022). https://doi.org/10.1155/2022/1862888
26. Kashyap, R.: Object boundary detection through robust active contour based method with global information. Int. J. Image Min. **3**(1), 22 (2018). https://doi.org/10.1504/IJIM.2018. 10014063
27. Kashyap, R.: Breast cancer histopathological image classification using stochastic dilated residual ghost model. Int. J. Inf. Retrieval Res. **12**(1), 1–24 (2021). https://doi.org/10.4018/ IJIRR.289655
28. Sakalle, A., Tomar, P., Bhardwaj, H., Bhardwaj, A.: Emotion recognition using portable EEG device. In: Solanki, A., Sharma, S.K., Tarar, S., Tomar, P., Sharma, S., Nayyar, A. (eds.) AIS2C2 2021. CCIS, vol. 1434, pp. 17–30. Springer, Cham (2021). https://doi.org/10.1007/ 978-3-030-82322-1_2

Impact of AI Infused Leadership on Subordinate Employee's Job Satisfaction: A Study Across Select Successful IT Companies in Bengaluru City

Rajani H. Pillai[1]([✉]) [ID], Aatika Bi[1] [ID], N. Nagesh[2] [ID], Deeksha Srinivasa[2] [ID], Roopa Adarsh[3] [ID], and Arpita Sastri[4] [ID]

[1] School of Commerce, Mount Carmel College, Autonomous, Bengaluru, Karnataka, India
{rajani.h.pillai,aatika.bi}@mccblr.edu.in
[2] Department of Commerce, Bengaluru City University, Bengaluru, India
[3] School of Humanities and Social Sciences, Mount Carmel College, Autonomous, Bengaluru, Karnataka, India
roopa.adarsh@mccblr.edu.in
[4] Department of Management Studies, Primus School of Management Studies, Bengaluru, India

Abstract. The objective of this study was to experimentally examine the nature and significance of AI-infused leadership and its impact on subordinate employee job satisfaction in information technology projects. The present study employs an exploratory research design and utilizes a quantitative data methodology. An intricately designed questionnaire was devised to gather the data. To determine the sample size, the Cochran Formula is used, using a known population, a 95% confidence level, and a 5% margin of error. The calculated sample size is 100 respondents. Only entry and middle level employees from the top 10 IT companies in Bangalore city, based on market capitalization, are included. Specifically, we evaluate 10 individuals from each organization who have been involved in successful projects. The study's sample is obtained by easy sampling. The questionnaire's reliability and validity were assessed using the Gaskins' master validity instrument, and it was confirmed. Data analysis in the study was conducted using SPSS Version 22 and AMOS Version 22 software. The incorporation of AI abilities in a leader's repertoire results in a significant 75% improvement in work satisfaction. Successful projects are characterized by leaders that provide ample AI-infused support to their subordinates, resulting in work satisfaction. Hence, enhancing the AI-integrated abilities of a leader is vital for the effective execution of initiatives. Moreover, the utilization of AI in leadership positions amplifies decision-making aptitude and streamlines procedures, hence augmenting efficiency and productivity. By using AI technology, leaders can effectively assess a larger volume of information and make decisions based on data, leading to improved results for both the team and the enterprise.

Keywords: AI infused leadership · Subordinate Employee's · Job Satisfaction · IT Projects

M. Botto-Tobar et al. (Eds.): ICAT 2023, CCIS 2050, pp. 156–166, 2024.
https://doi.org/10.1007/978-3-031-58953-9_12

1   Introduction

The definition and exploration of artificial intelligence (AI) have been the subject of ongoing discussions since the term was introduced during the Dartmouth Summer Research Project on Artificial Intelligence in 1956 [1]. This workshop is widely regarded as the first event in the area of AI. Numerous meanings have been put up throughout the years. In addition to the theoretical considerations surrounding the definitions of "intelligence" and "artificial intelligence", there exist significant practical and commercial incentives for establishing a shared definition. For instance, a widely acknowledged definition of AI facilitates the uniform quantification of investments in these technologies and facilitates the formulation of rules and the implementation of risk management methods [2]. Consequently, several international organizations have dedicated efforts to establishing a precise definition of artificial intelligence in recent years. For instance, the World Economic Forum suggests that AI refers to systems that operate by perceiving, analyzing data, acquiring knowledge, reasoning, and determining the most suitable course of action [3]. On the other hand, the OECD defines AI as a machine-driven system capable of making forecasts, offering suggestions, or making decisions that impact real or virtual environments, all based on a defined set of human objectives. For instance, this may be a system that provides online product recommendations, anticipates infrastructure problems for proactive maintenance, or determines the optimal route for an autonomous car. Although there are numerous variations of AI algorithms and systems, two commonly utilized in business involve the utilization of pre-established rules, potentially defined by humans, to generate predictions, recommendations, and decisions, and the acquisition of these "rules" (typically mathematical functions) through learning from data. Organizations have utilized the previous kind of artificial intelligence for an extended period of time.

Artificial intelligence (AI) has the potential to facilitate a new phase of human resource management, in which the integration of data analytics, machine learning, and automation may collaborate to enhance efficiency and produce superior results [2]. As AI technology progresses beyond automation to augmentation, firms are considering how AI technologies may enhance the function of human resources (HR) to benefit workers and job seekers. The objective is not just to save time, but also to deliver information, insights, and suggestions almost instantly. Furthermore, this is only the initial phase of implementing artificial intelligence in the field of human resources [3]. AI is increasingly recognized as an essential element of every contemporary organization's strategy [4]. The progress in IT/communications and internet is the main catalyst for worldwide economic growth and globalization. At the corporate level, it is becoming increasingly crucial in the reorganization and restructuring of business operations to adapt to heightened competition [5]. Researchers are recognizing that non-AI elements, such as managerial, organizational, and cultural challenges, are crucial in determining the success or failure of information technology initiatives [6]. These aspects are being examined alongside the important success factors of the projects. Effective leadership is crucial in any group setting. It is well recognized that professionals that use AI into their work require essential leadership skills to effectively oversee their team [7]. The integration of artificial intelligence (AI) into enterprises has a significant influence on the dynamics of leadership within the context of AI [8]. Artificial intelligence enhances decision-making by analyzing vast datasets, but it also presents the risk of overreliance, thereby diminishing human judgment [9]. The study conducted by AI on employee performance may overlook intangible leadership qualities [10]. Moreover, the application of AI in leadership gives rise to ethical concerns, including workplace surveillance and algorithmic biases [11]. With the increasing role of artificial intelligence in leadership, it is crucial for leaders to adapt their approach by giving priority to creating a distinct vision, fostering strong connections, and encouraging an innovative culture [12]. Leaders must stay updated and adaptable as artificial intelligence advances, skillfully overseeing its capabilities with human comprehension, ethical values, and emotional intelligence [13].

This study discusses the lack of empirical research in the IT project management literature regarding the importance of leadership for success. Additionally, it highlights the oversight of leadership researchers in recognizing the unique personality and vocational features of leaders that include artificial intelligence (AI). The objective of this study was to examine the nature and significance of AI-infused leadership and its impact on subordinate employee job satisfaction in information technology initiatives.

The first section of the study gives background for the study. The second section focusses on the review of literature. The research methods are specified in the third section and the fourth section presents the results of the study. The last section of this research concludes with limitations and scope for further research.

2 Review of Literature

The study employed a systematic literature review methodology to evaluate both background reviews and independent studies pertaining to the use of artificial intelligence in the field of leadership styles across the globe. A total of 64 studies were identified and selected for inclusion in the review based on the criteria of including only English studies published within the last fifteen years. A total of 54 pieces of literature were selected for the purpose of conducting a comprehensive evaluation of their quality, following the acquisition of the complete text of the respective research works. Four studies were excluded from the analysis due to iterative processes and concerns regarding their quality. The present study is grounded on a comprehensive review of 50 relevant scholarly sources pertaining to the subject matter.

The articles were sourced from reputed journals and were scrutinized to determine the level of quality exhibited by each study. Elsevier database, Routledge and CRC Press Taylor and Francis database. Emerald Group Publishing database, Springer Nature database and Sage database. Several supplementary articles were acquired from reputable academic databases such as Wiley, Academia, JSTOR, and Guildford Press.

2.1 AI Infused Leadership

The notion of AI-infused leadership in this study pertains to the knowledge and skills of leaders in the IT business about AI-infused abilities and technology [14]. The IT sector is seeing significant technical changes, necessitating executives to continually enhance their knowledge and understanding of these advancements [15]. Individuals working in the information technology sector possess distinct personality traits and occupational characteristics. These include a strong desire for independence, a high drive for achievement, loyalty to their profession and, to a lesser extent, their organization [16]. They also demonstrate a meticulous approach to their work, an affinity for logical thinking, a focus on project-based work, a non-linear career trajectory, a willingness to relocate, and a heightened awareness of and responsiveness to their work environment, among other qualities. Although they are primarily promoted to managerial roles based on their AI-enhanced capabilities, they often exhibit deficiencies in interpersonal and leadership skills [17]. This may be attributed to the narrow perspectives or blind spots resulting from their specialized training, or the absence of sufficient role models [18].

Recently, the literature on information technology and information systems project management has highlighted the significance of leadership as a crucial factor for achieving success [19]. Multiple studies have identified the crucial leadership qualities and skills that IT/IS project managers must possess to attain success. These include the capacity to effectively manage others, stress, emotions, bureaucracy, and communication, among other factors [20].

The concept of hybrid managers, who possess a combination of AI-integrated management and business skills, is gaining increasing popularity in the workplace [21, 22].

While there are several empirical studies examining the characteristics and importance of leadership in project management with artificial intelligence, there is a lack of study in this specific field [23]. [24] The author emphasizes those forward-thinking leaders that include AI into their practices focus on three key aspects: understanding the problem at hand, managing the exchange of ideas, and upholding high standards of quality. [25] study identifies successful leaders that integrate AI techniques as those who guide their team members towards optimal performance, manage and minimize disruptions within the organization, strategically facilitate the professional development of their subordinates, enhance individual productivity through collaborative teaming, and encourage self-directed management [26].

[6, 7, 10] Multiple studies have delineated the essential characteristics and competencies required of information systems project managers in the information technology sector. Prior scholars have emphasized the importance of possessing proficiency in several areas such as personnel supervision, technological oversight, stress mitigation, emotional regulation, organizational bureaucratic administration, and proficient communication skills for an AI manager [27]. According to the given information, the roles of managers incorporating AI are undergoing changes [28]. This change involves shifting the emphasis from only technical expertise to recognizing and valuing a wider array of leadership responsibilities, such as interpersonal abilities, strategic analysis, and business acumen, among other important qualities [29]. Consequently, in businesses where information plays a crucial role, leadership and IT are increasingly mutually reliant and must be effectively coordinated [30].

2.2 Research Gap

Because there is a paucity of empirical research on AI infused leadership, this study looked at general leadership literature and concentrated on the growing body of research on 'AI infused Leadership,' which is considered to be a new paradigm in leadership research.

2.3 Research Objectives

Objective - To analyse the impact of AI infused leadership on subordinate job satisfaction in the successful IT projects.

An awareness of how IT professionals may make better use of AI to increase productivity is an important part of the AI Infused leadership mix [31]. That is why successful AI infused leadership necessitates novel data, policies, and methods to promote the effective use of technological expertise in the advancement of IT project success. Those in the IT field sometimes take on expanded leadership roles without having the appropriate training. Without the right kind of technology leadership, this might lead to unwarranted inclusion and poor decision making. Job satisfaction among IT workers might fall as a result of these factors. Particularly in the information technology (IT) industry, which is crucial to the economy of our country, the use of technology is crucial. In this research, the investigation aims to find if AI infused leadership affects worker happiness in the information technology industry.

3 Research Methodology

Research Strategy: The current research is exploratory research and uses quantitative data approach [32].

Research Instrument: The Questionnaire consisting of 4 Parts - Information on the Demographic profile of the respondent (Multiple choices), Information on the Work profile of the respondent (Multiple choices), Questions related to elements of AI infused Leadership (LIKERT Scale-5 Points) Thite, M. [33] and Godfrey, Patrick [34] was used for the study. The data was collected using Interviews (Where ever possible) and Google forms.

Sample size: A Population of IT employees in Bangalore City which Around 15,00,000 Employees as on 2019 census is used to derive at the sample size using the Cochran Formula of Known Population [35] at 95% confidence level and 5% margin of error, sample size of 100 respondents. IT Employees in Bangalore city – Entry and Middle level employees (Top 10 IT Companies as per market cap) from each company (10 employees) who are part of successful projects are considered. The sample for the study is derived using convenient sampling [36].

Pilot study: [37] A pilot study using 30 IT employees was conducted to affirm the validity and reliability of the questionnaire. The scores for reliability for all constructs in the IT Employees research instrument were above .9 and below .95 indicating excellent reliability. The IT Employees questionnaire was deemed valid and reliable in the current model since all dimensions have been verified and all constructs meet the validity criteria.

The reliability and validity of the questionnaire was tested using the master validity tool by Gaskins and was affirmed [38].

Tools of Analysis: The study utilized SPSS Version 22 [39] and AMOS Version 22 software [40] for data analysis. The utilization of SPSS Version 22 and AMOS Version 22 software in research facilitates the effective examination of gathered data and the evaluation of inter-variable correlations. Using various software tools, the researchers employed statistical techniques such as factor analysis and structural equation modelling to enhance their comprehension of the variables that impact job satisfaction.

4   Results and Discussion

4.1   Demographic Profile of the Respondents

Male IT Employees account for the lion's share of the study's participants. Male respondents make up 73.5% of the sample, and Female IT Employees make up 26.5% of the technology sector. 41.9% of respondents (IT Employees) are between the ages of 31 and 40. 27.1% of IT Employees are between the ages of 41 and 50, while 11% of respondents are above the age of 50. It is encouraging to see that 20% of IT Employees are between the ages of 21 and 30. When asked about their experience in the IT projects, the majority of respondents (43.9%) stated that they have between 10 and 15 years of experience. 21.9% reported having about 15 years of experience, while 15.5% reported having five to ten years of experience. 18.5% said that they had between 0 and 5 years of experience.

4.2   Descriptive Statistics

The above descriptive statistics show that in terms of leadership, subordinates believe that their leaders have AI infused leadership trait with mean scores between 3.98 and 3.16. Subordinates perceive their leaders as having a strong sense of artificial intelligence and how it can be applied to their power. A medium score indicates that these leaders are adept at integrating AI into their decision-making processes and are able to effectively lead their teams in this rapidly evolving technological environment. Overall, the descriptive statistics indicate positive perceptions of AI-communicative leaders among subordinates (Tables 1 and 2).

Table 1. Descriptive statistics- AI infused leadership

Descriptive Statistics - AI infused Leadership		
My leader ………	Mean	Std. Deviation
has relevant AI infused knowledge	3.21	0.988
understands technology and domain	3.98	0.877
has knowledge of latest trends in technology and Artificial intelligence	3.61	0.781
has knowledge of latest trends in domain/industry	3.56	0.998
has AI related qualifications and skills	3.16	0.711

Table 2. Descriptive Statistics - Job satisfaction

Descriptive Statistics - Job satisfaction		
	Mean	Std. Deviation
I receive fair treatment and respect from my superiors	3.21	0.988
I am satisfied with the amount of supervision I receive from my superiors	4.01	1.055
I am satisfied with AI expertise received from my leader	3.68	0.881

In terms of Job satisfaction, the subordinate felt satisfied with the amount of supervision they receive from superiors with mean value of 4.01. A mean score of 3.68 indicates that employees in IT Firms are satisfied with AI expertise received from their leader. Overall, it can be concluded that subordinates feel well supervised and supported by their superiors in terms of job satisfaction. Furthermore, employees in IT organizations tend to be satisfied with the level of AI expertise provided by their leaders. This positive score indicates a healthy work environment and a strong leadership team in the organization.

4.3 Relationship Between AI Infused Leadership and Employee Job Satisfaction

In most successful projects, the AI infused leadership has played a significant role in the job satisfaction of the IT Employees. AI-embedded leaders have successfully leveraged intelligent technology to streamline processes and automate repetitive tasks, allowing IT staff to focus on more meaningful and challenging tasks. This not only increased their job satisfaction but also their productivity and morale. Additionally, AI-focused leadership has created a collaborative and inclusive work environment where employees feel empowered and valued for their contributions, further increasing overall satisfaction.

From the output of CFA [41], the model exhibited a strong fit to the data, as evidenced by the statistically significant Chi-Square value of 3375.414 with 178 degrees of freedom ($p < 0.01$). The Goodness of Fit Index (GFI) is 0.655, which falls below the required standards. The Root Mean Square Error Approximation (RMSEA) is 0.052, indicating that the model is approaching the desired fitness criteria. The diagram displayed below represents the visual representation of the results obtained from running the model. The standardized estimates for the relationships are also depicted in the diagram (Fig. 1).

As AI infused skills increase in the leader, the job satisfaction increases by 75% ($B = 0.746$, $b = 0.588$, $p => 0.05$). It is seen that the subordinates in successful projects get enough AI infused support from their leaders which makes them happy in the job. Therefore, improving the AI infused skills of leader is crucial to deliver projects successfully. In addition, the use of AI in leadership roles enhances decision-making capabilities and simplifies processes, increasing efficiency and productivity.

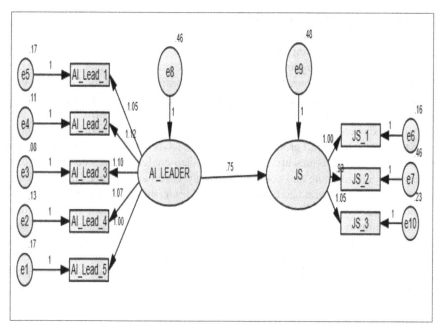

Fig. 1. Pictorial representation of structural relationship between variables

Table 3. Structural Relationship between variables

			Unstd Estimate	Std Es-timate	P
JS	<---	**AI_LEADER**	**0.746**	**0.588**	***
AI_Lead_5	<---	AI_LEADER	1	0.856	
AI_Lead_4	<---	AI_LEADER	1.069	0.895	***
AI_Lead_3	<---	AI_LEADER	1.102	0.935	***
AI_Lead_2	<---	AI_LEADER	1.12	0.916	***
AI_Lead_1	<---	AI_LEADER	1.048	0.867	***
JS_1	<---	JS	1	0.906	
JS_2	<---	JS	0.931	0.761	***
JS_3	<---	JS	1.052	0.882	***

Integrating AI technology enables leaders to analyze more information and make data-driven decisions, resulting in better outcomes for both the team and the organization Furthermore, AI-related skills in leadership foster a culture of about innovation and change develops. Investing in the development of communication skills is essential for success and job satisfaction in organizations (Table 3).

5 Suggestions and Conclusions

Due to its inability to account for the dynamism of the modern workplace, the present leadership literature fails to provide adequate guidance to technical managers. One such trend in IT projects is outsourcing, in which a substantial chunk of the IT project work is delegated to unaffiliated IT contractors that have little to no organizational allegiance. There has been another evolution in the form of global virtual teams, in which team members are dispersed throughout the globe and do not have the luxury of meeting in person to work on a difficult group assignment. The job is done via satellite connections around the world, and issues are resolved via video conferencing. The number of IT workers who telecommute and communicate only via email continues to rise. In such fast-paced contexts, the tried and true methods of leadership often fall short.

Knowledge workers in networked, boundary less, team-oriented, horizontal organizations dominate in the post-industrial world. In order to get the most out of these employees, beyond the scope of their contracts, it is essential to exercise strong leadership over them. This requires exceptional leadership abilities that take into account the swift transformations taking place in today's workplace. We now live in a period of "discontinuity" and "hyper-competition," meaning that no one-leadership paradigm can be said to be suitable in every situation. As a result, studies of leadership need to pay more attention to the interplay between different groups of employees. This research contributes to that goal by concentrating on the backbone workers of the information age, by pointing out gaps in the existing literature on AI-infused leadership, and by proposing a model that expands upon those gaps.

The findings have substantial implications for the selection and training of information technology project managers, since they need to provide AI infused support and play an acceptable 'role model' to subordinates.

The findings of this study points in the direction of additional investigation into the development of theoretically and empirically proven model for development of AI infused project leadership. Future research should take into account the most recent technological and organizational developments.

From the study, it is evident that project leaders need to have sufficient AI infused know-how and they also need to be aware of the latest technology trends in the industry to lead and guide the team. These skills will help leaders to guide team to solve AI infused problems in the project and increase the satisfaction level of team.

Present and future engineers and scientists need more than AI infused expertise to make a meaningful contribution to society. To accomplish this lofty objective, it is not enough to just provide students with a solid technical education; rather, we must also instill in them the drive, perseverance, bravery, cooperation, and leadership qualities that will allow them to effectively put their training to use. There is a need for more emphasis on developing cooperation and leadership abilities in engineering programs, although this is increasingly being addressed by more and more schools. Furthermore, engineering as a whole is seeing significant shifts.

References

1. Martin, A.-S., Freeland, S.: The advent of artificial intelligence in space activities: new legal challenges. Space Policy **55**, 101408 (2021). https://doi.org/10.1016/j.spacepol.2020.101408
2. Rajendra, R.: Artificial intelligence for business. SB, Springer, Cham (2019). https://doi.org/10.1007/978-3-319-97436-1
3. Yawalkar, M.V.V.: A study of artificial intelligence and its role in human resource management. Int. J. Res. Anal. Rev. **6**(1), 20–24 (2019)
4. Quaquebeke, N.V., Gerpott, F.H.: The now, new, and next of digital leadership: how artificial intelligence (AI) will take over and change leadership as we know it. J. Leadersh. Organ. Stud. **30**, 265–275 (2023)
5. Brobey, C.: Leadership style perceptions, race, and career advancement of black information technology professionals. Ph. D. thesis, University of the Cumberlands, Cumberlands, Northern England (2021)
6. Vidic, Z., Burton, D.: Developing effective leaders: motivational correlates of leadership styles. J. Appl. Sport Psychol. **23**(3), 277–291 (2011)
7. Smith, A.M., Green, M.: Artificial intelligence and the role of leadership. J. Leadersh. Stud. **12**(3), 85–87 (2018). https://doi.org/10.1002/jls.21605
8. Peifer, Y., Jeske, T., Hille, S.: Artificial intelligence and its impact on leaders and leadership. Procedia Comput. Sci. **200**, 1024–1030 (2022). https://doi.org/10.1016/j.procs.2022.01.301
9. Petrat, D.: Attitude towards artificial intelligence in a leadership role. In: Black, N.L., Neumann, W.P., Noy, I. (eds.) IEA 2021. LNNS, vol. 223, pp. 811–819. Springer, Cham (2022). https://doi.org/10.1007/978-3-030-74614-8_100
10. Sun, Z.: Artificial leadership: an artificial intelligence approach. PNG UoT BAIS **3**(12), 1–7 (2018)
11. Awosola, I.: What effect does technology have on a responsive leadership style? In: Exploring Ethical Problems in Today's Technological World. IGI Global, pp. 23–44 (2022)
12. Alblooshi, M.A.J.A., Mohamed, A.M., Yusr, M.M.: Moderating role of artificial intelligence between leadership skills and business continuity. Int. J. Prof. Bus. Rev. **8**(6), e03225 (2023). https://doi.org/10.26668/businessreview/2023.v8i6.3225
13. Wang, Y.: Artificial intelligence in educational leadership: a symbiotic role of human-artificial intelligence decision-making. J. Educ. Adm. **59**(3), 256–270 (2021)
14. Sarkis, E., Pallotta, V.: Leadership in the artificial intelligence era. STRATEGICA, 224 (2020)
15. Tiago, I.R.: The influence of artificial intelligence leadership on employee ethical decision-making. Ph. D. thesis, The Catholic University of Portugal, Lisbon, Portugal (2021)
16. Canbek, M.: Artificial Intelligence Leadership: Imitating Mintzberg's Managerial Roles: Business Management and Communication Perspectives in Industry 4.0. IGI Global, pp. 173–187 (2020)
17. Dhamija, P., Chiarini, A., Shapla, S.: Technology and leadership styles: a review of trends between 2003 and 2021. TQM J. **35**(1), 210–233 (2023)
18. Eriksson, M., Djoweini, C.: Artificial intelligence's impact on management: a literature review covering artificial intelligence's influence on leadership skills and managerial decision-making processes. Ph. D. thesis, School of Industrial Engineering and Management, Stockholm, Sweden (2020)
19. Odugbesan, J.A., Aghazadeh, S., Qaralleh, R.E.A., Sogeke, O.S.: Green talent management and employees' innovative work behavior: the roles of artificial intelligence and transformational leadership. J. Knowl. Manage. **27**(3), 696–716 (2023). https://doi.org/10.1108/JKM-08-2021-0601
20. Zhou, J., Liu, Y., Zhang, P.: Artificial intelligence knowledge transfer and artificial intelligence new product development quality under knowledge leadership. In: Zheng, X., Parizi, R.M.,

Hammoudeh, M., Loyola-González, O. (eds.) CSIA 2020. AISC, vol. 1146, pp. 783–791. Springer, Cham (2020). https://doi.org/10.1007/978-3-030-43306-2_110

21. Björkman, I., Johansson, S.: What impact will Artificial Intelligence have on the future leadership role (2017)
22. Milton, J., Al-Busaidi, A.: New role of leadership in AI era: educational sector. In: SHS Web of Conferences, vol. 156, p. 09005. EDP Sciences (2023)
23. Dhamija, A., Chatterji, N.: Artificial intelligence: the missing link between leadership and knowledge management. In: Managerial Issues in Digital Transformation of Global Modern Corporations, pp. 210–221. IGI Global (2021)
24. Naqvi, A.: Responding to the will of the machine: leadership in the age of artificial intelligence. J. Econ. Bibliography 4(3), 244–248 (2017)
25. Björkman, I., Johansson, S.: What impact will Artificial Intelligence have on the future leadership role?–a study of leaders' expectations (2018)
26. Almarzooqi, A.: Towards an artificial intelligence (AI)-driven government in the United Arab Emirates (UAE): a framework for transforming and augmenting leadership capabilities. Ph. D. thesis, Pepperdine University, Malibu, United States (2019)
27. Sagnières, B.: Leadership competencies in the presence of artificial intelligence. Ph. D. thesis, HEC Montréal, Montréal, Canada (2022)
28. Hao, M., Lv, W., Du, B.: The influence mechanism of authentic leadership in artificial intelligence team on employees' performance. J. Phys. Conf. Ser. 1438(1), 012022 (2020)
29. Leal, C.M.S.: Algorithmic aversion in artificial intelligence co-leadership and the impact of metaphors and comparisons. Ph. D. thesis, The Catholic University of Portugal, Lisbon, Portugal (2023)
30. Anghel, D.: New perspectives for human and artificial intelligence interactions for leadership e-recruitment. Societies 13(3), 55 (2023). https://doi.org/10.3390/soc13030055
31. April, K., Dalwai, A.: Leadership styles required to lead digital transformation. Effective Executive 22(2), 14–45 (2019)
32. Swedberg, R.: Exploratory research. In: Elman, C., Gerring, J., Mahoney, J. (eds.) The production of knowledge: Enhancing progress in social science, pp. 17–41. Cambridge University Press (2020). https://doi.org/10.1017/9781108762519.002
33. Thite, M.: Identifying key characteristics of technical project leadership. Leadersh. Organ. Dev. J. 20(5), 253–261 (1999)
34. Godfrey, P.: Building a technical leadership model. INCOSE Int. Symp. 26(1), 757–772 (2016)
35. Halim, H., Hasnita, H.: Determining sample size for research activities: the case of organizational research. Selangor Bus. Rev. 2(1), 20–34 (2017)
36. Sedgwick, P.: Convenience sampling. BMJ 347(oct25 2), f6304–f6304 (2013). https://doi.org/10.1136/bmj.f6304
37. In, J.: Introduction of a pilot study. Korean J. Anesthesiol. 70(6), 601–605 (2017)
38. Sürücü, L., Maslakci, A.: Validity and reliability in quantitative research. Bus. Manage. Stud. Int. J. 8(3), 2694–2726 (2020)
39. Bala, J.: Contribution of SPSS in social sciences research. Int. J. Adv. Res. Comput. Sci. 7(6), 250 (2016)
40. Ong, M.H.A., Puteh, F.: Quantitative data analysis: choosing between SPSS, PLS, and AMOS in social science research. Int. Interdisc. J. Sci. Res. 3(1), 14–25 (2016)
41. Hoyle, R.H.: Confirmatory factor analysis. Handbook of Applied Multivariate Statistics and Mathematical Modeling, pp. 465–497. Academic Press (2000)

Uncovering AI Potential Techniques for Infectious Disease: A Comprehensive Exploration of Surveying, Classifying, and Predicting Models

Shivendra Dubey[✉], Dinesh Kumar Verma, and Mahesh Kumar

Department of Computer Science and Engineering, Jaypee University of Engineering and Technology, Guna, Madhya Pradesh 473226, India
shivendrashivay@gmail.com

Abstract. The virus primarily spread during immediate touch with contaminated people, and while researchers are still investigating other transmission, pathways physical touch has been considered a more likely mode. Traditional diagnosis methods had been become ineffective due to the rapid rise in infections. Researchers have created deep learning algorithms to deliver quick and precise COVID-19 diagnoses to solve the machine learning problem. The study comprises open COVID-19 datasets from various countries, and is separated into ML including the DL method. The paper provides a detailed description and comparison of the metrics used for evaluating the diagnosis procedures. For diagnosing COVID-19 and forecasting outbreaks, Convolution Neural Network is the considerably extensively utilized deep learning method, whereas the SVM approach is the most used ML algorithm. Future research in DL and ML policies toward COVID-19 diagnostics will be guided and inspired by this work.

Keywords: Accuracy · COVID-19 · Deep Learning · Machine Learning · SVM

1 Introduction

The COVID is a infectious disease brought on by SARS-COV-2 virus. The WHO initially discovered it in Wuhan, Hubei, China, on December 31, 2019, and on January 30, 2020, it was designated a worldwide outbreak. That marked the second pandemic recognized by the WHO, with the first being the H1N1 Influenza in 2009 [1]. The virus primarily spread during immediate touch with contaminated people, and while researchers are still investigating other transmission, pathways physical touch has been considered a more likely mode. Some patients also have muscle discomfort, exhaustion and a diminution of smell or taste in addition to the typical COVID-19 symptoms of a flu-like illness, dry coughing and breathing difficulties. Additionally, around 10% of patients have gastrointestinal symptoms such as diarrhoea. The infection can spread up to 6 feet away by particles breathed while speaking or sneezing, so social distance could reduce the chance of infection. However, not all COVID-19 cases show apparent symptoms [2].

M. Botto-Tobar et al. (Eds.): ICAT 2023, CCIS 2050, pp. 167–177, 2024.
https://doi.org/10.1007/978-3-031-58953-9_13

There are so many diagnostic methods for COVID-19 including Polymerase Chain Reaction to detect the virus's proteins, next-generation sequencing, and imaging tests like Computed Tomography (CT) scans and chest X-rays. CT scans are often favoured as they provide more detailed information about the patient's condition and are quicker. At the same time, X-rays offer results at a lower cost with less radiation exposure. Both methods have limitations, such as the potential for skull bones to impact brain CT scans or the lack of 3D images with X-rays [3].

Medical imaging tests such as Computed Tomography Scans and X-radiation are frequently utilized for diagnosing COVID-19 [6, 7]. COVID-19 patients have their X-rays, including CT scans; analyzed using a variety of AI approaches, including DL and ML [15].

1. Supervised Learning [1, 2].
2. Unsupervised Learning [3, 8].

Deep Learning techniques could use to identify coronaviruses, forecast viral infection, and diagnose viruses. The most well-known Deep Learning techniques are:

1. Convolutional Neural Network (CNN) [4, 5].
2. Deep Neural Network (DNN) [6, 7].
3. Recurrent Neural Network (RNN) [8, 9].
4. Generative Adversarial Networks (GANs) [1, 3].

The current work could help us get the data points on the well-regarded public collection of data points of COVID-19, which other researchers can use. Additionally, this article will assist academics and healthcare practitioners to comprehend the upcoming developments of DL and ML and their impact on COVID-19 diagnosis. This document also provides solutions to the following questions:

1. What DL and ML methods are employed during diagnosing COVID-19?
2. Exist any standard data sets that are openly accessible that can be used to test Machine Learning and Deep Learning methods?
3. What indicators are most crucial for assessing ML and DL techniques?
4. Is there a complete program for the diagnosis of COVID-19?
5. Researchers belonging to which nation publishes the majority of the work on DL and ML methods in support of diagnosing COVID-19?
6. Which ML or DL approaches best assesses many performance metrics for COVID-19 diagnosis?

2 Protocols for the Selection of Studies Related to Covid19

These studies are chosen based on the most relevant terms, which included 'COVID-19 along with ML and DL.' Only papers in the English language were selected and online resources such as; Springer, IEEE Xplore, Elsevier, and others were used. Finding research about the COVID-19 pandemic was the preliminary phase, and we discovered 251 papers. Concurrent with the release of this result in April 2021, research into ML, including DL methods considering such COVID-19 outbreak, is being done. These three keywords (i.e., COVID-19, ML, and DL) were used in various permutations using the

'AND' operator; 'COVID-19' Duplicate papers eliminated in the second phase. In the third stage, articles were chosen, for checking depending on titles and abstracts, although they ignored publications with topics outside our field. Only approximately 85 papers were chosen and moved on to the next phase after rejecting more than 100 articles. We scanned each document in step four to confirm its topic was within the designated scope. As a consequence, ten items were eliminated. Finally, 80 articles on ML and DL tactics considering regulating COVID-19 are also combined and figured out in a query as illustrated in Fig. 1.

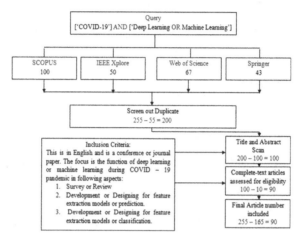

Fig. 1. A flowchart of the studies' inclusion and query criterion

2.1 Covid19, Machine Learning as Well as Deep Learning Methods

Due to the coronavirus's widespread infection, conventional COVID-19 detection techniques have also been improved with the help of DL, including ML methods.

Whereas COVID-19 identification, ML techniques like supervised and unsupervised learning have been explored, as detailed in this section and Fig. 2. Furthermore, for COVID-19 identification, multiple DL technologies have been employed, which will be further detailed and discussed in subsequent sections. The hybrid strategies for diagnosing COVID-19 infections combine deep learning and machine learning.

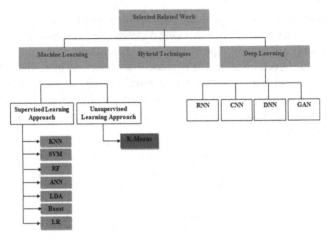

Fig. 2. Categorization of the related works

2.2 Machine Learning Methodologies

Machines are trained to carry out activities independently via machine learning which teaches them how to carry out tasks. Data analysis is one form that entails creating prototypes that let systems and machines learn from experience and put together calculations. Through detecting COVID-19, machine learning analyses the information of CT scan pictures and X-ray input pictures and extracts identifying traits from it. These characteristics determine whether forecasting such an input picture is impure or standard cases that will deliver [2]. Usually, ML approaches utilized as much as COVID-19 identification includes supervised learning methods and unsupervised learning strategies. In Fig. 3, the COVID-19 ML study is shown.

2.3 Deep Neural Network

Compared to the DL models that did not incorporate data augmentation, the acquired results showed improved detected accuracy, testing duration and logarithmic loss. An automated illness detection system was created [2]. The technique made it easier for medical professionals to identify COVID-19 and quickly delivered accurate results, indicating a decreased risk of deadliness. These used CNN to get deep functions and LSTM to identify the extracted elements. The apparatus has 4575 X-ray data on it, including 1525 COVID-19 data. The test findings revealed that the suggested method had a 99.4% accuracy rate, a 99.9% specificity rate, a 99.2% sensitivity rate, and an F1 score of 98.9%. Introducing an intrusive and educational online examination replica powered by real-time data and CNN with adaptive algorithms [5].

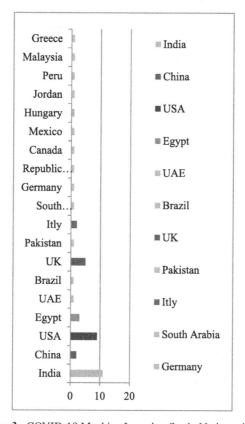

Fig. 3. COVID-19 Machine Learning Study Nation wise

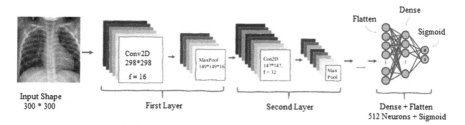

Fig. 4. Stages Deep learning algorithm for COVID-19 diagnosis [7]

Figures 4 and 5 illustrate an instance with deep learning methods of COVID-19 disease and publications among several nations respectively [7]. The suggested method has an 86.66% accuracy rate for identifying COVID-19 patients. They may employ pneumonia, coronavirus and typical cases, to recognize COVID-19 against chest X-radiation pictures [13].

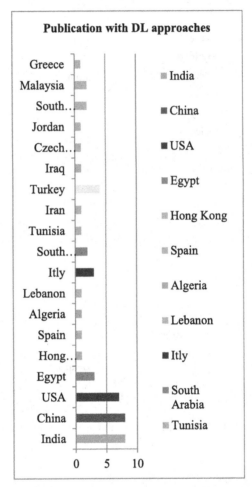

Fig. 5. Number of DL publications in different countries for COVID-19

2.4 Hybrid Approach Merging Deep Learning and Machine Learning

X-ray imagery of COVID-19 is a pulmonary indication, was employed in an iteratively pruned DL model [7]. Using learning the different feature values of COVID-19, this approach combined a standard CNN with an ImageNet-trained model. Afterwards, the newly learned information was used by categorizing the victims, like COVID-19 virus disorders, pneumococcal disease, or typical instances. The investigational suggested approach performs admirably along a 99.72% AUC and 99.01% accuracy. These labelled data do not adequately supplement the information used in COVID-19 training. The explanation for this was that COVID-19 has features with viral lung infections. They included feebly labelled X-ray organisms connected to bacteria or viruses pneumonia to the training data set's initial component, which is the one important data set [1]. After selecting these images trained a CNN algorithm on them and compared the results to those of a model that had not been trained using more data. They used six collections of the dataset in the assessment. When identifying COVID-19 infections as bacterial pneumonia during training, the data augmentation with poorly labelled data beats the base data with no augment [4].

3   COVID 19 Datasets

Obtaining a fine collection of data points for training, testing, and evaluating suggested algorithms is problematic for employing ML including DL techniques. As a result, this part includes the most often used contemporary COVID-19 collection of data points, which has varying properties, data formats, and sizes, such as X-ray or CT scans.

Table 1. Public Datasets

Dataset	Dataset Type	Uniqueness	Achievement
(NCBI) database (DNA sequence data) [5]	COVID-19 virus sequence	5000 different sequences of viral genomic (61.8 million bp)	Technique 1: Percentage of 72.7, Technique 2: Percentage of 68.7, Technique 3: Percentage of 91.45
World Health Organization [2]	'Coronavirus disease (COVID-19) situation reports	Infection rates by temperature in different Chinese provinces	Accuracy Situation 1: Percentage of 80.6, Scenario 2: Percentage of 85.2, Scenario 3: Percentage of 99.9
First dataset: (the pneumonia) database; Second dataset: is COVID-19 images [6]	chest x-ray picture	1,675 normal cases and 216 COVID-19 make up the first dataset. 1,341 normal cases and 219 COVID-19 make up the second dataset	Accuracy Case 1: Percentage of 96.09 Case 2: Percentage of 98.09
COVID-19 epidemiological data [7]	Time series data	Instances of COVID-19 infection in several nations (Russia, Brazil, India, Indonesia, and Peru)	Specificity Percentage of 94.30 Sensitivity Percentage of 93.34, Accuracy: Percentage of 94.99

(continued)

Table 1. (*continued*)

Dataset	Dataset Type	Uniqueness	Achievement
Indian COVID-19 dataset [8]	Time series data	Reports on the incidence of COVID-19 in India	Situation 1: Percentage of 97.82, Situation 2: Percentage of 98, Case 3: Percentage of 96.66 Situation 4: Percentage of 97.50

Table 1 shows a complete example of various collections of data points and how to access them. These data points were chosen from the text using an elegant query to collect similar studies. Through finding the most relevant publications, a keyword combination including DL and ML as well as COVID-19 diagnostic was employed. The articles received from the question are subjected to screening and filtering techniques by picking just the diagnoses of COVID-19 with the collection of data points and removing an additional collection of data points, such as the detection of the mask.

The results of machine learning research are not currently used in a fully real-time system [2]. DL and ML technology allow researchers to develop a real-time system recognizing the COVID-19 virus. Various researchers have used many evaluation measures described in Table 2.

Table 2. Evaluation Measures

Measure	Equation
Precision [12]	$\text{Precision} = \frac{Ta}{Ta+Fa}$
Recall [7]	$\text{Recall} = \frac{Ta}{Ta+Fr}$
Accurac [11]	$\text{Accuracy} = \frac{Ta+Tr}{Ta+Fa+Tr+Fr}$
Specificity [9]	$\text{Specificity} = \frac{Tr}{Tr+Fr}$
G_Mean [10]	$\text{GM} = \sqrt{Specificity * Sensitivity}$
F1-Score [15]	$\text{F1} - \text{Score} = 2*\frac{Precision*Recall}{Precision+Recall}$
Mean absolute error [5]	$\text{MAE} = \frac{1}{N}\sum_{t=1}^{N} et$
Root mean square error [4]	$\text{RMSE} = \sqrt{\frac{1}{N}\sum_{i=1}^{n} 1*\frac{di-fi}{\sigma i}}$
Mean absolute percentage error [4]	$\text{MAPE} = \frac{1}{N}\sum_{1}^{t} 1 * \frac{At-Ft}{At}$

(*continued*)

Table 2. (*continued*)

Measure	Equation
Root Mean squared log error [10]	RMSLE = $\sqrt{\frac{1}{N}\sum_{1}^{N}1*\left[(loglog\,(xi+1)-loglog\,(x\prime i+1))\right]^2}$
Logarithmic loss [14]	Logloss $=\frac{1}{N}\sum_{i=1}^{N}1*[Yi.\left(y\prime i\right)+(1-yi)(1-y\prime i)]$
Receiver operating characteristics [3]	ROC $=\int_{a}^{b}1f(x)dx$
Area under curve [10, 12]	ROC $=\int_{a}^{b}1f(x)dx$
Testing the execution time [6]	TET
Matthews correlation coefficient [12]	MCC $=\sqrt{\frac{x^2}{N}}$
Average time for COVID-19 detection [6]	M $=\frac{1}{N}*\sum_{j=1}^{N}1*t$

4 Outcomes of the Study

Most research looks at chest imaging to predict COVID-19 infection. This further research the organs impacted by the virus since they may aid in viral identification and lower the risk of infection. Be mindful of this because the virus is considered in a late, harsh illness period when it penetrates the patient's lung. In contrast, a past infection phase is a moderate infection. There are no indications of illness in the viral carrier [3]. The resource that motivates future researchers to investigate COVID-19 issues from different viewpoints such as:

a. **Patient's history record:** The ML and DL algorithms may be modified to forecast COVID-19 patients with historical record restrictions (e.g., chronic diseases).
b. **The impact of the COVID-19**: Vaccine pharmaceutical formulations against victim recovery or body chemistry can be tracked and observed using DL and ML technologies.
c. **The COVID-19 disease life cycle:** DL and ML may be used to track the progression of the COVID-19 virus in the body. Determine the crucial infected cases using CT scans, ultrasound pictures, and X-rays.
d. Other ML and DL methods, such as COVID-19, include the reinforcement learning method, which could boost the effectiveness using ML and DL methods.
e. **Using the IOT:** This approach for COVID-19 monitoring requires little manual labour. Using a cloud server; may be made possible through effective sensor networking. The technology to monitor senior care isolated strength observation.
f. **Gene expression:** By pinpointing the uttermost instructive genes linked with all infectivity, the genetic mutations generated primarily by identified COVID-19 cases can be compared for scientific purposes. These genes are extractable, and the ML and DL algorithms explain how they affect the chance of viral infection or the intensity of affected individuals.

g. **The effects of disease on chemistry in the body:** A set of data points containing information on COVID-19 infection and the alterations to the body's chemistry is required (e.g., RNA sequence, blood group, oxygen level, etc.). Such information can support adopting alternative patient diagnosis approaches, which can support the development of unique methods for identifying contaminated people.

5 Conclusions

This research has undertaken a detailed assessment of DL, and ML approaches to detect and recognize the epidemic of COVID-19. The most significant goal of this Learning is to describe prior investigations and their applicability to COVID-19. These examined studies are chosen from various open and reputable educational records, such as the MDPI, IEEE, Elsevier, Springer, and other databases. These publications are filtered via numerous filters with Dl and ML approaches to removing duplicate concepts with important material connected to COVID-19 disease. In conclusion, China does have the most COVID-19 basis DL research compared to India, which has the most ML research based on the dataset. Typically, techniques- Deep Learning including machine learning are ordinary analysis and discussion on all aggregated COVID-19 research. Machine learning investigation is separated into these two types: unsupervised and supervised Learning. Moreover, only some researchers employed DL or ML to predict the outcome. For COVID-19 diagnosis and epidemic prediction, LDA, SVM, LR, KNN, Boost, ANN, K-means, and RF are utilized as ML algorithms, and GANs, CNN, RNN, and DNN, as DL algorithms. In conclusion, CNN is the multiple often utilized deep learning method as much as diagnosing COVID-19 and predicting outbreaks, while SVM is the prevalent machine learning method. Future research in DL and ML policies toward COVID-19 diagnostics will be guided and inspired by this work.

Acknowledgements. The authors express their gratitude to the Jaypee University of Engineering Technology, located in Guna, Madhya Pradesh, India, for providing them with infrastructural support. Additionally, the authors extend their thanks to all members of the DPMC for their valuable guidance and support. Their contributions were instrumental in the success of the research project, and the authors acknowledge their efforts with deep appreciation.

Authors' Contributions. All authors have equal contribution.

Funding. Not applicable.

Availability of Data and Material. Data and material are available on request.

Compliance with Ethical Standards.

Ethical Approval. - This article does not contain any studies with human participants or animals performed by any of the authors.

Research Involving Human Participants and/or Animals. - Not applicable.

Informed Consent. - All participants received and signed a written informed consent before entering a study.

Conflicts of Interest/Competing Interests. - Not applicable.

References

1. Sohrabi, C., et al.: World Health Organization declares global emergency: a review of the 2019 novel coronavirus (COVID-19). Int. J. Surg. **76**, 71–76 (2020)
2. Varanasi, R., et al.: Comparative effectiveness of pre-identified homeopathic medicines in asymptomatic COVID-19 individuals receiving standard care—an open-label, randomized, controlled exploratory trial. Homeopathy **111**(04), 252–260 (2022)
3. Hamed, A., Sobhy, A., Nassar, H.: Accurate classification of COVID-19 based on incomplete heterogeneous data using a K NN variant algorithm. Arab. J. Sci. Eng. **46**, 8261–8272 (2021)
4. Agarwal, V., Lohani, M.C., Bist, A.S., Harahap, E.P., Khoirunisa, A.: Analysis of deep learning techniques for chest x-ray classification in context of covid-19. ADI J. Recent Innov. **3**(2), 208–216 (2022)
5. Dubey, S., Verma, D.K., Kumar, M.: Severe acute respiratory syndrome Coronavirus-2 GenoAnalyzer and mutagenic anomaly detector using FCMFI and NSCE. Int. J. Biol. Macromolecules **258**, 129051 (2023)
6. Comito, C., Pizzuti, C.: Artificial intelligence for forecasting and diagnosing COVID-19 pandemic: a focused review. Artif. Intell. Med. **128**, 102286 (2022)
7. Mercaldo, F., Belfiore, M.P., Reginelli, A., Brunese, L., Santone, A.: Coronavirus covid-19 detection by means of explainable deep learning. Sci. Rep. **13**(1), 462 (2023)
8. Barstugan, M., Ozkaya, U., Ozturk, S.: Coronavirus (covid-19) classification using CT images by machine learning methods. arXiv preprint arXiv:2003.09424 (2020)
9. Yang, H., Wang, L., Xu, Y., Liu, X.: CovidViT: a novel neural network with self-attention mechanism to detect Covid-19 through X-ray images. Int. J. Mach. Learn. Cybern. **14**, 1–15 (2022)
10. Minaee, S., Kafieh, R., Sonka, M., Yazdani, S., Soufi, G.J.: Deep-COVID: predicting COVID-19 from chest X-ray images using deep transfer learning. Med. Image Anal. **65**, 101794 (2020)
11. Sufian, A., Ghosh, A., Sadiq, A.S., Smarandache, F.: A survey on deep transfer learning to edge computing for mitigating the COVID-19 pandemic. J. Syst. Architect. **108**, 101830 (2020)
12. Roy, S., et al.: Deep learning for classification and localization of COVID-19 markers in point-of-care lung ultrasound. IEEE Trans. Med. Imaging **39**(8), 2676–2687 (2020)
13. Soni, S., Dubey, S., Tiwari, R., Dixit, M.: Feature based sentiment analysis of product reviews using deep learning methods. Int. J. Adv. Technol. Eng. Res. (IJATER) (2018)
14. Tripathi, A., Chourasia, U., Dubey, S., Arjariya, A., Dixit, P.: A survey: optimization algorithms in deep learning. In: Proceedings of the International Conference on Innovative Computing & Communications (ICICC) (2020)
15. Dubeya, S., Kumar, M., Verma, D.K.: Machine learning approaches in deal with the COVID-19: comprehensive study. ECS Trans. **107**(1), 17815 (2022)

A Survey: Detection of Heart-Related Disorders Using Machine Learning Approaches

Kapil Dev Raghuwanshi$^{(\boxtimes)}$ and Shruti Yagnik

Department of Computer Science and Engineering, Indus University, Ahmedabad, Gujrat, India
dev2988@gmail.com, shrutiyagnik.ce@indusuni.ac.in

Abstract. Heart-related illnesses often known as CVDs (cardiovascular diseases) seem to be the leading cause of mortality globally in recent years. Consequently, a precise, workable, and trustworthy technique is necessary to recognize this disorder before time and begin the suitable treatment course. In this automated analysis of vast and complex health datasets, numerous machine learning methods are employed to scrutinize the information. Various machine learning techniques that have been developed by researchers are now being used by healthcare professionals to aid in the detection of heart-related disorders. Proposed study examines several models based on different methodological approaches, assessing the functionality of each. The Naive-Bayes model, SVM model (Support Vector Machines model), KNN model (K-Nearest Neighbor Model), DT model (Decision Trees Model), Ensemble models, and Supervised learning techniques based on RF model (Random Forest Model) are highly favored by researchers.

Keywords: SVM · KNN · Heart Disease · Random Forest · Decision Tree

1 Introduction

Heart disease remains a leading cause of death worldwide, accounting for a significant number of fatalities each year. The deterioration of cardiac muscle can lead to heart disease. Additionally, the inability of the heart to control blood flow characterizes heart failure. Coronary artery disease (CAD) is another name for heart disease [1]. A lack of blood flow to the arteries can lead to CAD. Symptoms such as cardiac arrest, high blood pressure, hypertension, chest pain etc., might be used to identify heart syndrome.

Chest pain, shortness of breath, and fainting are typical symptoms. Congenital disabilities, alcohol, diabetes, high blood pressure, medications, and smoking are all causes of heart disease [2]. Sometimes, infections that damage the cell membranes of the heart can also cause symptoms, including skin rashes, tiredness, fever, and dry cough. Bacteria, parasites, and viruses are the root causes of heart infections. Here, we discuss about the various types of heart disease [2].

M. Botto-Tobar et al. (Eds.): ICAT 2023, CCIS 2050, pp. 178–188, 2024.
https://doi.org/10.1007/978-3-031-58953-9_14

1.1 Angina

Angina is a condition that can have different patterns of symptoms depending on the severity of the underlying coronary artery disease. For example, stable angina is characterized by predictable chest pain or discomfort that occurs during physical exertion or emotional stress and typically subsides with rest.

1.2 Coronary Heart Disease

Atherosclerosis is the underlying process that causes the buildup of plaque in the coronary arteries in CHD. It is a complex process that involves inflammation, lipid metabolism, and immune system activation. Risk factors such as smoking, high blood pressure, and diabetes can contribute to the development of atherosclerosis by damaging the endothelial cells that line the arteries and promoting the deposition of cholesterol and other lipids in the arterial wall. As the plaque builds up, it can narrow the arteries and reduce blood flow to the heart muscle, leading to symptoms of CHD. In addition to lifestyle modifications and medical treatments, there is ongoing research into new therapies for atherosclerosis, including novel drugs that target inflammation and immune system pathways.

1.3 Unstable Angina

Unstable angina is more unpredictable and can occur at rest or with minimal exertion, and may be a sign of an impending heart attack. In addition to chest pain, angina can also cause shortness of breath, nausea, sweating, and dizziness. Treatment for angina may include lifestyle modifications, medications, and in some cases, invasive procedures such as angioplasty or bypass surgery.

1.4 Heart Failure

Heart failure is a serious condition in which the heart is unable to pump enough blood to meet the body's needs. This can happen due to a variety of underlying causes, including coronary artery disease, high blood pressure, heart valve disease, or previous heart attack. Symptoms of heart failure can include shortness of breath, fatigue, swelling in the legs and ankles, and rapid or irregular heartbeat.

1.5 Heart Attack

Heart attack are abnormal sounds heard during the heartbeat cycle and are usually detected during a routine physical examination. They can be caused by a variety of conditions, such as valve disorders, congenital heart disease, or infections. Some murmurs may be benign and require no treatment, while others may indicate underlying heart problems and require further investigation.

Table 1. Common datasets elements

S. No.	Code of variable	Variable values	Variable description
1	CP	0 = Atypical 1 = Typical 2 = Asymptotic 3 = Non-angina	Chest Pain
2	AGE	25 – 75	Age of the people
3	EXANG	1 = Yes 0 = No	Exercise Induced Angina
4	SEX	0 = Female 1 = Male	Gender
5	FBG	1 = True 0 = False	Fasting Blood Glucose
6	CHOL	125–565	Serum Cholesterol Level
7	OLD PEAK	0.0–6.3	ST depression induced by exercise related to rest
8	TRESTB PS	93–200	Resting Blood Pressure
9	THALACH	71–202	Maximum Heart Rate Achieved
10	REST ECG	0 = Normal 1 = STT Wave Abnormalities 2 = Left Ventricular Hypertrophy	Resting Electrocardiographic Results

1.6 Congenital Heart Conditions

Heart defects that are present at the time of birth are referred to as congenital heart conditions or birth defects of the heart. These conditions can affect the structure of the heart, the way it works, or both. They can range from mild to severe and can cause a variety of symptoms, including shortness of breath, and fatigue.

There are too many analytics processes available to identify cardiac disease these days, including deep learning, data mining, and machine learning methods. Therefore, this work will give a basic overview of machine learning approaches. Here, we learned about machine learning resources, and also learn various datasets in this [1, 2]. Certain risk variables are used to make predictions about heart disease as shown in Table 1. Blood pressure, gender, cholesterol, age, chest pain, occurrence of heart disease in one or more family members, smoking, diabetes, heart rate, alcohol, and being overweight are risk factors.

2   The Used Techniques and Approaches

There are so many techniques used to analyze heart disease, some of the methods discussing below.

2.1   K – Nearest Neighbor

The K-Nearest Neighbor rule a nonparametric method for classifying patterns was first developed [4]. Among the many classification methods available, the K-Nearest Neighbor algorithm stands out as one of the simplest yet most effective approaches. The approach is usually applied in classification tasks where there is a lack of prior information about the data distribution, and it refrains from making any assumptions about the data. With this approach, the data object where a response variable is absent is located together with the k nearest sample points as in the training dataset. The mean values of those sample points are then applied to that data point.

2.2   Support Vector Machine

When a pre-defined response variable is present, SVM is a popular supervised machine learning technique that can serve as both a classifier and a predictor. By analyzing the feature space, a hyperplane is identified to differentiate between categories for the purpose of classification.

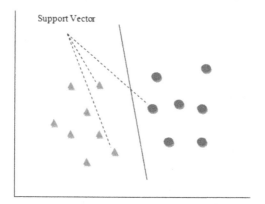

Fig. 1. Support Vector Machine

The SVM framework represents the training data points as samples in the feature space, where samples from different classes are separated by the largest possible distance [3]. During testing, the data samples are plotted on the same map within the feature space and categorized based on which side of the gap they fall into, as depicted in Fig. 1.

2.3 Naïve Bayes

The well-known Bayes Theorem is based on the simple yet powerful classification technique identified as Naive Bayes. It presupposes that predictors are independent of one another, which means that the traits or features shouldn't be related to each other in any way. Regardless of whether there is reliance, each of these characteristics or attributes still individually affects the likelihood, which is why it is referred to as naïve [5].

$$P\left(\frac{A}{B}\right) = \frac{P\left(\frac{B}{A}\right)P(A)}{P(A)} \tag{1}$$

where;

$P\left(\frac{A}{B}\right)$ = Posterior Probabilities

$P\left(\frac{B}{A}\right)$ = Chances

P (B) = Predictor prior probabilities

P (A) = Class prior probabilities

2.4 Decision Tree

As a supervised learning technique, the decision tree approach is a useful method for classification and regression, as illustrated in Fig. 2. Most of the classification-related issues are addressed by this strategy; both categorical and continuous qualities are performed with ease. Depending on the most important predictors, DT algorithm splits the crowd into more than two related subgroups [3].

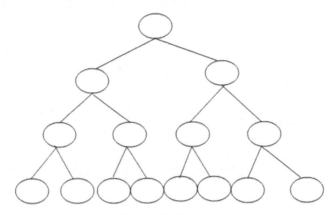

Fig. 2. Decision Tree

The entropy of every individual feature is primarily calculated through the algorithm called the Decision Tree model. Those features or determinants with the best information gain or perhaps the minimum entropy are subsequently employed to segregate the dataset. Iteratively apply these two measures to remain property.

$$\text{Entropy} = \sum_{(i=1)}^{c} -P_i P_i \; \text{Gain}(S, A) = \text{Entropy}(S) - \sum_{v \in values(A)} \frac{|S_v|}{|S|} Entropy(Sv) \qquad (2)$$

2.5 Random Forest

Another well-liked supervised algorithm for machine learning is Random Forest, as shown in Fig. 3. Although both classification and regression objectives could be accomplished using this method, classification tasks often yield better results. The Random Forest approach, as the name implies, takes numerous decision trees into account before producing an output. As a result, it is essentially a collection of decision trees.

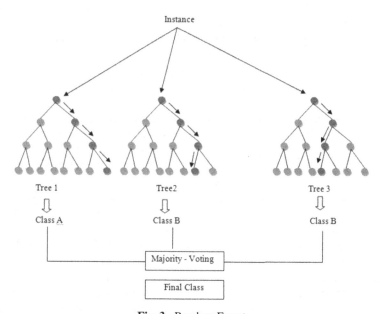

Fig. 3. Random Forest

That method is predicated on the idea that far more trees will eventually lead to the correct answer. In regression, a simple mean of each outcome from every decision tree is taken, but for classification, a voting method is used to determine the class. It performs effectively with big datasets with plenty of dimensions [6].

3 Literature Review

Healthcare facilities have utilized diverse machine learning algorithms to explore disease analysis and prediction. The objective of the presented hybrid method is to enhance the accuracy of cardiovascular disease prediction by utilizing machine learning techniques to identify crucial components. A few well-known design methods are used to produce the prediction model, composed of different highlighted mixtures [2]. A methodology developed for a cardiovascular disease prediction model using HRFLM, which has an 88.7% precision level. The healthcare professionals were trained on various data mining algorithms and prediction techniques, including Linear Regression, K-Nearest Neighbor, Support Vector Machine Model, Logistic Regression Model, Neural Network Model, and Vote, which have become popular recently due to their effectiveness in detecting and predicting heart disease. This investigation aims to explain how decision trees and Naive Bayes classifiers were employed in examination, particularly in the heart disease prediction system [1].

According to some research that examined the application of the predictive data mining method on the same dataset, the decision tree outperformed the Bayes classification model. Researchers utilized the Multi-Layer Perceptron Method (MLP) - a type of neural network algorithm - to train and test the dataset [7]. The layer for input, the other for output, or rather various hidden units between the output and input layers are just a few of the many levels that make up this algorithm. These hidden layers connect each input node to an output layer node. This link has some assigned weights. Bias, or identical additional input with weight b, is applied toward the nodes to balance the number of neurons. Depending on the circumstance, the connection between the nodes might be either feedforward or feedback. This report provides a prediction system for cardiac arrest by employing artificial intelligence techniques with explicit recurrent neural systems.

The model was constructed using deep learning [8] to anticipate the chances that a patient will encounter heart-related diseases. RNN is an extremely innovative characterization method that applies Deep Learning methodology in ANN. The paper goes into great detail about the main elements of the framework and the underlying assumptions. The suggested method employs deep learning and data mining to get accurate, error-free outcomes. The growth of a special type of prediction system for heart attack is guided by and measured against the findings of this study. Again, in a model created for heart disease prediction using Machine Learning [25, 26], the likelihood that the causes of heart disease will increase is predicted (diabetes, circulatory strain, high cholesterol, current smoking, etc. As a result, it is challenging to identify heart illness. Several neural algorithms and data mining algorithms have been used to determine how bad heart disease is among people. Being confounded by CHD disease, it is important to approach it carefully. An unanticipated death could occur if an earlier detection is not made, leading to heart difficulties. In the realm of medical science, data mining techniques are employed to discover and understand diverse metabolic pathways and their associated algorithms, a technique that allows the algorithm to profit from previous studies on information and modeling without really being explicitly specialized. Machine learning creates reasoning reliant on historical data.

A machine-learning model was developed using classification methods to predict cardiac issues in males [9]. Within this article, comprehensive insights are presented concerning cardiac health issues, including their distinguishing features, prevalent forms, and related medical conditions. The tool used is WEKA, a valuable platform for data mining in biomedical disciplines. The major available WEKA platforms—Artificial Neural Networks, Naive Bayes, and Decision Trees—are used to forecast cardiovascular illness. C4.5, CART, J48, CHAID, Naive Bayes Techniques, and ID3 Algorithms are examples of Decision Trees commonly employed in prediction methods.

To simplify the study of complicated and huge data, [10] a proposal for a prediction system model using machine learning methods included a health datasets variety. To assist healthcare professionals and specialists in diagnosing heart-related illnesses, researchers have increased their use of many machine learning algorithms in recent years. Scientists favor supervised methods for modeling, such as KNN, SVM, DT, Naive Bayes, ensemble models, and RF models. To automate the enormous study and complex data frameworks are used to analyze multiple medical datasets. Many researchers have recently begun using a few more algorithms for machine learning and approach various medical datasets to simplify examining large and complicated data.

4 Findings

Various researchers have used different machine learning technologies to analyze and predict heart disease; some of the outcomes from this research are discussed in Table 2.

Table 2. Several researchers' methods for predicting heart disease

Authors	Technologies Used	Dataset	Year	Accuracy
Xu, S. et al.	Evaluation of the CFS Subset Using a BFS and enhanced RF Framework	People's Hospital (PKU) and Cleveland	2017	Dataset Test with People's Hospital: 97% and CHDD Test: 91.6%
S. M. M. Hasan	DT (ID3), Gaussian Naive Bayes, RF, and LR	Cleveland	2018	Logistic regression with 92.76%
Amin, Ul	Feature Selection Using SVM, ANN, KNN, LR, DT, NB and mRMR, LASSO, and RF Relief	Cleveland	2018	Logistic regression with Relief: 89%

(*continued*)

Table 2. (*continued*)

Authors	Technologies Used	Dataset	Year	Accuracy
S. Mohan	"LM (Linear Method)," RF join an "HRFLM"	Cleveland	2019	88.7%
A. N. Repaka	Sequential Minimal Optimization "Navies Bayesian," Parallel Homomorphic Encryption Algorithm, and Multi-Layer Perception "Bayes Net," Advanced Encryption Standard "AES"	UCI Repository	2019	89.77% with Navies Bayesian
S. Bashir	LR, DT, RF, Naïve Bayes, Logistic regression, and SVM	UCI Repository	2019	84.85% with FS/MR with Logistic Regression
J. P. Li	LASSO, mRMR, KNN, NB Relief, ANN, SVM, DT and LR	Cleveland	2020	92.37% with FCMIM-SVM
Shah, D.	Naive Bayes, KNN, RF, and DT	Cleveland	2020	90.78% with KNN
N. L. Fitriyani	LR, NB, SVM, MLP, RF, and DT	Cleveland and Statlog	2020	98.40% with Cleveland 95.90% with Statlog
A. Singh	LR, KNN, SVM, and DT	UCI Repository	2020	87% with KNN
Rani, P.	adaboost classifiers, NB, SVM, random forest, and LR	Cleveland	2021	86.60%
Katarya, R.	Naive Bayes, LR, SVM, MLP, KNN, RF, DT, DNN, and ANN	UCI Repository	2021	95.60% with Random Forest
M. Kavitha	The Hybrid of DT and RF	Cleveland	2021	88.70% with Hybrid Model

5 Conclusion

According to the review above, machine learning algorithms have enormous potential for detecting cardiac disorders and cardio ailments. Each of the algorithms mentioned above has done incredibly well in some situations while failing miserably in others. We developed machine learning methods and examined their attributes to determine the best. Each method has produced a distinct outcome in a variety of circumstances. Subsequent analysis shows that the forecasting algorithm for cardiac diseases only achieves minimal accuracy; hence, further complicated models are required to improve the detection of early cardiovascular disease accuracy. We will develop new methodologies for accurate, low-cost, and simple, early heart disease prediction.

References

1. Nikhar, S., Karandikar, A.M.: Prediction of heart disease using machine learning algorithms. Int. J. Adv. Eng. Manage. Sci. **2**(6), 239484 (2016)
2. Mohan, S., Chandrasegar, T.: Srivastava Gautam Effective heart disease prediction using hybrid machine learning techniques. IEEE Access **7**, 81542–81554 (2019)
3. Pouriyeh, S., et al.: A comprehensive investigation and comparison of machine learning techniques in the domain of heart disease. In: 2017 IEEE Symposium on Computers and Communications (ISCC). IEEE (2017)
4. Silverman, B.W., Christopher Jones, M.: E. Fix and J.L. Hodges (1951): an important contribution to nonparametric discriminant analysis and density estimation: commentary on fix and hodges (1951). Int. Statist. Rev./Revue Int. Statist. **1989**, 233–238 (1951)
5. Pahwa, K., Kumar, R.: Prediction of heart disease using hybrid technique for selecting features. In: 2017 4th IEEE Uttar Pradesh Section International Conference on Electrical, Computer and Electronics (UPCON). IEEE (2017)
6. Xu, S., et al.: Cardiovascular risk prediction method based on CFS subset evaluation and random forest classification framework. In: 2017 IEEE 2nd International Conference on Big Data Analysis (ICBDA). IEEE (2017)
7. Gavhane, A., et al.: Prediction of heart disease using machine learning. In: 2018 Second International Conference on Electronics, Communication and Aerospace Technology (ICECA). IEEE (2018)
8. Kishore, A., et al.: Heart attack prediction using deep learning. Int. Res. J. Eng. Technol. (IRJET) **5**(04), 2395–2472 (2018)
9. Krishnan, S., Geetha, S.: Prediction of heart disease using machine learning algorithms. In: 2019 1st International Conference on Innovations in Information and Communication Technology (ICIICT). IEEE (2019)
10. Ramalingam, V.V., Dandapath, A., Karthik Raja, M.: Heart disease prediction using machine learning techniques: a survey. Int. J. Eng. Technol. 7.2.8, 684–687 (2018)
11. Hasan, S.M.M., et al.: Comparative analysis of classification approaches for heart disease prediction. In: 2018 International Conference on Computer, Communication, Chemical, Material and Electronic Engineering (IC4ME2). IEEE (2018)
12. Haq, A.U., et al.: A hybrid intelligent system framework for the prediction of heart disease using machine learning algorithms. Mobile Inf. Syst. **2018**, 1–21 (2018)
13. Repaka, A.N., Ravikanti, S.D., Franklin, R.G.: Design and implementing heart disease prediction using naives Bayesian. In: 2019 3rd International Conference on Trends in Electronics and Informatics (ICOEI). IEEE (2019)
14. Riyaz, L., Butt, M.A., Zaman, M., Ayob, O.: Heart disease prediction using machine learning techniques: a quantitative review. In: Khanna, A., Gupta, D., Bhattacharyya, S., Hassanien, A.E., Anand, S., Jaiswal, A. (eds.) International Conference on Innovative Computing and Communications. AISC, vol. 1394, pp. 81–94. Springer, Singapore (2022). https://doi.org/10.1007/978-981-16-3071-2_8

15. Shah, D., Patel, S., Bharti, S.K.: Heart disease prediction using machine learning techniques. SN Comput. Sci. **1**(6), 345 (2020). https://doi.org/10.1007/s42979-020-00365-y
16. Fitriyani, N.L., et al.: HDPM: an effective heart disease prediction model for a clinical decision support system. IEEE Access **8**, 133034–133050 (2020)
17. Singh, A., Kumar, R.: Heart disease prediction using machine learning algorithms. In: 2020 International Conference on Electrical and Electronics Engineering (ICE3). IEEE (2020)
18. Rani, P., et al.: A decision support system for heart disease prediction based upon machine learning. J. Reliab. Intell. Environ. (2021)
19. Katarya, R., Meena, S.K.: Machine learning techniques for heart disease prediction: a comparative study and analysis. Health Technol. **11**, 87–97 (2021)
20. Kavitha, M., et al.: Heart disease prediction using hybrid machine learning model. In: 2021 6th International Conference on Inventive Computation Technologies (ICICT). IEEE (2021)
21. Dubeya, S., Kumar, M., Verma, D.K.: Machine learning approaches in deal with the COVID-19: comprehensive study. ECS Trans. **107**(1), 17815 (2022)
22. Soni, S., et al.: Feature based sentiment analysis of product reviews using deep learning methods. Int. J. Adv. Technol. Eng. Res. (IJATER) (2018)

Technological and Other Motivating Factors Behind Purchase Intention for Organic Processed Food

Tanveer Kaur$^{(\boxtimes)}$ ⓘ and Anil Kalotra

University School of Business, Chandigarh University, Punjab, India
ratantanveer@gmail.com

Abstract. Growing knowledge of the organic diet as a healthy food alternative has spread around the world. The idea that organic food doesn't contain dangerous chemicals like nonorganic food has begun to gain widespread acceptance. More customers are turning to natural products as a result of the rising incidence of food contamination caused by the use of chemical pesticides and fertilisers in agriculture. More ecologically concerned consumers are gravitating toward organic foods. As a result, the organic food business worldwide is expanding at a pace of 20–22% yearly. Consumers' lifestyles have evolved in recent years, and dining out has become commonplace. From a health perspective, the consumer is prepared to pay more for high-quality goods, particularly food products. New industry opportunities for producers and merchants have emerged as a result of promising customers a shift in mind set. Enhancing public health and protecting the environment both depend on organic agriculture. Therefore, encouraging organic farming will benefit customers as well as farmers by meeting consumer demands for high-quality food and environmentally friendly food production. This conceptual study lists 11 key elements that have a significant impact on customer intentions to buy organic goods. Further, this research investigates the impact of technology as a motivating factor behind consumers' purchase intention for organic processed food. As the food industry experiences rapid advancements in technology, including digital platforms, e-commerce, and information-sharing tools, understanding how these technological elements influence consumer choices in the context of organic processed food becomes crucial.

Keywords: Purchase Intention · Perception · Organic Food Products · Attitude · Technological Factors · Motivational Factors

1 Introduction

Policymakers and society as a whole are becoming more concerned about food safety nowadays. People's attitudes about organic food items, environmental issues, and food safety have all seen substantial shifts over the past few decades. Organic farming not only protects the environment but also uses fewer toxic chemicals. Organic food is typically thought to be healthier [1]. Therefore, it is not unexpected that interest in

M. Botto-Tobar et al. (Eds.): ICAT 2023, CCIS 2050, pp. 189–196, 2024.
https://doi.org/10.1007/978-3-031-58953-9_15

foods grown organically is at an all-time high among consumers and governmental organisations. IFOAM's 2010 research indicates that the market for organic processed foods worldwide has been expanding significantly. The market for organic processed food was worth US$ 15 billion in 1999, US$ 54.1 billion in 2009, and US$ 59.1 billion in 2010. The anticipated rise is 23 percent [2].

2 Methodology

A literature review served as the conceptual study's technique. To determine the elements that encourage or impede customers' intents to make purchases of organic products, researchers studied the literature on related topics and studies. The parameters in this research are established from a review of 30 papers in the literature.

3 Research Objective

Finding the driving forces (technological and motivational) behind people's decisions to buy organic processed food is the major goal of the article based on the literature research.

4 Factors Impacting Decisions to Buy Organic Processed Food

Eleven characteristics were identified as influencing consumers' decisions to purchase organic processed foods through a literature review. The following subsections go into further information about these eleven criteria.

Concern Towards Environment
One of key drivers of every product purchase is concern for environment. It has been demonstrated by several research that organic agriculture is less harmful to the environment. According to a study by Ling, green customers' purchase of organic products was favourably connected with their environmental attitude and self-efficacy [3]. Previous research by Tobler et al. on customers in England found a correlation between consumers' attitudes, desire to engage in real-world behaviours related to green food, and concern for making a positive contribution to the environment [4]. Taiwanese consumers' views toward buying organic products are influenced by their healthy lifestyles, favourable environmental attitudes, and health consciousness [5].

Concern for Health
One of the most significant drivers of customer apprehension regarding buying organic processed food is determined to be health. Customers are well aware of the nutritional value of the meals they eat. Consumer attitudes regarding organic processed food are influenced by health concerns. Numerous research have demonstrated that health is key factor in decision to purchase organic processed foods [6]. Parents are now more worried about the health of their kids. She also believes that organic processed food is high-priced than non-organic food by between 30 and 40 percent [7]. A study conducted in Bangalore

city supported Swati's results that consumers strongly believe organic processed food items are safe & healthful to consume. Research in Egypt discovered that desire to live a healthy lifestyle was the main driver of the purchase of organic processed food, and desire to pay. In a study, it was discovered that healthy eating and living were excellent predictors of attitudes toward organic processed food. The health value was further established as a good predictor when compared to other parameters [8].

Concern for Nutrition Value
Consumers are particularly interested in nutrition that is crucial to their bodies and what kinds of foods include large amounts of nourishment. Nutritional value, sensory quality, and food safety were all the subject of several earlier studies. Crops produced organically have been shown to have more nutrients [9].

Concern Towards Native Farmers
One significant aspect influencing customers' decision to purchase organic products is their concern for the welfare of their local farmers. In their 2013 study, Pugliese et al. looked at how Lebanese organic consumers interacted with local goods and organic processed foods. Additionally, it was shown that farmers' markets had key role in the beneficial association between non-organic & organic processed food products. The research confirms results from earlier studies showing that consumers who purchased organic items were far more inclined to buy them from local markets [10].

Concern for Quality
Value for money is referred to as quality; when one pay premium price, one anticipate higher quality. In general, consumers who buy organic products are less price sensitive & more inclined toward quality. Bangalore city found that customers associate organic processed food goods with product quality and pricing. Quality and affordability were the main motivators for customers in Izmir to purchase organic processed food items, according to an analysis [11]. It was discovered that there was a stronger correlation between price and quality than with other criteria. Consumer attitudes concerning impediments to the uptake of organic products were surveyed. All inhabitants of the Iranian province of Golestan's Gorgan city were included in the target population. Institutional hurdles (16.75%), feed quality barriers (14.54%), cultural barriers (14.28%), & economic barriers (10.43%) were the four primary impediments identified by the results [12].

Availability
The demand of organic products is vital elements influencing customer buying behaviour, according to previous study. The accessibility of organic processed food products is the most important driving factors that led to purchase of organic processed food, according to a study conducted in Denmark between 2008 and 2009 with goal of gaining insight into purchase of organic processed food products & investigating key parameters that influences their buying intention. The customers were able to easily get organic processed food thanks to the products' exposure & obvious refelection of their organic certification, which led to frequent purchases of organic processed food items [13].

Concern Towards Animal Welfare

It is discovered that buying organic processed food is influenced significantly by animal welfare. Concerns regarding how animals are fed, bred, and cared for are raised by consumers. Customers that buy organic products are worried about the biosphere in addition to the environment and their health. Animal welfare was revealed to be a significant factor in food choice in his research in Taiwan. The study identified a number of significant favourable attitudes regarding organic processed food, one of which being the substantial effect of animal rights problems. Animal welfare is first driver of organic processed food purchases in the UK and Germany [14].

Concern for Safety

Consumers are switching from traditional to organic processed food items because of two extremely essential factors: trust and safety. Consumers are searching for safer food options due to rising food and health safety violations. For a food that is trustworthy and safer and contains less pesticides and dangerous substances, a consumer is prepared to pay a high price [15].

Demographics

Family members, reference groups, & other individuals can also influence buyers. Studies have revealed that individual characteristics like gender, age, income & education level can influence consumer behaviour. Mervin & Velmurugan discovered that a consumer's attitude toward organic processed food products is positively correlated with monthly income, gender, place of family status, residence, length of consumption, amount of knowledge about organic processed food products, & health status [16].

Another study corroborated the finding which consumers' intentions to buy organic processed food and willingness to pay are significantly influenced by education. With 200 respondents, looked at variables impacting the propensity to buy organic goods in Kuala Lumpur. The study found six elements that influence motivation, including knowledge & health awareness, education, government support & policy, concerns for the environment, and attitudes, perceived values, & habits. The research emphasised importance of each of these criteria in relation to how organic processed food buyers choose to make purchases. Knowledge and education were determined to have the most impact. The most essential factor for predicting the desire to purchase organic processed food is knowledge, according to research [17].

Attitude and its Effect Towards Organic Processed Food

The mentality of the consumer is a significant element in whether they choose to buy organic processed food. Environmental concern was the second-strongest correlation between consumer views of organic processed food items and their propensity to purchase them. The results revealed that consumers of organic processed food are relatively lesser price sensitive, trust in quality, & seek out information at the place of purchase as well as through newspapers and publications. According to the findings, client loyalty to organic processed food goods was significantly influenced by how much they valued such products [14].

Understanding about Organic Processed Foods and Purchase Intention
We may generate greater interest the more we know. Consumer knowledge and information are key factors in their purchasing decisions. Knowledge seems to be essential for the successful advertisement of organic processed foods. This emphasises the bare minimum necessity of comprehending consumers' convictions on the value of organic processed food. According to several research, understanding how food is produced or produced would improve consumer attitudes and raise the possibility that people will embrace these meals [12, 13, 18, 19].

5 Technology as a Motivating Factors Behind Purchase Intention for Organic Processed Food

Information Accessibility and Transparency
Technology enables consumers to access a wealth of information about the origins, production methods, and nutritional value of organic processed foods. Websites, mobile applications, and QR codes on packaging provide details about certifications, farming practices, and supply chain transparency. This information empowers consumers to make informed choices aligned with their values [20].

Digital Marketing and Social Media
Digital marketing campaigns and social media platforms are powerful tools for promoting organic processed foods. Brands leverage these channels to communicate their sustainability initiatives, ethical practices, and unique product attributes. Consumer engagement through social media influencers and user-generated content fosters a sense of community and trust, influencing purchase intentions [20].

e-Commerce and Online Shopping Platforms
The convenience of online shopping platforms accelerates the adoption of organic processed foods. E-commerce allows consumers to explore a diverse range of products, read reviews, and make purchases without physical constraints. Subscription models and personalized recommendations further enhance the shopping experience, encouraging repeat purchases and brand loyalty.

Mobile Applications and Loyalty Programs
Mobile applications from organic food retailers often offer loyalty programs, discounts, and personalized recommendations. These features not only enhance user experience but also incentivize consumers to choose organic processed foods over conventional alternatives [21]. The ease of mobile transactions contributes to the overall convenience and satisfaction of the purchasing process.

Blockchain Technology for Traceability
Blockchain technology enhances traceability in the supply chain, assuring consumers of the authenticity of organic claims. With a transparent and immutable ledger, consumers can verify the journey of their food from farm to table, reinforcing trust in the organic certification process and motivating purchase decisions [22].

Augmented Reality (AR) and Virtual Reality (VR)

AR and VR technologies are increasingly used to create immersive experiences for consumers. In the context of organic processed food, these technologies can be employed to provide virtual farm tours, interactive educational content, and engaging storytelling, fostering a deeper connection between consumers and the origins of their food [23].

Sustainability Tracking Tools

Technology allows for the development of apps and tools that enable consumers to track their environmental impact through their food choices. These tools may calculate carbon footprints, water usage, or other ecological metrics associated with organic processed foods, aligning with the growing interest in sustainable and eco-friendly consumption [20].

6 Discussion and Conclusion

According to the literature review, a number of factors affect consumers' intentions to purchase organic processed food. In total, 11 significant variables were found in this study.

More health-conscious consumers choose the foods that have the highest nutritional value. Due to its advantages and favourable effects on the environment, demand for organic processed food is continuously rising across the world. Environmental protection, health, animal rights, promoting local farmers, safety, & quality are the main variables that appear to affect the desire for organic processed food consumption. However, past research has revealed that the perceived obstacles to not buying organic processed food are a high price, hassle, and lack of knowledge [24].

According to past studies, each nation has unique important aspects that affect its citizens' opinions about buying organic processed food, both positively and negatively. Marketing departments will be better able to position their items to appeal to organic buyers if they have a deeper awareness of their characteristics and factors [25].

To advertise organic processed food as being safer for society, better for health, and more nutritious, policymakers need create an effective marketing plan. In order to create better marketing strategies and policies, extra research may be employed to better understand customers [26]. Most importantly, it might be used to compare how factors such as location and price affect customer intentions to purchase organic processed food. The decision-making process for marketing operations dealing with organic products might benefit from having a thorough awareness of various market sectors [27].

References

1. Hamm, U.: A re organic consumers preferring or avoiding foods with nutrition and health claims. Food Qual. Prefer. **30**, 68–76 (2013)
2. Mervin, R., Velmurugan, R.: Consumer's attitude towards organic food products. Discovery **3**(7), 15–18 (2013)
3. Shamsollahi, A., Chong, C.W., Nahid, N.: Factors influencing on purchasing behavior of organic foods. Hum. Soc. Sci. Res. **1**(2), 93–104 (2013)

4. Rousseau, S., Vranken, L.: Green market expansion by reducing information a symmetry: evidence for labeled organic food products. Food Policy **40**, 31–43 (2013)
5. Raghavan, N., Mageh, R.: A study on consumers' purchase intentions towards organic products. Indian J. Res. **2**(1), 111–114 (2013)
6. Manohar, S.J., Devaruand, S.D.B., Arundathi, S.V.: Consumer perception towards organic food products: an exploratory study in Bangalore using factor analysis. Int. J. Manage. Res. Rev. **2**(1), 1733–1747 (2012)
7. Radhika, P., Ammani, P., Seema: Eating healthy-consumer perception of organic foods in twin cities. Int. J. Market. **1**(2), 67–72 (2012)
8. Ozguven, N.: Organic foods motivation factors for consumers. Procedia-Soc. Behav. Sci. **62**, 661–665 (2012)
9. Mohamed, M.A., Chymisand, A., Shelaby, A.A.: Determinants of organic food consumption in Egypt. Int. J. Econ. Bus. Model. **3**(3), 183–191 (2012)
10. Padiya, J., Valla, N.: Profiling of organic food buyers in Ahmedabad city: an empirical study. Pacific Bus. Rev. Int. **5**(1), 19–26 (2012)
11. Kumar, S., Ali, J.: Analyzing the factors affecting consumer awareness on organic foods in India. In: Symposium ID: 282, Prepared for presentation at 21st Annual IFAMA World Forum and Symposium on the Road to2050: Sustainability as a Business Opportunity (2012)
12. Hjelmar, U.: Consumers' purchase of organic food products. A matter of convenience and reflexive practices. Appetite **56**, 336–344 (2011)
13. Amarnath, B., Vijayudu, G.: Rural consumers' attitude towards branded packaged food product. Asia-Pacific J. Soc. Sci. **3**(1), 147–159 (2011)
14. Perrini, F., Castaldo, S., Misani, N., Tencati, A.: The impact of corporate social responsibility associations on trust in organic products marketed by mainstream retailers: a study of Italian consumers. Bus. Strategy Environ. **19**, 512–526 (2010)
15. Chen, M.F.: Attitude towards organic foods among Taiwanese as related to health consciousness environmental attitudes and the mediating effects of a healthy lifestyle. British Food J. **111**(2), 165–178 (2010)
16. Salleh, M.M., Ali, S.M., Harun, E.H., Jalil, M.A., Shaharudin, M.R.: Consumer's perception and purchase intentions towards organic food products: exploring attitude among academician. Can. Soc. Sci. **6**(6), 119–129 (2010)
17. Sadati, S.A.: Survey consumer attitude toward barriers of organic products(OP) in Iran: a case study in Gorgan city. World Appl. Sci. J. **8**(11), 1298–1303 (2010)
18. Smithand, S., Paladino, A.: Eatingc leanand green? Investigating consumer motivations towards the purchase of organic food (2009)
19. Essoussi, L.H., Zahaf, M.: Exploring the decision-making process of Canadian organic food consumers. J. Cetacean Res. Manag. **12**(4), 1352–2752 (2009)
20. Sihombing, S.O.: Predicting environmentally purchase behaviour. A test of the value-attitude-behaviour hierarchy. In: The 2nd Indonesian Business Management Conference, Jakarta (2007)
21. Wijaya, T.: Model of consumer's buying intention towards organicfood: a study among mothers in Indonesia. In: International Conference on Economics, Business and Marketing Management. IPEDR, vol. 29, p. 174 (2012)
22. Bawa, S.S., et al.: A study of consumer satisfaction towards fast moving consumer goods. Webology **18**(4) (2021). http://www.webology
23. Kaur, T., Singhal, S.: Empirical study of consumer perception towards organic products. J. Xi'an Univ. Archit. Technol. **12**(3), 5657–5672 (2020)
24. Batte, M.T., Hooker, N.H., Haab, T.C., Beaverson, J.: Putting their money where their mouths are: consumer willingness to pay for multi-ingredient, processed organic food products. J. Sci. Direct. **32**(2), 145–159 (2007)

196 T. Kaur and A. Kalotra

25. Ajzen, I.: Nature and operation of attitudes. Ann. Rev. Psychol. **52**, 27–58 (2001)
26. Reganold, J.P., Glover, J.D., Andrews, P.K., Hinman, H.R.: Sustainability of three apple production system. Nature **410**, 926–930 (2001)
27. Gupta, L., Kaur, T.: To examine the roadmap of organic farming in India. Shodhasamhita, Vol. IX, Issue II (2022)

Conversational AI-Based Technological Solution for Intelligent Customer Service

Alessandro Chumpitaz Terry[✉], Liliana Yanqui Huarocc, and Daniel Burga-Durango

Universidad Peruana de Ciencias Aplicadas Lima, Lima, Perú
{u201822524,u201822475,pcsidbur}@upc.edu.pe

Abstract. Virtual assistants are used to complement user navigation and experience through e-commerce platforms and online services. Several studies show that customer experience is significantly improved when virtual assistants exhibit human-like attention and provide personalized recommendations tailored to individual preferences and needs. To achieve this, the assistant can make use of Natural Language Processing, which enables understanding of human language along with responses. This study develops a virtual assistant focused on conversational AI which is implemented in a poultry retail's website to improve customer experience. To validate the benefits of the implementation, we collected feedback from a group of 58 customers in the city of Lima that interacted with the virtual assistant. In this way, results showed that the virtual assistant generated a positive impact on customer service with an average of 83.66% across dimensions such as usability, functionality, and customer satisfaction.

Keywords: Conversational AI · Virtual Assistant · Voice Assistant · Conversational Agent · Customer Service

1 Introduction

Communicating with customers through live conversational technologies has shown to be an increasingly popular way of delivering quality customer service in various digital environments [1]. Consequently, many companies are interested in having an integration with virtual assistants on their digital channels and ecommerce with the objective of boosting sales of products or services to have better opportunities in comparison between the competition of their market segment. In this way, companies will not only benefit from making sales, but also generate a positive impact with the user experience and customer service. However, this technology is still developmental stage and is not yet available in a form that caters to the distinct needs of market segments [2].

According to [3], only 28% of Peruvian companies have implemented virtual technologies in their commercial processes, primarily attributed to a deficiency in knowledge and capacity for virtual customer service. Likewise, there exists a pressing need for Peruvian companies to familiarize themselves with overarching principles for effective AI development and utilization. Among these principles, the consideration of delay time stands out, as the tardy adoption of cutting-edge technologies may hinder their

M. Botto-Tobar et al. (Eds.): ICAT 2023, CCIS 2050, pp. 197–210, 2024.
https://doi.org/10.1007/978-3-031-58953-9_16

impactful integration, like trends observed in other countries. Additionally, guidelines encompass the engagement of stakeholders and capital investment in AI, crucial aspects for advancing AI initiatives in both Peru and the broader Latin American context.

Due to continuous advances in artificial intelligence with emphasis in natural language processing, conversational AI guarantees a normal voice interaction between humans and computers [4]. Within this framework, the voice assistants and chatbots are considered as conversational agents and can support the user with the completion of different tasks [5]. This technology has applications in many areas where it can replace humans by engaging in dialogues to provide information, conduct transactions, and participate in conversations [7]. The deployment of conversational agents holds the potential for significant positive impacts, enhancing customer satisfaction. Thus, digital agents are deemed capable of meeting customer expectations and fulfilling their needs. In the end, the customer decides to continue with the service or make a purchase [6].

According to [8] and [9], numerous companies have incorporated conversational agents into core customer service processes, particularly in accounting and medical attention. However, a substantial portion of customers reports negative feedback regarding their experiences with conversational AI-based solutions. Instances such as providing inaccurate answers for specific tasks contribute to disparities between user expectations and system performance. Moreover, negative responses from conversational agents have the potential to adversely impact user interactions, influencing purchase intentions [10]. Therefore, there remains a notable scope for enhancement in conversational agents within e-commerce platforms. Such improvements could serve as a distinctive feature for organizations dedicated to elevating the quality of their customer service, as highlighted in [11].

In Sect. 2, pertinent information derived from related work about conversational AI for customer service is presented. Section 3 defines examples of technology and the developmental process of conversational AI. Section 4 shows the process of validation of the developed solution. Section 5 analyses the statistics results with graphics and tables. In Sect. 6, principal findings about results, limitations and future relative jobs and investigations are introduced.

2   Related Works

2.1   Conversational AI-Based Technological Solutions

Studies have been conducted on the development of a virtual assistant, as detailed in [12]. The focus of this research was the creation of a web-based assistant tailored for online banking services, utilizing artificial intelligence for natural language understanding. This assistant underwent testing across Google Home and Assistant, involving both spoken and text interactions. Results demonstrated that assistant have a practical and lasting utility. Furthermore, the study revealed that assistants consistently provide responses to users at a superior level, showcasing heightened reliability and speed when compared to conventional methods.

In the study conducted by [13], a conversational AI was integrated with an animated avatar from SitePal was implemented within a museum setting. It utilized Dialogflow for command processing, the Google Cloud text-to-speech API for voice synthesis, and Natural Language Processing through the RASA NLU App. Notably, the system achieved an impressive 3-s response time, with an average human-computer interaction duration of 3 min and 26 s.

In [14] and [8], an extensive assessment of the impact of virtual assistants on customer service was conducted. Survey findings indicate that providing assistants aligned with customer expectations positively influences customer experience and satisfaction. Another study [14] demonstrated that the main reason a virtual assistant can have a positive impact on a business is its consideration of factors that customers can perceive, especially in terms of information and service quality, perceived enjoyment, perceived usefulness, perceived ease of use, satisfaction, and continuance intention.

2.2 Technologies that Support Development of Virtual Assistant

The selection of appropriate software for accurate data processing in virtual assistant systems and ensuring user-friendly interfaces is crucial [15]. Notably, various studies and successful cases have employed specific tools for this purpose:

- **Rasa NLU y Rasa Core**: Rasa's Stack platform integrates Natural Language Understanding (NLU) and machine learning processes to facilitate the creation of an automated chatbot for placing orders, handling requests, and managing returns in a virtual library [16].
- **Intent Recognition Providers**: The Xatkit framework is dedicated to model driven engineering (MDE) and offers open-source application integrations with capabilities for interpreting and converting voice to text, similar to Lex and Microsoft Bot Framework [17].
- **Third party applications**: The study conducted benchmarking of three third-party applications, especially Microsoft LUIS, IBM Watson and Dialogflow. These applications were selected for their utility in designing conversational agents, and the investigation included an analysis of their precision levels and performance under a substantial number of simultaneous queries [18].
- **Domain-specific language (DSL)**: Another essential consideration for the development of a virtual assistant is the integration with Character User Interface (CUI) through three packages: intentions package, behavior package, and a runtime package. This approach facilitates the implementation of a multi-functional agent [19].

3 Method

This project was developed with the purpose of achieving a good and effective customer experience in an e-commerce's website. A virtual assistant was designed to assist users with core processes of the website, including product selection, making a complaint, and information requests. The focus was finding effective methods to aid customers in their future orders and to ensure an overall satisfying experience with the website. For that reason, various technological resources were employed for research, development, testing, and analysis processes.

The implementation utilized major platforms and frameworks, including Spring Boot, Google Dialogflow, Eclipse IDE, Node.js, PostgresSQL and Railway App Deployment.

3.1 Architecture of the Project for the Development

The primary objective of this study is to develop a virtual assistant capable of responding to user requests made through human voice. To achieve this, the project involves capturing user speech and converting it into text, followed by the identification of user requests based on this text. Subsequently, a response is generated on the website, accompanied by the reproduction of a voice contextualized with displayed response. The final solution comprises a virtual assistant integrated into an ecommerce. To map all the components of this solution, both a logical architecture and a physical architecture were designed.

The logical architecture illustrates the functionalities and relationships among the software components within the solution. In Fig. 1, users can access a web page developed in Java and HTML programming languages, utilizing the Spring Boot framework and Eclipse's development environment. This web page, deployed on the Railway App, interfaces with PostgreSQL database. Besides that, the page leverages APISs and functionalities from the conversational AI framework, including actions such as 'Speech-to-text' and 'Text-to-speech'. Furthermore, the virtual assistant on the page has the capability to respond to user queries, provide information about products, offer business-related insights, make suggestions, and execute various other features available on the web page.

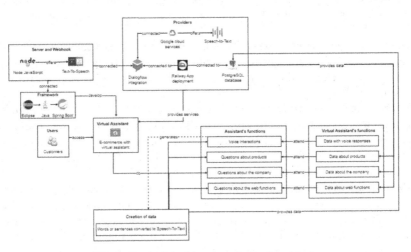

Fig. 1. Logical Architecture of virtual assistant.

The physical architecture delineates the tangible components that support the solution. As illustrated in Fig. 2, the implementation involves the use if a personal computer or tablet with an internet connection. Additionally, dedicated environments for both development and production are depicted. Both environments will use a web service, an app service and one database.

3.2 Benchmarking and Choosing Criteria of the Framework

Before the development of the application, a careful framework selection process was undertaken for the virtual assistant. Using the information of [18], we evaluated

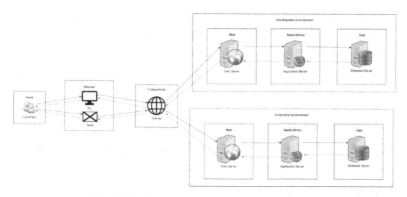

Fig. 2. Physical Architecture of virtual assistant.

four potential options: Google Dialogflow, IBM Watson Assistant, Amazon Lex, and Microsoft Bot Framework.

In determining the optimal framework, crucial criteria were considered, encompassing cost/benefits analysis, integration options with other platforms, user support, active community engagement, learning curve, machine learning capabilities, and deployment viability. Each criterion was assessed on a scale from 1 to 7, where 1 represented 'Very bad' and 7 indicated 'Very Good'.

Table 1 shows the score assigned for all the proposed frameworks, with Google Dialogflow as the winner because it had the most integrations and a friendly environment.

Table 1. Final Frameworks score based on criteria.

Criteria/Framework	Google Dialogflow	IBM Watson Assistant	Amazon Lex	Microsoft Bot Framework
Cost-benefit	7	6	6	4
Integration with other platforms	7	7	7	7
Learning curve	7	6	6	4
Support and Community	7	7	4	6
NLP incorporation	7	7	7	7
Deployment	7	7	7	7
Development environment	6	6	7	4
Application interface via voice	7	7	7	7
Total Score	55	53	51	46

Based on the criteria presented in [18], which provides detailed explanations and statistics regarding the functionality and interaction of their solution, an implementation of a chatbot assistant featuring a native web page application developed in Java and HTML. Utilizing this information, the potential interaction and integration of a web page with the software and hardware infrastructure frameworks were evaluated.

3.3 Web Implementation

The development of the Virtual Assistant required understanding and integration of the technological components described in the previous section. Figure 3 shows a segment of the website's code and resources structure, constructed upon the MVC pattern (Model, View, and Controller). In this context, a poultry consumables website was replicated as the environment for implementing the virtual assistant. The e-commerce platform was developed using Java programming language and a Spring Boot application framework, all within the Eclipse Integrated Development Environment (IDE).

Fig. 3. Eclipse IDE with Spring Boot app.

The database architecture was systematically designed to function as an information repository for electronic commerce, employing the PostgresSQL database management system. This systematic approach was adopted with the principal aim of facilitating testing of the virtual assistant incorporated within the e-commerce platform.

3.4 Virtual Assistant Implementation

Following the development of the website, the construction of the virtual assistant within the context of e-commerce was initiated using Dialogflow. This configuration was specifically designed to recognize requests related to poultry consumables. In the initial phase, we formulated intents and entities within Dialogflow. These intents correspond to diverse user requirements on the website, encompassing the provision of additional information about the company, display of detailed product information, presentation of delivery service coverage, product searches based on category, general product searches, assistance with user sign-in or login processes in the e-commerce platform, and the collection of user feedback and suggestions concerning products, or the website at large as illustrated in Fig. 4.

Fig. 4. Virtual Assistant Intents in Dialogflow

3.5 Virtual Assistant Integration

Following the completion of the website and the Dialogflow agent, the integration of both components was undertaken. The main component for the integration is a Node.js web server. Initially, the Speech-to-text API is used to convert the user's voice request from the website into text. Subsequently, the Dialogflow package is utilized to process the user's request and present a result that aligns with the user's inquiry.

Thus, the two solutions can collaborate to provide an enhanced navigation of the poultry's website with a virtual assistant employing Natural Language Processing. In other words, when the customer requests an action, such as searching for a product, the virtual assistant can execute the task (e.g., list all the products in the "Egg" category), demonstrating the capability to perform similar actions with other examples.

Finally, the app deployment process was initiated. Railway App Deployment was selected for its straightforward setup, offering hosting services for the website and its database, along with providing a unique domain name for integrating the Node.js server. Figure 5 illustrates the website with the integrated virtual assistant, enabling access for all users with an internet connection and a web browser.

Fig. 5. Web page with the virtual assistant.

4   Experimental Setting

In this section, the objective is to conduct testing on the virtual assistant to assess its performance and determine customer approval. A set of diverse question was formulated, organized based on dimensions as outlined in Table 2.

The objective is to assess dimensions such as usability, functionality, and customer satisfaction, as well as the alignment of the virtual assistant's functions with the main goal of this project: enhancing the quality of customer service within e-commerce platforms in Peruvian companies in the retail sector.

Table 2. Dimensions and Affirmations about the Virtual Assistant.

Dimension	Affirmation
Usability	Based on my own belief, it was easy to interact with the virtual assistant I was able to communicate with the virtual assistant using Natural Language The language that uses the virtual assistant was understandable
Functionality	The virtual assistant gave me fast responses to my requests The information that the virtual assistant match with my requests The responses that I got with the virtual assistant gives to me was error-free The virtual assistant was available all the time
Customer Satisfaction	The experience that I obtain with the virtual assistant was pleasant and satisfactory I will be using this virtual assistant to complete my requests in the web site I will recommend this virtual assistant to my friends, relatives, and acquaintances

To measure if the affirmation previously shown was accurate or not, the methodology of Likert's Scale methodology was employed. As illustrated in Table 3, the Likert's

Scale comprises 5 points, each assigned with an individual score. This scale facilitates the scoring of statements, enabling the calculation of average scores and subsequent result analysis. A questionnaire was created using Google Forms, incorporating all the questions for conducting the acceptance test with the users.

Table 3. Likert's Scale.

Score	Message
5	Strongly Agree
4	Agree
3	Neutral
2	Disagree
1	Strongly Disagree

First, the reliability of the dimension results was assessed using the Coefficient of Cronbach's Alpha [20]. This measure aided in evaluating the internal consistency of the questionnaire. The Coefficient of Cronbach's Alpha is determined by variables such as the number of items (K), the sum of variance for all the items ($\sum S_i^2$), and the variance of sum for all the items (S_t^2).

$$\alpha = \frac{K}{K-1}\left[1 - \frac{\sum S_i^2}{S_t^2}\right] \qquad (1)$$

In interpretating the values of the Coefficient of Cronbach's Alpha values [21], a predetermined range of values from Table 4 was employed. The objective was to demonstrate that the final results in each dimension be equal to or greater than 0.70 on Cronbach's Alpha, indicating a satisfactory level of internal consistency.

Table 4. Relativity Range and the respective Coefficient of Cronbach's Alpha.

N°	Coefficient of Cronbach's Alpha	Relativity level
1	More than 0.90	Excellent
2	0.80 – 0.89	Good
3	0.70 – 0.79	Acceptable
4	0.6 – 0.69	Questionable
5	0.5 – 0.59	Poor
6	Less than 0.59	Unacceptable

Utilizing the SPSS with the numbers of items, the obtained Cronbach's Alpha values for each dimension were as follows:

- For the "Usability" dimension, Cronbach's Alpha was 0.88, indicating "Good reliability" and internal consistency, making it correct and applicable for acceptance tests.
- For the "Functionality" dimension, Cronbach's Alpha was 0.78, suggesting "Acceptable reliability" and internal consistency, making it correct and applicable for acceptance tests.
- For the "Customer Satisfaction" dimension, Cronbach's Alpha was 0.87, denoting "Good reliability" and internal consistency, making it correct and applicable for acceptance tests.

Secondly, an important e-commerce retail service (Avinka SA., located in "Las Casuarinas" urbanization) was selected, and permission was obtained to conduct the investigation on-site. Volunteers within a physical location of a poultry company's store were recruited, and the functionality of the virtual assistant was explained to them. The acceptance test involved the interaction of volunteer clients with the virtual assistant through a website interface, followed by a comprehensive questionnaire designed to capture their feedback and insights. A total of 58 participants, comprising 36 women and 22 men within the age range of 15 to 64 years, were included in the study.

Lastly, the results of each dimension were analyzed using an equation related to the percentage of customer perceptions about each dimension (D_X). This value is derived from variables including the sum of the frequency of each affirmation ($\sum f_r$), the maximum score obtained for the dimension (P_{max}), the total sample of responses (n) and the value of the Liker's Scale (*Scale*).

$$D_X = \frac{(\sum f_r x Scale)}{(P_{max} x n)} \tag{2}$$

In the final results, the objective was to achieve a minimum percentage of 80% in customer perceptions for each dimension.

5   Results

After fulfilling the acceptance with customers at the poultry consumables store, the results obtained in each dimension are as follows:

5.1   Usability Dimension

Figure 6 illustrates the percentage of customers perception regarding the usability of the virtual assistant, with 50.57% of respondents completely agreeing, and 36.21% expressing agreement. The results indicate a positive perception of customers concerning the design and ease of use of the developed virtual assistant.

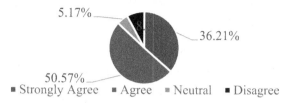

5.17%

36.21%

50.57%

▪ Strongly Agree   ▪ Agree   ▪ Neutral   ▪ Disagree

Fig. 6. Percentage of Customer Perception Regarding Solution Usability.

According to Table 5, the percentage of customer perceptions regarding the usability dimension was 82.99%, surpassing the targeted acceptance threshold of 80%.

Table 5. Usability dimension results.

Scale	Level of Satisfaction	f_r A1	f_r A2	f_r A3	$\sum f_r$
5	Strongly Agree	21	23	19	63
4	Agree	29	25	34	88
3	Neutral	4	3	2	9
2	Disagree	4	7	3	14
1	Strongly Disagree	0	0	0	0

5.2 Functionality Dimension

Figure 7 illustrates the percentage of customer perception regarding the functionality of the virtual assistant, with 42.67% of respondents completely agreeing, while 36.64% expressing agreement. The results indicate a positive perception of the precision of the responses provided by the virtual assistant to the client's requests.

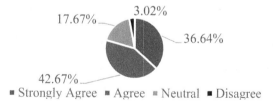

17.67%   3.02%

36.64%

42.67%

▪ Strongly Agree   ▪ Agree   ▪ Neutral   ▪ Disagree

Fig. 7. Percentage of customer perception regarding solution functionality.

According to Table 6, the percentage of customer perceptions regarding the usability dimension was 82.59%, surpassing the targeted acceptance threshold of 80%.

Table 6. Functionality dimension results.

Scale	Level of Satisfaction	f_r A4	f_r A5	f_r A6	f_r A7	$\sum f_r$
5	Strongly Agree	23	17	22	23	85
4	Agree	27	25	26	21	99
3	Neutral	4	16	7	14	41
2	Disagree	4	0	3	0	7
1	Strongly Disagree	0	0	0	0	0

5.3 Customer Satisfaction Dimension

Figure 8 illustrates the percentage of the degree of customer perception regarding the satisfaction with the virtual assistant, with 47.70% of respondents completely agreeing and 35.06% expressing agreement. The results indicate the client's positive perception of the experience and satisfaction with the use of the virtual assistant.

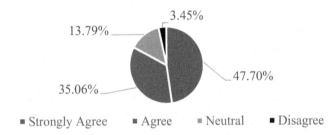

Fig. 8. Percentage of Customer Satisfaction Perception Regarding the Solution.

According to Table 7, the percentage of customer perceptions regarding the customer satisfaction was 85.40%.

Table 7. Customer satisfaction dimension results.

Scale	Level of Satisfaction	f_r A8	f_r A9	f_r A10	$\sum f_r$
5	Strongly Agree	29	31	23	83
4	Agree	22	14	25	61
3	Neutral	4	10	10	24
2	Disagree	3	3	0	6
1	Strongly Disagree	0	0	0	0

6   Conclusion

This study represents the implementation of Artificial Intelligence with Natural Language Processing in the form of a virtual assistant. It is integrated into a poultry's consumables store to improve customer service in navigating the website. This demonstrates significant progress in the technologies used to automate business processes to increase value for customers. Provides an objective idea of the positive impact that technology has on optimizing customer service on digital platforms.

Based on the results of the acceptance test described in the previous section, it is deduced that the virtual assistant generated a positive impact and a good level of acceptance among customers, achieving an 83.66% acceptance rate across the dimensions of usability, functionality, and customer satisfaction overall. This suggests that the virtual assistant aligns with client expectations and enhances the quality of customer service in the retail context.

Some limitations in this implementation included functions such as the purchasing and payment of products. While these are integral processes for an e-commerce's retail website, the focus of this research was solely on the customer service process.

This study allows further development of new research related to Intelligent Human Computer Interfaces and Artificial Intelligence applications. Future investigations might explore the extension of implementing conversational AI solutions into domains beyond customer service or employing alternative technologies to enhance performance.

References

1. Gestión, D.: IBM: inteligencia artificial ya no es opcional para empresas en escenario posCOVID|TECNOLOGIA|GESTIÓN. Diario Gestión (2021). https://gestion.pe/tecnologia/ibm-inteligencia-artificial-ya-no-es-opcional-para-empresas-en-escenario-poscovid-noticia/
2. Albrieu, R., Rapetti, M., Brest López, C., Larroulet, P., Sorrentino, A.: Inteligencia artificial y crecimiento económico. Oportunidades y desafíos para Perú. CIPPEC (2018)
3. El Comercio, D.: IA: el 28% de empresas en el Perú ha implementado la inteligencia artificial, según informe de IBM|España|México|Colombia|TECNOLOGIA|EL COMERCIO PERÚ (2022). https://elcomercio.pe/tecnologia/actualidad/ia-el-28-de-empresas-en-el-peru-ha-implementado-la-inteligencia-artificial-segun-informe-de-ibm-espana-mexico-colombia-noticia/?ref=ecr
4. ¡Asistentes virtuales de IA, IA conversacional y chatbots explicados! (2022). Retrieved August 20, 2022. https://aisera.com/chatbots-virtual-assistants-conversational-ai/
5. Behera, R.K., Bala, P.K., Ray, A.: Cognitive chatbot for personalised contextual customer service: behind the scene and beyond the hype. Inf. Syst. Front. **2021**, 1–21 (2021). https://doi.org/10.1007/S10796-021-10168-Y
6. Guzman, A.L.: Voices in and of the machine: Source orientation toward mobile virtual assistants. Comput. Hum. Behav. **90**, 343–350 (2019). https://doi.org/10.1016/J.CHB.2018.08.009
7. Quiroz Martinez, M.A., Mayorga Plua, S.E., Gomez Rios, M.D., Leyva Vázquez, M.Y., Plua Moran, D.H.: Chatbot for technical support, analysis of critical success factors using fuzzy cognitive maps. Commun. Comput. Inf. Sci. **1388**, 363–375 (2021). https://doi.org/10.1007/978-3-030-71503-8_28/COVER

8. Brill, T., Munoz, L., Miller, R.: Siri, Alexa, and other digital assistants: a study of customer satisfaction with artificial intelligence applications. J. Mark. Manag. **35**(15–16), 1401–1436 (2019). https://doi.org/10.1080/0267257X.2019.1687571

9. Adam, M., Wessel, M., Benlian, A.: AI-based chatbots in customer service and their effects on user compliance. Electron. Mark. **31**(2), 427–445 (2021). https://doi.org/10.1007/S12525-020-00414-7/FIGURES/7

10. Tran, A.D., Pallant, J.I., Johnson, L.W.: Exploring the impact of chatbots on consumer sentiment and expectations in retail. J. Retail. Consum. Serv. **63**, 102718 (2021). https://doi.org/10.1016/J.JRETCONSER.2021.102718

11. Falcón, D.: Comercio electrónico en el Perú - 2017|Blogs|GESTIÓN (2017). https://gestion.pe/blog/innovaciondisrupcion/2017/03/comercio-electronico-en-el-peru-2017.html?ref=gesr

12. Doherty, D., Curran, K.: Chatbots for online banking services. Web Intell. **17**(4), 327–342 (2019). https://doi.org/10.3233/WEB-190422

13. Duguleană, M., Briciu, V.A., Duduman, I.A., Machidon, O.M.: A virtual assistant for natural interactions in museums. Sustainability **12**, 6958 (2020). https://doi.org/10.3390/SU1217 6958

14. Matveev, A., et al.: A virtual dialogue assistant for conducting remote exams. In: Conference of Open Innovation Association, FRUCT, 2020-April, pp. 284–290 (2020). https://doi.org/10.23919/FRUCT48808.2020.9087557

15. Fernandes, T., Oliveira, E.: Understanding consumers' acceptance of automated technologies in service encounters: drivers of digital voice assistants adoption. J. Bus. Res. **122**(September 2020), 180–191 (2021). https://doi.org/10.1016/j.jbusres.2020.08.058

16. Bagchi, M.: Conceptualising a library chatbot using open source conversational artificial intelligence. DESIDOC J. Libr. Inf. Technol. **40**(06), 329–333 (2020). https://doi.org/10.14429/DJLIT.40.06.15611

17. Daniel, G., Cabot, J., Deruelle, L., Derras, M.: Xatkit: a multimodal low-code chatbot development framework. IEEE Access **8**, 15332–15346 (2020). https://doi.org/10.1109/ACCESS.2020.2966919

18. Abdellatif, A., Badran, K., Costa, D.E., Shihab, E.: A Comparison of natural language understanding platforms for chatbots in software engineering. IEEE Trans. Softw. Eng. **48**(8), 3087–3102 (2020). https://doi.org/10.1109/TSE.2021.3078384

19. Planas, E., Daniel, G., Brambilla, M., Cabot, J.: Towards a model-driven approach for multi experience AI-based user interfaces. Softw. Syst. Model. **20**(4), 997–1009 (2021). https://doi.org/10.1007/S10270-021-00904-Y/FIGURES/10

20. Oviedo, H.C., Campo-Arias, A.: Metodología de investigación y lectura crítica de estudios Aproximación al uso del coeficiente alfa de Cronbach Title: An Approach to the Use of Cronbach's Alfa (2005)

21. George, D., Mallery, P.: SPSS for Windows Step by Step: Answers to Selected Exercises. A Simple Guide and Reference, 63 (2003). https://books.google.com/books/about/SPSS_for_Windows_Step_by_Step.html?hl=es&id=AghHAAAAMAAJ

Detecting the Use of Safety Helmets
on Construction Sites

Jorge Cordero$^{(\boxtimes)}$ (iD), Luisa Bermeo, Luis Barba-Guaman (iD), and Guido Riofrio

Universidad Técnica Particular de Loja, San Cayetano Alto, Loja, Ecuador
{jmcordero,lfbermeo,lrbarba,geriofrioutpl}@utpl.edu.ec

Abstract. Occupational safety in construction sites is a vital topic due to the inherent risks associated with this type of work environment. This research provides a practical and effective solution to monitor compliance with safety standards. Therefore, it helps improve safety and minimize risks associated with not wearing safety helmets, such as head injuries and fatalities. The system is non-intrusive and can be easily integrated into existing surveillance systems. Moreover, it provides notifications to the administrator in case of non-compliance to enforce safety regulations. During the evaluation process, a set of video sequences recorded in real-world scenarios was used. The results obtained, mainly with the nano model, show that the system achieved a high level of precision with a score of 0.93, as well as an acceptable recall of 0.62. Regarding the F1 score, it has a score of 0.81.

Keywords: Safety Helmet Detection · Computer Vision · Deep Learning · Industrial Safety · Accident Prevention

1 Introduction

In recent years, vision-based systems for monitoring compliance with safety standards in various environments have gained significant importance. The use of safety helmets in industrial and construction environments is a critical measure to prevent serious and fatal head injuries. However, manual monitoring of their use can be difficult and may result in an insufficient compliance rate [1]. To address this issue, vision-based algorithms are increasingly being used to monitor the use of safety helmets in a variety of applications [2].

The International Labor Organization (ILO) estimates that approximately 2.3 million workers worldwide die each year from illnesses or accidents occurring at construction sites, equating to over 6,000 deaths per day. These numbers are periodically updated by the ILO, and recent updates indicate an increase in accidents and illnesses [3]. According to [4], the authors highlight that among various personal protective gear used in construction, the safety helmet is regarded as an essential tool for ensuring worker safety on site.

The aim is to reduce the rate of occupational accidents caused by the misuse of safety equipment on construction sites through the use of image processing techniques and occupational safety concepts. This will be achieved by implementing artificial vision algorithms that aid in monitoring the use of safety helmets. Safety helmets are essential safety factors, as they can reduce injuries from blows and occasionally prevent severe accidents, although they do not prevent accidents from occurring. Wearing helmets helps prevent approximately 85% of injuries caused by falls.

Artificial vision can offer a solution to this issue by allowing for automatic and real-time monitoring of the use of safety helmets. Recent literature has studied the use of artificial vision techniques to monitor the use of safety helmets [1, 5–7]. However, despite the acknowledged utility of artificial vision in safety monitoring, as noted in existing literature, important challenges remain in developing effective and reliable systems. This is particularly true in creating targeted, robust solutions that can operate effectively in the dynamic and complex environments of construction sites.

This investigation developed a system for monitoring safety helmet usage using artificial vision techniques. A deep learning model was used to identify whether an individual is wearing a safety helmet. This research not only contributes to the technological advancements in artificial vision systems but also holds substantial implications for improving workplace safety practices and reducing occupational hazards in the construction industry. The system's results were compared with those of manual monitoring to evaluate its effectiveness.

Results demonstrate that the system can accurately detect and classify safety helmet usage with high precision and speed. Furthermore, the system shows good generalizability to different environments and situations. These results suggest that the system can be a valuable tool for enhancing workplace safety and preventing injuries. The rest of the article is divided as follows: in Sect. 2, related work is described; the methodology implemented is described in Sect. 3; proposed work is described in Sect. 4; the results and discussion are shown in Sect. 5; and, finally, the conclusions and future work are presented in Sect. 6.

2 Related Work

Several studies have proposed various methods and techniques for detecting the use of safety helmets by those who should wear them while performing their activities. These studies have explored YOLO's ability to accurately detect and classify helmets in environments like those evaluated in this research. For instance, [5] proposed a computer vision-based method for safety helmet detection and classification among construction workers, leveraging a convolutional neural network (CNN) and a feature fusion approach to achieve high precision and generate real-time reports. Similarly, [8] developed a safety helmet detection system for construction workers based on a YOLO algorithm. They proposed a new dataset for safety helmet detection in construction sites and compared their method with various state-of-the-art algorithms.

In construction environments, [9] presented a safety helmet detection system for workers in hazardous environments, using deep learning algorithms. They proposed a new dataset consisting of images captured in various industrial environments and demonstrated the effectiveness of their approach in detecting safety helmets with high precision. Moreover, [10] presented a system for monitoring the usage of safety helmets through the use of proximity sensors and a mobile application. This system allows supervisors to monitor real-time use of safety helmets by workers and receive alerts in case they are not properly using them. Other studies have developed systems for monitoring the usage of safety helmets in construction by utilizing computer vision and YOLO in various versions as the baseline. The results showed a satisfactory accuracy and a high detection speed [7, 11–15].

In [16] proposed a computer vision-based surveillance system to detect the presence and appropriate use of safety helmets in an industrial environment. They employed a deep neural network to detect helmets and classify whether they were being used appropriately or not. The results demonstrated a high detection and accurate classification rate of the system. Several studies in the field of occupational safety have highlighted the significance of wearing proper personal protective equipment such as safety helmets. Nevertheless, monitoring the consistent use of this equipment can pose a challenge in industrial settings.

These studies demonstrate the ability of computer vision to monitor the use of safety helmets in various environments. However, there is still a need to develop more accurate and reliable systems that can be applied across a wide range of industrial and construction environments. In this regard, the use of computer vision technologies to monitor the use of safety helmets has recently been explored. For instance, [17] presented a deep learning approach to monitor the use of safety helmets in a factory. This system employs a You Only Look Once (YOLO) and a Region-based Convolutional Neural Network (RCNN) as a deep learning model to detect the usage of safety helmets.

The CRoss-Industry Standard Process for Data Mining (CRISP-DM) methodology has demonstrated excellent performance in projects of computer vision. For example, in [18], they applied this methodology to identify leading safety indicators in construction sites, enhancing safety, and preventing accidents.

Finally, these studies demonstrate the usefulness of computer vision technologies in monitoring the use of safety helmets and compliance with safety standards in various environments. The proposed system for detecting the use of safety helmets in industrial and outdoor activity environments uses YOLOv8 with high accuracy and computational efficiency to detect the use of safety helmets.

3 Methodology

This section describes the methodology used to carry out the study, focusing on CRISP-DM, a widely used methodology for deep learning projects. The process consists of six stages: Business Understanding, Data Understanding, Data Preparation, Modeling, Evaluation, and Deployment.

3.1 Business Understanding

The research was primarily conducted to fulfill the objective of developing a system for detecting the use of safety helmets at construction sites. The system can be used to enforce safety regulations and prevent accidents among construction workers.

The initial stage of the project is critical. The problem was identified, along with the expected requirements and benefits. The objectives were carefully planned and executed to ensure project success. Adequate resources and efforts were allocated to build a solid foundation and a clear direction towards the goals.

3.2 Data Understanding

To identify the case of construction workers, a dataset available on Kaggle was utilized, consisting of 5000 images in PASCAL VOC format, classified by helmet, person, and head. To utilize the data effectively and ensure the accuracy of the final model, the images were converted into YOLO format using Python scripts to facilitate their adaptation to the artificial vision algorithm.

3.3 Data Preparation

The dataset was split into three groups: 80% for training, 10% for validation, and 10% for testing, to ensure YOLO algorithm functions properly. Furthermore, an additional set of training images was added to enhance the process.

4 Proposed Work

This section describes the other three stages of CRISP-DM for detecting the use of safety helmets using YOLOv8.

4.1 Modeling

The YOLOv8 architecture was used for training the models. Google Colab's online platform was used to develop training scripts, and ClearML was used to track the process. Various models were used for safety helmet detection according to the context: The "medium" model was used for images, the "small" model for pre-recorded videos, and the "nano" model for real-time videos. Each model has distinct characteristics and processing speeds, justifying their specific selection and use in each situation.

Figure 1 shows the Google Colab environment with the parameters used for training, such as image size (imgz), number of iterations (epochs), batch size (batch), device used (device), training project (project), and the assigned name for the project (name). This allowed for the subsequent implementation of models for the safety helmet recognition system.

The architecture of the safety helmet detection system was defined. Figure 2 displays the interconnection of key components for training and detection. For training purposes, Kaggle data and the YOLOv8 object detection algorithm were used.

The system was called SafemetSpotter. SafemetSpotter uses a client-server architecture, where the backend employs Flask, a lightweight Python framework, to serve the application, and YOLOv8 to utilize the trained models. The model's prediction is sent to the frontend through Flask. The frontend is developed with VUE 3, offering a straightforward interface to upload images/videos or use the webcam. It consumes the

▾ YOLO

```
[ ] model = YOLO(model_name)

    Downloading https://github.com/ultralytics/assets/releases/download/v0.0.0/yolov8s.pt to yolov8s.pt...
    100%|██████████| 21.5M/21.5M [00:00<00:00, 164MB/s]
    2023-04-18 16:53:43,127 - clearml.model - INFO - Selected model id: b4c445d7479e4a088bafca22c12bf53b


[ ] results = model.train(

        data='/content/datasets/worker_helmet.yaml',
        imgsz=416,
        epochs=100,
        batch=32,
        device=0,
        cache='ram',
        project=clearml_project_name,
        name=clearml_task_name
        )
```

Fig. 1. Training parameters.

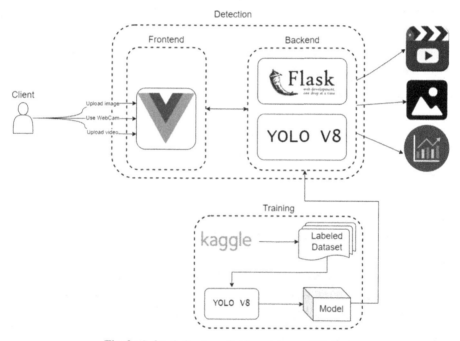

Fig. 2. Safety helmet monitoring system architecture.

backend endpoints and displays the images, videos, or streams where the safety helmet is detected. If there is a real-time video, a notification will appear indicating if the safety helmet is being used or not.

The system's architecture is designed to be both scalable and flexible. The system can be implemented in either one or multiple cameras, depending on the construction site's size. The YOLO algorithm can be trained with additional data to improve its accuracy over time. The user interface can be customized to include additional features such as analysis and historical data reports.

Figure 3 displays the main view of the system, highlighting its key components and the result obtained based on the system's architecture. The detection button is located on the navigation bar. Furthermore, the first component includes relevant information for the end-user, explaining the system's functionality in a clear and concise manner, with the aim of enhancing their comprehension.

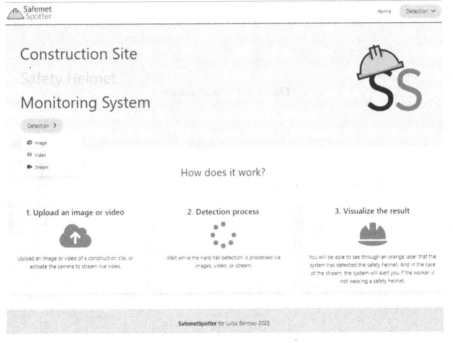

Fig. 3. Main view of SafemetSpotter.

The vision-based system described in this document is a scalable and flexible solution to enhance safety in construction sites. The system employs a combination of hardware and software components to detect the use of safety helmets and provide real-time information to relevant personnel. The system is designed to be user-friendly and intuitive, with potential for customization and additional features in the future.

4.2 Evaluation

During the evaluation phase of trained models, performance metrics provided by ClearML in the plots section are used. These metrics allow the evaluation of the model's performance and effectiveness in the field of artificial intelligence and machine learning. Some of the most common metrics include accuracy, recall, F1-score, and precision. These metrics analyze aspects such as accurate classification, identification of positive and negative cases, and minimization of false positives and false negatives. Together, these metrics provide a balanced evaluation of the model's precision and recall.

The confusion matrix is a key tool for evaluating the performance of a classification model. It displays correct and incorrect predictions for each class in a visual format. The rows represent the true classes, while the columns represent the predicted classes by the model. The correct predictions, i.e., true positives (TP), are found on the main diagonal. These predictions are particularly relevant for evaluating the model as they indicate a precise classification of each class instance.

Figure 4 displays the confusion matrix of the "medium" model using the ClearML platform. This matrix evaluates three classes: "Head", "person", and "helmet" classes are evaluated respectively. True positives (TP) are highlighted in red since they are the most relevant results for evaluating the model.

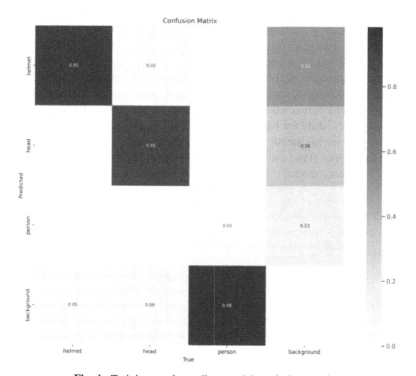

Fig. 4. Training result, medium model confusion matrix.

Table 1 shows the observation matrix for the three classes: helmet, head, and person. This matrix identifies the values of TP (True Positive), TN (True Negative), FP (False Positive), and FN (False Negative). These values are essential to evaluate each model using metrics such as precision, recall, F1 score, and accuracy.

Evaluation metrics are essential to measure the performance of a classification model when correctly classifying positive and negative instances. These metrics allow comparison and selection of the best model for the specific problem.

Table 1. Results divided into four categories, medium model.

Classes	TP	TN	FP	FN
Helmet	0.95	2.48	0.05	0.53
Head	0.90	2.64	0.11	0.36
Person	0.02	2.88	0.98	0.13
Background	0.00	1.89	1.00	1.12

Figure 5 shows the results of the evaluated metrics for the selected classes (helmet, head, and person). These metrics are recommended to analyze the trained model's performance. Precision for helmet class: 0.93 (nano model), 0.94 (small model), 0.95 (medium model). Precision for head class: 0.89 in all models. High precision implies an error rate of only 0.7% in predictions. This is valid for all models. The helmet class recall is 0.62 (nano model), 0.61 (small model), and 0.64 (medium model). The head class recall is 0.74 (nano model), 0.73 (small model), and 0.71 (medium model). There is only a 0.38% error in predictions. This is valid for all models. The F1-Score for helmet class is 0.74–0.77, while for head class it is 0.79–0.81. The prediction error stands at only 0.26%. This is consistently achieved across each model. The accuracy ranges from 0.83–0.86 for helmet class, and from 0.86–0.9 for head class. The accuracy for person class is 0.72 for nano model, 0.73 for small model, and 0.72 for medium model.

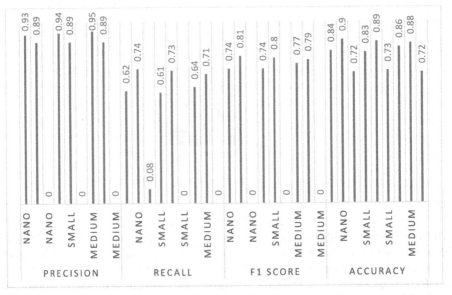

Fig. 5. Evaluation results of the metrics (Precision, Recall, F1 Score and Accuracy) of the three models (Nano, Small and Medium).

Figure 6 displays the precision-recall curve used to evaluate the model's performance in binary classification. In particular, the precision and recall variation with decision threshold is observed in order to select an optimal threshold and adjust the model for better performance. The results obtained via the medium model in the tests were as follows: precision for the helmet class 0.97, precision for the head class 0.91, precision for the person class is 0.016. In conclusion, there is a high precision value for the main helmet class with approximately 3% of false detections.

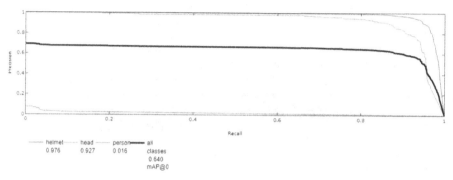

Fig. 6. Precision-recall curve, medium model.

4.3 Deployment

The implementation of computer vision model enables analysis of real-time or pre-recorded video. The system can detect the use of safety helmets in video transmissions and send alerts to site administrator or security officer in case of non-compliance.

During the deployment or implementation phase of the safety helmet monitoring system for construction sites, Vue3 was used for the client and Flask for the server. The server implemented YOLOv8 trained models (nano, small, and medium). Flask was used as the primary framework for developing the API and web services in the backend. Routes and controllers were created in Flask to handle client requests related to helmet recognition. Vue3 was chosen to build the user interface on the frontend, allowing for image and video uploading as well as webcam usage. Real-time notifications were also implemented to inform the user about the status of the helmet recognition process.

The backend is responsible for the internal functionality of the application and plays a key role in the safety helmet recognition system. It receives images and videos from the client, processes them with helmet recognition algorithms, stores the results, and manages the business logic related to the detection of safety helmets. Using Flask, the server is configured to listen and respond to client requests.

SocketIO library was used for real-time detection and the YOLO v8 nano model is loaded in memory for optimal response times. Endpoints for loading and predicting the model are created for each video frame using sockets. The model was chosen based on accuracy, capacity, and response time. Since smooth real-time video performance is paramount.

The frontend, also known as the client-side, uses Vue3 due to its exceptional performance. Its main objective is to provide a pleasant and intuitive user interface. In this interface, users have the option to upload images, pre-recorded videos, or use their computer's webcam as shown in Fig. 7.

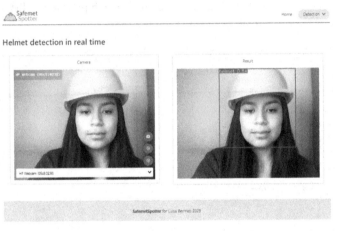

Fig. 7. System performing helmet detection via streaming.

The system comprises of three main components: a camera, an artificial vision algorithm, and a user interface. The camera is placed on the construction site and captures images of individuals present in the location. These images are then processed by the computer vision algorithm to detect the presence of safety helmets on individuals. The results of this processing are displayed on the user interface, which provides real-time information to the staff responsible for enforcing safety regulations at the construction site.

The interface is designed to be user-friendly and intuitive, with clear visual indicators of the presence or absence of safety helmets on people. The interface includes an alert system that notifies relevant personnel when individuals are detected without safety helmets. The alert system can be customized to send notifications via email, text message, or other means based on personnel preferences.

5   Results and Discussion

Performance tests were conducted after implementing detection and training components into the main system architecture. Images were loaded and the YOLOv8 algorithm was used during these tests to perform detection. Tests were conducted in various scenarios, such as front views, rear views, overhead views, with images and videos of low, medium, and high resolution, as well as in both daylight and nighttime conditions. In Fig. 8, the algorithm detected that the persons on the right and left of the image are indeed wearing safety helmets, with a Precision of 0.89. However, the person in the center can be visually observed as not wearing a safety helmet, and the algorithm failed to detect it.

These results demonstrate the good performance of the implemented architecture, by providing accurate and effective detections regarding the use of safety helmets.

Fig. 8. Detection of safety helmet use among construction workers using front view.

The system monitors live video transmissions and notifies law enforcement or security officers in case of non-compliance, making it an effective tool in enforcing helmet laws and reducing the risk of head injuries. The approach highlights the potential of computer vision and deep learning techniques in addressing safety concerns in construction.

Fig. 9. Detection of safety helmet use among construction workers from posterior view.

Figure 9 demonstrates the detection of helmet use by three construction workers from a rear view. The obtained accuracy exceeds 0.86, demonstrating the system's capacity for precise identification of compliance with helmet use. However, there are limitations in precise detection under extreme lighting and angle conditions despite the promising findings of this study, which can affect the accuracy of helmet use detection.

Fig. 10. Detection of safety helmet use in workers using video.

Figure 10 shows the detection of safety helmets on video. In the image, there are ten workers, and the system was able to accurately detect the workers wearing safety helmets. In the background of the video, it can be observed that two workers are not following the regulation, thus, the system generates the corresponding alert. It's important to note that the detection of helmets depends on their position and lighting quality. Furthermore, as the algorithm is trained on a larger set of images, the precision of object detection will increase.

A tool for usability analysis is the System Usability Scale (SUS), which helps determine a system's accuracy, functionality, effectiveness, and satisfaction. The SUS (shown in Table 2) is a questionnaire with ten items, each with five scale steps. The odd-numbered items have a positive tone; the tone of the even-numbered items is negative. The SUS scoring method requires participants to provide a response to all ten items. Responses range from strongly agree to strongly disagree. If for some reason participants can't respond to an item, they should select the center point of the scale. Thus, overall SUS scores range from 0 to 100 [19].

The fundamental goal of usability testing is to help developers produce more usable products. Usability testing remains a central way of determining whether users accomplish their goals. Usability testing helps determine user satisfaction with the system, including complexity, ease of use, dialogue flow functioning, consistency, reliability, and integration [20].

Table 2. The SUS adapted version to evaluate the usability of systems.

	Items	Strongly disagree			Strongly agree	
		1	2	3	4	5
1	I think that I would like to use this system frequently.	☐	☐	☐	☐	☐
2	I found the system unnecessarily complex.	☐	☐	☐	☐	☐
3	I thought the system was easy to use.	☐	☐	☐	☐	☐
4	I think that I would need the support of a technical person to be able to use this system.	☐	☐	☐	☐	☐
5	I found the various functions in this system were well integrated.	☐	☐	☐	☐	☐
6	I thought there was too much inconsistency in this system.	☐	☐	☐	☐	☐
7	I would imagine that most people would learn to use this system very quickly.	☐	☐	☐	☐	☐
8	I found the system very cumbersome to use.	☐	☐	☐	☐	☐
9	I felt very confident using the system.	☐	☐	☐	☐	☐
10	I needed to learn a lot of things before I could get going with this system.	☐	☐	☐	☐	☐

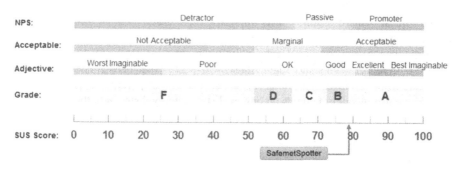

Fig. 11. SUS scores for the system.

A usability score of 79 was obtained by applying the SUS questionnaire to evaluate the implemented practical case. Figure 11 shows the obtained scores and illustrates user perception on the satisfaction level of the system which is rated as 'Good'. The result reflects that the customer experience is influenced by their capability to use technology, given that many of the people who interacted with and evaluated the usability of the system were workers who struggle to adopt new technologies. Overall, the system proved to be acceptable; therefore, it is useful, easy to use, and can be implemented in construction companies.

6 Conclusions and Future Work

In today's world, institutions place high value on research and solutions aimed at detecting the use of safety helmets. This study demonstrates that construction sectors can utilize safety helmet detection systems to prevent injuries that may lead to severe head injuries or worker fatalities. The challenge lies in adopting the integration of these innovative systems to comply with safety regulations.

The computer vision-based system developed allows for highly accurate identification of safety helmet usage in real-time video transmissions of construction workers. These findings have vital implications for the safety of construction workers, as they can aid in ensuring compliance with safety regulations and preventing accidents.

The implemented solution was based on the use of a web server, which allowed for efficient communication and the obtaining of visible results. The CRISP-DM methodology was effectively used in developing the SafemetSpotter system, achieving the main objective of supervising the use of safety helmets on construction sites through the analysis of pre-recorded images and videos, as well as real-time videos. This solution represents a significant advancement in improving occupational safety by providing an effective tool for monitoring and ensuring compliance with safety protocols in the workplace.

YOLOv8 algorithm is notable for its speed and ease of model learning, as well as its high precision and speed, among other evaluated criteria. In particular, it demonstrated a remarkable ability to detect safety helmets in real-time, achieving a noteworthy level of precision in the nano model, with a score of 0.93.

SUS questionnaire usability tests allow for the measurement of system satisfaction. According to the results, the implementation of the helmet recognition system is widely accepted, encouraging construction companies to integrate it to effectively monitor compliance with safety regulations.

Future work will investigate other scenarios, such as transportation environments, to monitor the use of safety helmets among cyclists, motorcyclists, and other individuals engaging in various outdoor activities.

References

1. Huang, L., Fu, Q., He, M., Jiang, D., Hao, Z.: Detection algorithm of safety helmet wearing based on deep learning. Concurr. Comput. Pract. Experience **33**(13), e6234 (2021). https://doi.org/10.1002/cpe.6234
2. Sanjana, S., Shriya, V.R., Vaishnavi, G., Ashwini, K.: A review on various methodologies used for vehicle classification, helmet detection and number plate recognition. Evol. Intell. **14**, 979–987 (2021)
3. Poongodi, K., Shivakrishna, P., Murthi, P.: Studies on the Factors Influencing Occupational Accidents on Health Hazards of Labours in Thermal Power Plant Construction. In: Vilventhan, A., Singh, S.B., and Delhi, V.S.K. (Eds.) Advances in Construction Materials and Management, pp. 117–135. Springer Nature Singapore, Singapore (2023)
4. Wong, T.K.M., Man, S.S., Chan, A.H.S.: Critical factors for the use or non-use of personal protective equipment amongst construction workers. Saf. Sci. **126**, 104663 (2020). https://doi.org/10.1016/j.ssci.2020.104663
5. Hayat, A., Morgado-Dias, F.: Deep learning-based automatic safety helmet detection system for construction safety. Appl. Sci. **12**(16), 8268 (2022). https://doi.org/10.3390/app12168268
6. Paneru, S., Jeelani, I.: Computer vision applications in construction: Current state, opportunities a challenges. Autom Constr. 132, 103940 (2021). https://doi.org/10.1016/j.autcon.2021.103940

7. Zhou, F., Zhao, H., Nie, Z.: Safety helmet detection based on YOLOv5. In: 2021 IEEE International Conference on Power Electronics Computer Applications (ICPECA), pp. 6–11 (2021)
8. Lee, J., Lee, S.: Construction site safety management: a computer vision and deep learning approach. Sensors. **23**(2), 944 (2023). https://doi.org/10.3390/s23020944
9. Wang, H., Hu, Z., Guo, Y., Yang, Z., Zhou, F., Xu, P.: A real-time safety helmet wearing detection approach based on CSYOLOv3. Appl. Sci. **10**(19), 6732 (2020). https://doi.org/10.3390/app10196732
10. Colombo, S., Lim, Y., Casalegno, F.: Deep vision shield: assessing the use of HMD and wearable sensors in a smart safety device. In: Proceedings of the 12th ACM International Conference on PErvasive Technologies Related to Assistive Environments, pp. 402–410. Association for Computing Machinery, New York, NY, USA (2019). https://doi.org/10.1145/3316782.3322754
11. Han, K., Zeng, X.: Deep learning-based workers safety helmet wearing detection on construction sites using Multi-scale features. IEEE Access. **10**, 718–729 (2022). https://doi.org/10.1109/ACCESS.2021.3138407
12. Chen, J., Deng, S., Wang, P., Huang, X., Liu, Y.: Lightweight helmet detection algorithm using an improved YOLOv4. Sensors **23**(3), 1256 (2023). https://doi.org/10.3390/s23031256
13. Kisaezehra Muhammad Umer Farooq, M.A.B.A.K.K.: Real-time safety helmet detection using Yolov5 at construction sites. Intell. Autom. Soft Comput. **36**, 911–927 (2023). https://doi.org/10.32604/iasc.2023.031359
14. Chen, K., Yan, G., Zhang, M., Xiao, Z., Wang, Q.: safety helmet detection based on YOLOv7. In: Proceedings of the 6th International Conference on Computer Science and Application Engineering. Association for Computing Machinery, pp. 1–6 New York, USA (2022). https://doi.org/10.1145/3565387.3565418
15. Fang, W., Love, P.E.D., Luo, H., Ding, L.: Computer vision for behaviour-based safety in construction: a review and future directions. Adv. Eng. Inf. **43**, 100980 (2020). https://doi.org/10.1016/j.aei.2019.100980
16. Li, Y., Wei, H., Han, Z., Huang, J., Wang, W.: Deep learning-based safety helmet detection in engineering management based on convolutional neural networks. Adv. Civil Eng. **2020**, 1–10 (2020). https://doi.org/10.1155/2020/9703560
17. Anushkannan, N.K., Kumbhar, V.R., Maddila, S.K., Kolli, C.S., Vidhya, B., Vidhya, R.G.: YOLO Algorithm for helmet detection in industries for safety purpose. In: 2022 3rd International Conference on Smart Electronics and Communication (ICOSEC), pp. 225–230 (2022). https://doi.org/10.1109/ICOSEC54921.2022.9952154
18. Poh, C.Q.X., Ubeynarayana, C.U., Goh, Y.M.: Safety leading indicators for construction sites: a machine learning approach. Autom. Constr. **93**, 375–386 (2018). https://doi.org/10.1016/J.AUTCON.2018.03.022
19. Lewis, J.R.: The system usability scale: past, present, and future. Int. J. Hum. Comput. Interact. **34**, 577–590 (2018)
20. Lewis, J.R., Sauro, J.: Usability and user experience: Design and evaluation. In: Salvendy, G., Karwowski, W. (eds.) Handbook of Human Factors and Ergonomics, pp. 972–1015. Wiley (2021). https://doi.org/10.1002/9781119636113.ch38

Preventing Diabetes: Substituting Processed Foods and Nutritional Chatbot Assistance

Pablo Solano[1], Víctor Herrera[1], Victoria Abril-Ulloa[2],
and Mauricio Espinoza-Mejía[2,3(✉)]

[1] Faculty of Engineering, University of Cuenca, Cuenca, Ecuador
{pablo.solanoc98,victor.herrera}@ucuenca.edu.ec
[2] Technologies Applied to Health Research Group, Faculty of Medical Sciences,
University of Cuenca, Cuenca, Ecuador
{victoria.abril,mauricio.espinoza}@ucuenca.edu.ec
[3] Computer Science Department, University of Cuenca, Cuenca, Ecuador

Abstract. Type 2 Diabetes Mellitus (T2DM) is one of the biggest threats to Ecuador's health. The intake of processed foods has been linked to a higher risk of T2DM. This paper proposes FoodSub, a mobile application to recommend substitutes for processed foods using the NOVA Classification. Nutrient-based food clustering is used to identify substitute pairs between processed and unprocessed foods. The recommendations are supported and personalized using a knowledge graph that contains foods, dietary guidelines, and user information. In addition, a chatbot is implemented to answer simple questions about foods. This chatbot is developed using a Large Language Model (LLM) to query the knowledge graph. The mobile application and the chatbot are evaluated in terms of usability; both perform well, but there is room for improvement. Additionally, the recommendations' performance is evaluated through expert verification. The recommendations perform well when issues like food transformation processes, flavor, context, or meal time are not relevant. Future work will consider the enhancement of the chatbot and the improvement of substitute recommendations for the relevant cases.

Keywords: Processed Foods · Clustering · Knowledge Graph · Chatbot

1 Introduction

According to the "Instituto Nacional de Estadísticas y Censos" (INEC) [17], in Ecuador, diabetes mellitus was the third cause of death in 2020 (8,025 deaths) and 2021 (5,564 deaths). Type 2 Diabetes Mellitus (T2DM) is the most common type of diabetes, and it comprises more than 90% of diabetes cases worldwide [31]. As per [11], diets that include highly processed foods imply a greater risk of acquiring T2DM. Moreover, the work in [12] indicates that a qualitative classification based on processing level is essential for people to make healthier choices to prevent T2DM.

© The Author(s), under exclusive license to Springer Nature Switzerland AG 2024
M. Botto-Tobar et al. (Eds.): ICAT 2023, CCIS 2050, pp. 226–240, 2024.
https://doi.org/10.1007/978-3-031-58953-9_18

The work [28] revises many processed food classification systems. The NOVA classification system is the most widely published. NOVA [21] categorizes foods into four groups: (1) unprocessed and minimally processed foods; (2) processed culinary ingredients; (3) processed foods; and (4) ultra-processed foods, with this last group being a major issue for health. However, [13] suggests that some globalized and industrialized processed foods (NOVA Group 3) could also contribute to overweight and obesity (T2DM-related conditions). Therefore, our main goal is to develop a mobile app recommending substitutions for processed foods (NOVA groups 3 and 4).

To the best of our knowledge, there are no works that offer suggestions for processed food alternatives using the NOVA classification. In fact, no work was discovered that truly offered suggestions for alternatives to processed foods. However, there are two approaches to suggesting appropriate meal substitutes. The first approach uses unsupervised machine learning methods to cluster similar foods and recommend substitutes within the same cluster [4,24]. On the other hand, the second approach focuses on ingredient substitution within recipes, using methods like a word embedding model [23], or exploiting semantic information from a knowledge graph [29].

In our approach, the solution involves employing nutrient-based clustering, utilizing a combination of a Self-Organizing Map (SOM) and K-means, similar to the approach presented in [24]. However, in this work, the substitutions are made based on the NOVA classification and not on a custom categorization like in [24]. Additionally, all food items used in this work are adapted to the Ecuadorian context. The goal is to recommend foods that have a lower processing level (foods in NOVA groups 1, 2, or 3) and that can be eaten on their own.

The substitution recommendations are meant to prevent T2DM in Ecuadorian adults. A knowledge-based approach could be used to generate proper recommendations using the information from a food knowledge graph like [14]. There are other works like [7], which presents a knowledge graph that considers concepts of Chinese food and medicine and maps them with user information, or like [1], which includes dietary guidelines information from sources like the American Diabetes Association[1] (ADA) into its knowledge base. However, works like [7,14] are more focused on recipes (or dishes) and ingredients, and none of these works take the NOVA classification system into account.

The aim of this work was to build a knowledge graph containing general and health information of users, as well as nutritional information of Ecuadorian foods to offer personalised and contextualised recommendations; replacing processed and ultra-processed products with natural foods in order to prevent diseases such as diabetes in the medium or long term, as in the works [1,7], considering that so far there are no similar works related to the substitution of products using the NOVA classification. Additionally, this work implements a chatbot to query general and nutritional information about foods. The main challenge is to implement an adequate Natural Language Processing (NLP) technique to extract information from the knowledge graph based on natural lan-

---

[1] https://diabetes.org/.

guage prompts. Simple Knowledge Graph Question Answering (KGQA) is an adequate technique to solve this problem.

For instance, in [14], a QA system can answer simple questions, comparative questions, and constraint questions about recipes, ingredients, and nutrients. Besides, there are other QA systems that focus on the food safety field, such as [25,26]. Most of the KGQA methods described in the previous works use specific NLP tasks to solve individual problems such as mention detection, entity disambiguation, and relationship detection. As per [10], Large Language Models (LLMs) have been utilized to handle a large range of applications instead of training specialized models for specific tasks. Therefore, a LLM could be used to handle most of the KGQA tasks.

In this work, a KGQA method is developed to answer simple, natural language questions about foods, their nutrients, general product information, and ingredients when applicable. The proposed method uses a template matching approach to tackle mention detection and entity disambiguation tasks by generating Cypher queries with the GPT-3.5-turbo model[2], like in the work [9]. However, to tackle the entity disambiguation task, the Neo4j full-text search indexes[3] are applied to relevant entities.

The rest of the paper is organized into three sections. Section 2 presents the materials and methods used in this work. Section 3 describes and discusses the results obtained in the evaluation of the proposed app and chatbot. The results of the expert verification of the substitute recommendations are also shown. Finally, Sect. 4 draws final conclusions and provides future work lines.

2   Materials and Methods

2.1   Data

This work utilized a pre-existing SQL database from the "Technologies Applied to Health Research"[4] team. Two datasets were used as sources to generate this database. The first source consisted of a database collected in 2019 that holds records about processed and ultra-processed products sold by supermarkets in Ecuador [22]. The data includes attributes like the name of the product, its brand, ingredients, the information for each nutrient either per 100 g, its portion, or the volume, etc.,according to the INFORMAS protocol mentioned in [22]. The second source is a table of the food chemical composition elaborated in [15]. These data hold the nutritional information (micronutrients and macronutrients) of more than a thousand unique products, expressed in either 100 g or 100 ml.

The database itself has differing amounts of detail as the two sources did not use the same approach or purpose for gathering and storing their information. The first source provided a complete set of data for each product, but the second source

---

[2] https://platform.openai.com/docs/models/gpt-3-5.

[3] https://neo4j.com/docs/cypher-manual/current/indexes-for-full-text-search/.

[4] This research team is made up of professors from the Faculties of Engineering and Medical Sciences at the University of Cuenca.

just provided the product names and information on the related nutrients. As a result, data preparation and learning processes were defined by this restriction.

2.2 Foods Clustering and Distance Matrix

Data Preparation and Variable Selection. Data extraction involved SQL queries and Python processing through Jupyter Notebooks. Standardization into a common reference (100 g) was achieved by calculating nutrient quantities using densities from the FAO, INFOODS databases [6], and the Aqua-Calc tool[5]. The selection of usable nutrients was based on the results and methods used in [24], which identified eight key nutrients for further investigation. Five of these eight nutrients were found to be significantly present in the database. Three additional nutrients, cholesterol, sugar, and sodium, were added to the analysis as they were essential for similarity analysis and the dietary requirements of people with TD2M, as recommended by nutritionists. The chosen nutrients were energy, protein, fats, carbohydrates, fiber, cholesterol, sodium, and sugars.

Statistical analysis was applied to determine which variables did not offer helpful information for future analyses. The distribution of nutrients in the dataset was asymmetric; the removal of outliers was considered, but to preserve the insightful data that could be used for recommendations and substitutions, a log transformation was applied to all variables.

Correlation analysis revealed relationships between sugars and carbohydrates, and between energy, carbohydrates, and fats. For simplicity, only energy was retained due to its association with both carbohydrates and fats. Sugar was retained despite its lower correlation with carbohydrates.

SOM Configurations for Visualization and Reduction of Dimensions. To uncover hidden patterns and structures in the dataset, SOM was performed over selected variables. The number of neurons was calculated using $5\sqrt{N}$ (N being equal to the number of records we have on our dataset), as indicated in [30]. This number considers the computational complexity and the fact that clustering is going to be performed over the results.

The search for the optimal configuration for a two-dimensional lattice containing the specified number of neurons was conducted. The topographic error and quantization error were calculated for each type of lattice and neighborhood function. The configuration with the lowest average value was selected as shown in [3], taking into account both topographic error and quantization error. The best result was a 14 by 17 rectangular lattice with a Gaussian neighborhood function, with a topographical error of 0.0974 and a quantization error of 0.3488. A visual representation of the SOM results can be seen in Fig. 1-a, where a heatmap representing the relative distribution of each variable is shown. Darker colors represent relatively small values, while lighter values represent relatively large values.

---

[5] https://www.aqua-calc.com/page/density-table.

Clustering of the SOM. Once the optimal SOM configuration was found, BMUs were clustered with K-means. If two food items have different BMUs but have the same cluster, they are good substitutes.

K-means was chosen for this process due to its noise reduction properties when applied to the results of SOM. The Davies Bouldin Score was calculated for different numbers of clusters. The lowest score achieved was 17 partitions, indicating the optimal clustering solution. The Silhouette Score was also calculated, whose results consistently support the Davies-Bouldin Score, reaching its best score at 17 partitions, aligning with the data size, number of neurons used in SOM, and expected number of clusters.

The K-means algorithm was applied to group BMUs together, with each BMU colorized and numbered with the cluster it falls into (see Fig. 1-b). To determine which cluster each food item belongs to, the clusterization results were mapped to each food in the dataset. Each BMU had a cluster, and each food had a BMU, so basically, each food had a cluster.

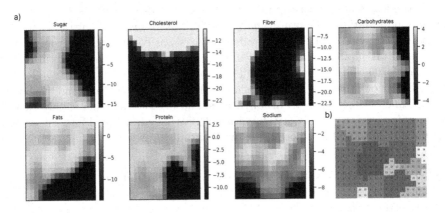

Fig. 1. Foods Nutrient Based SOM-Kmeans Clustering. a) Nutrients Component Planes. b) SOM Clustering.

A thorough trial-and-error process was employed to optimize the learning and clustering process. Various configurations were tested, including different permutations of skewed variables and retaining correlated variables. Expert evaluation of substitution pairs helped identify promising configurations for making recommendations across the dataset.

Distance Matrix. Finally, once a cluster is identified for every processed and unprocessed food, the distance between a food item and every other member of the same cluster is used as our recommendation metric. This intra-cluster distance allows us to identify the nearest (most appropriate) food that can be recommended for a specific food item. So an additional process was run where the Euclidean distance was measured between the nutritional information in each pair of items in each cluster. The result was a distance matrix that holds the measure of distance between food items that fall in the same cluster; this link is the basis of our recommendation system.

2.3 Foods, Dietary Guidelines, and Users Knowledge Graph

Figure 2 shows the knowledge graph model used in this work. The graph model captures the entities, attributes, and implicit relationships of the original database described in Sect. 2.1. In addition, entities and relationships regarding dietary guidelines and users are also included. The main entities and relationships of the proposed knowledge are divided into three main topics: Foods, Dietary Guidelines, and Users.

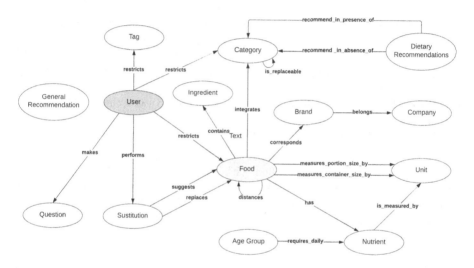

Fig. 2. Model for the Knowledge Graph used in this work.

Foods. The information from the original SQL database (see Sect. 2.1) was extracted in CSV files via SQL queries. The graph was populated using Python scripts (Jupyter Notebooks) and the Py2neo[6] Neo4j client library. The Food nodes contain information like name, portion size, container size, number of servings per container, sugar-salt-fat traffic light label, product density, and its NOVA group. All foods have information on the Nutrient nodes that compose them. There are different Category nodes that relate to different types of food. Additionally, when applicable, the Ingredient, the Brand, and the Company nodes related to food items are described via their corresponding relationships.

---

[6] https://py2neo.org/2021.1/.

Dietary Guidelines. This work takes into account dietary recommendations from three major sources: the ADA Standards of Care in Diabetes [8], the "Diabetes mellitus tipo 2 Guía de Práctica Clínica (GPC)" [19] from the "Ministerio de Salud Pública del Ecuador" (MSP), and the "Documento Técnico de las Guías Alimentarias Basadas en Alimentos (GABA) del Ecuador" [20] from the MSP and Food and Agriculture Organization (FAO). CSV files containing guidelines concerning T2DM prevention were manually generated and loaded to the graph. This was done to build three different node labels. First, General Recommendation nodes contain general recommendation messages for users based on their Body Mass Index (BMI) and T2DM risk (calculated using the modified FINDRISC questionnaire from [19]). Second, Dietary Recommendation nodes contain dietary recommendation messages to give to users depending on the category of the substitute they choose to replace processed food with, since TD2M is a disease related to an excess of carbohydrates and a lack of fiber, these facts are modeled through advisable or avoidable categories of foods as in [20]. Finally, Age Group nodes allow for modeling the recommended daily percentages or values for certain critical nutrients depending on the user's age group. Personalized daily values in grams are computed for the users considering their Total Daily Energy Expenditure (TDEE), which is calculated using the Resting Metabolic Rate (RMB) and then multiplied by the corresponding Physical Activity Level (PAL). In addition, an energy deficit is applied depending on the user's BMI (¿24.9).

Users. The users can be identified with the User nodes. These nodes store basic user information such as ID (internal app ID), names, email, sex, birth year, weight, height, PAL, FINDRISC score, and BMI value. Additionally, users can restrict Food, Category, and Tag (tags to search in ingredient and food names) nodes using the restricts relationship.

2.4   FoodSub: System Architecture

This work aimed to provide individualized suggestions for healthier food choices by developing a mobile app that allows users to browse and search processed products, find nutritional information, and receive personalized recommendations. The system architecture for the mobile app was designed using a client-server architecture, with a frontend built using React Native and a backend built using Node.js and Express. Firebase was used for authentication, ensuring secure storage of user credentials and authentication states. The OpenAI API was also utilized to enhance the user experience with intelligent conversational abilities. A RESTful API was used to establish communication between the frontend and backend, handling data storage and retrieval in the Neo4j knowledge graph.

2.5   Processed Foods Substitution Method and Recommendation

Figure 2 from Sect. 2.3 illustrates the distances relationship between Food nodes. This relationship indicates substitute pairs ranked by the distance metric obtained from the clustering distance matrices described in Sect. 2.2. The recommendations are meant to discourage the consumption of all foods in NOVA Group 4 and some foods in NOVA Group 3, so only the pairs in which the original food is part of one of the previous NOVA Groups and the substitute has a lower NOVA Group are considered. Additionally, the is_replaceable relationship between Category nodes can help enhance the recommendations since foods from a replaceable category can be recommended first as well (e.g., to replace foods in the Sausages category, the substitutes are preferred to be part of the Meats and Derivatives category). An example illustrating the top 5 food substitutes for an ultra-processed food is shown in Table 1.

Table 1. Top 5 Food Substitutes for "Tuna Loin Pieces in Soy Oil" (NOVA Group 4), part of the "Canned Meat" category.

Recommended Substitute	Category	NOVA Group	Distance
Trout	Fish and Seafood	1	0.072750540
Salmon	Fish and Seafood	1	0.086335694
Beef (Steak)	Meats and Derivatives	1	0.088917534
Tuna Canned in Water	Fish and Seafood	3	0.089548968
Beef (High Fat without Bone)	Meats and Derivatives	1	0.089985500

The recommendations can be personalized using the knowledge graph information. For a given user, unwanted substitutes can be filtered using the restricts relationship between User nodes and Food, Category, or Tag nodes. In addition, to help the users make a better decision, reference values for the intake contributions to their daily requirements are displayed to them for each recommended food. Additionally, when users accept a substitute suggestion, some general and dietary messages to improve their diets are shown. Figure 3 shows an example in which a determined user requested substitute foods using the FoodSub mobile application.

2.6   Nutritional Information Chatbot

The Nutritional Information Chatbot can answer basic questions about food nutritional values, comparisons, ingredients, and general information about food products. In this work, the following intentions are included:

- How much [nutrient] does a [food] have?
- How many calories does a [food] have?
- What has more [nutrient], a [food] or a [food]?
- What has more calories, a [food] or a [food]?
- Tell me the ingredients of [food].
- Give me general information about the [food].
- What can replace a [food]?

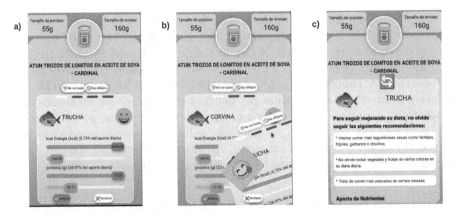

Fig. 3. FoodSub App Screenshots. a) The app suggests substitutes and shows nutritional values. b) The user browses the suggested substitutes and accepts one. c) The app provides general and dietary messages.

The chatbot was developed using a template-matching approach. First, Cypher queries are generated from natural language questions using the GPT-3.5-turbo model in the OpenAI Chat Completion API[7]. The API is provided with a prompt consisting of the user question and "training" input-output examples. The provided examples consist of Natural Language Question - Cypher Query pairs that refer to foods, nutrients, node labels, and relationship names from the knowledge graph. All the Cypher statements use full-text index queries. The results are returned based on a matching score, so the best-matching entry is put first. Next, the generated Cypher statements are executed to query the knowledge graph. The queries are designed to return JSON responses. Once the response is obtained, the API is prompted with a different task: to generate a human-readable answer from a JSON object. Finally, the answer is displayed to the user. Figure 4 summarizes the chatbot workflow with an illustrative example.

3   Results and Discussion

This section describes and discusses the results obtained in the evaluation of the proposed mobile app and chatbot. Both were evaluated in terms of usability using the System Usability Scale (SUS) questionnaire [5] and the Chatbot Usability Questionnaire (CUQ) questionnaire [16], respectively. Additionally, this work aimed to evaluate the food substitute recommendations' performance through the expert verification.

3.1   Evaluation Participants

The evaluation was conducted with students and teachers from Ecuadorian universities and other volunteers. This was done considering that universities are

---

[7] https://platform.openai.com/docs/api-reference/chat.

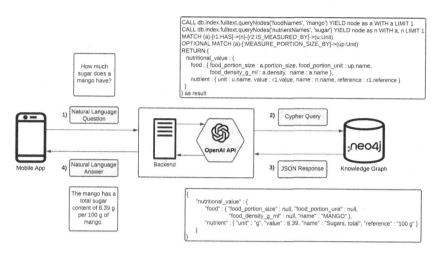

Fig. 4. Chatbot Workflow and Example.

ideal environments for health promotion, as certified by several studies that demonstrate the effectiveness of establishing public health promotion programs in these spaces [18].

The evaluation was carried out in face-to-face and virtual sessions. After a brief introduction and after using the app, all of the participants were invited to fill out both of the corresponding questionnaires (SUS and CUQ). A total of 57 participants filled out the SUS questionnaire to evaluate the FoodSub app's usability. However, only 32 participants completed the CUQ questionnaire to evaluate the chatbot's usability. The number of participants by their characteristics (sex and age group) as they registered in the app is described as follows: 16 (male, 18–29), 38 (female, 18–29), 2 (male, 30–59), 1 (female, 30–59).

3.2   FoodSub: Usability Evaluation with SUS

The SUS is a widely used usability assessment tool that uses a 10-item Likert scale survey to measure user opinions on system usability, effectiveness, and learnability. The analysis revealed that users had a generally favorable opinion of the system's usability, with an average score of 79.12, indicating a positive user experience. This score is higher than the acceptable score of 68, which is typical for similar systems in comparable domains [2]. The system exceeded expectations and efficiently satisfied users' needs.

The SUS questionnaire's individual items can be examined to gain more information about specific usability facets. Some items about the need for technical support and the need to know a lot of things before usage scored near neutral values. This suggests that more training and understanding of nutritional terms are required before using the system. Overall, the SUS survey results show that users have a favorable opinion of the system's usability.

3.3 Chatbot: Usability Evaluation with CUQ

This work utilized the CUQ questionnaire to evaluate the usability of a chatbot developed for the mobile application. The questionnaire, consisting of 16 items, was designed for chatbots and asked participants to rate their agreement on the chatbot's benefits and drawbacks on a scale of 1 to 5. The CUQ allowed the assessment of the overall usability of the chatbot; some items' scores suggested that some users thought the chatbot did not understand them well and that the chatbot seemed unable to handle errors or mistakes, which helped to identify areas that required attention. Even so, the average score of the 16 items was 78.1; given that this questionnaire is comparable to the SUS, this indicates high satisfaction and confirms that users had a good experience with the chatbot.

3.4 Expert Verification for Substitution Recommendations

This work aimed to evaluate the accuracy of substitute recommendations using expert verification. A sample of 67 foods (from NOVA groups 4 and 3) was used along with information from seven anonymous users to generate a record of food substitute recommendations. Each user was randomly assigned a maximum of 11 foods, and a maximum of 5 substitute recommendations were generated for each food. The resulting CSV file contained 318 substitute recommendations, with 65 out of 67 foods having at least one substitute. Three nutrition experts were given the list of suggested food substitutes for verification. The experts evaluated the recommendations based on accuracy, relevancy, and appropriateness, which are metrics taken from the work of [1], but adapted as follows:

1. **Accuracy:** It measures how good the food suggested as a substitute for the original food is.
2. **Relevancy:** Regarding general and dietary recommendation messages, it measures if they contain words, phrases, and concepts familiar to the user.
3. **Appropriateness:** It measures if the recommendation would produce a positive and encouraging user outcome.

The experts were divided into two groups: (1) a doctor of biochemistry and pharmacy with a Ph.D. in nutrition and metabolism; (2) a nutritionist and a recently graduated student of nutrition and dietetics. The main results of the expert verification in both groups are presented in Table 2.

Table 2 reveals that Group 1 has slightly higher satisfaction rates for the accuracy, relevancy, and appropriateness of substitute recommendations compared to Group 2. However, the difference between satisfaction rates can be larger for specific food categories, such as "Preparations of National and Multinational Chains." This suggests that the substitute recommendations' performance may be difficult to evaluate due to the subjective nature of the experts' judgments.

The discrepancy in expert nutritional recommendations can be attributed to factors such as experience, acquired knowledge, and academic training [27]. Thus, the interpretation of nutritional recommendations can be subjective and

Table 2. Expert Verification Satisfaction Rates by Original Food Category. For the sake of brevity, categories with n ¡ 10 recommendations are consolidated in Others.

Category	Total	Group 1			Group 2		
		Acc.	Rel.	App.	Acc.	Rel.	App.
Drinks	39	58.97%	76.92%	41.03%	66.67%	74.36%	61.54%
Cookies	35	71.43%	91.43%	62.86%	62.86%	45.71%	40.00%
Bakery and Pastry Products	35	71.43%	91.43%	68.57%	68.57%	28.57%	25.71%
Dairy	25	52.00%	100.00%	52.00%	60.00%	88.00%	56.00%
Breakfast Cereals, Bars, Granola	25	40.00%	100.00%	32.00%	32.00%	64.00%	04.00%
Snacks	20	95.00%	100.00%	95.00%	80.00%	100.00%	80.00%
Chocolates	20	55.00%	95.00%	50.00%	65.00%	55.00%	45.00%
Prepared Foods	16	12.50%	100.00%	12.50%	00.00%	00.00%	00.00%
Ice Creams	10	60.00%	100.00%	60.00%	70.00%	70.00%	70.00%
Sausages	10	80.00%	100.00%	80.00%	30.00%	60.00%	30.00%
Canned Meat	10	80.00%	90.00%	80.00%	50.00%	80.00%	50.00%
Cereals and Derivatives	10	70.00%	100.00%	70.00%	80.00%	30.00%	10.00%
Preparations of National and Multinational Chains	10	90.00%	90.00%	90.00%	00.00%	40.00%	00.00%
Others	53	35.85%	94.34%	43.40%	47.17%	60.38%	41.51%
Overall	318	58.18%	93.40%	55.03%	54.09%	57.86%	39.31%

depend on the professional or expert in nutrition. However, expert verification allows them to provide feedback, which can be valuable for improving substitute recommendations. The main issue identified is that some suggested substitutes do not have the same food transformation processes, flavor, context, or meal time as the original food. These issues become relevant when analyzing the results of the verification by experts for individual categories of foods. For example, substitute recommendations for "Snacks" food items are less likely to be affected by the stated issues, as a snack can be directly replaced with a single food item like a fruit. However, in the "Prepared Foods" category, substitute recommendations that replace these food items are more likely to be affected by the stated issues.

For the relevant cases, the research team determined that there were not enough substitute foods in the original database for the specific categories where discrepancies were found. Additionally, the products offered as replacements did not have the same characteristics in terms of preparation but had similar macronutrient content, such as protein, but without an excess of critical nutrients that can be harmful to health (salt, fat, or sugars).

4   Conclusions and Future Work

This work introduces FoodSub, a mobile app that allows users to recommend food substitutes for preventing T2DM in the Ecuadorian context using the NOVA Classification. The app and its chatbot were evaluated for usability using the SUS and CUQ questionnaires, showing good performance. However, there is room for improvement in this regard. Some suggestions for the mobile app flow and graphic user interface were made to make the app more intuitive. Technical issues related to the chatbot's ability to handle errors and unexpected inputs were identified. Additionally, expert verification revealed that the recommendations perform well in cases where food transformation processes, flavor, context, or meal time are not relevant. However, there is room for improvement in cases where these issues are relevant.

Future work will focus on enhancing the chatbot and the substitute recommendations in the relevant cases. We planned to include a more powerful LLM, such as GPT-4[8], to enhance the chatbot through more sophisticated prompts and to consider the use of a LLM-oriented framework like LangChain[9] to improve the chatbot's capacity for handling errors and unexpected inputs. Substitute recommendation improvements will involve expanding the knowledge graph to include more food items and categories; integrating information about food transformation processes, flavor, context, and meal time; and exploring the use of Explainable AI to provide more detailed information on substitute recommendations.

Acknowledgements. This work is part of the research project "2021_030_UPS_ESPINOZA_MAURICIO", supported by the Vice-Rectorate for Research of the University of Cuenca.

References

1. Alian, S., Li, J., Pandey, V.: A personalized recommendation system to support diabetes self-management for american indians. IEEE Access **6**, 73041–73051 (2018). https://doi.org/10.1109/ACCESS.2018.2882138
2. Alonso-Mencía, J., Castro-Rodríguez, M., Herrero-Pinilla, B., Alonso-Weber, J.M., Rodríguez-Mañas, L., Pérez-Rodríguez, R.: ADELA: a conversational virtual assistant to prevent delirium in hospitalized older persons. J. Supercomput. (2023). https://doi.org/10.1007/s11227-023-05352-7
3. Tu, A.L.: Improving feature Map Quality of SOM based on adjusting the neighborhood function. In: Almusaed, A., Almssad, A., Hong, L.T., (eds.) Sustainability in Urban Planning and Design. IntechOpen (2020). https://doi.org/10.5772/intechopen.89233
4. Baek, J.W., Kim, J.C., Chun, J., Chung, K.: Hybrid clustering based health decision-making for improving dietary habits. Technol. Health Care **27**(5), 459–472 (2019). https://doi.org/10.3233/THC-191730
5. Brooke, J.: SUS A- a quick and dirty usability scale. In: Usability Evaluation In Industry, pp. 189–194 (1996). CRC Press
6. Charrondiere, R., Haytowitz, D., Stadlmayr, B.: FAO/INFOODS Density Database version 2. FAO, Italy (2012). URL https://www.fao.org/3/ap815e/ap815e.pdf
7. Chi, Y., Yu, C., Qi, X., Xu, H.: Knowledge management in healthcare sustainability: a smart healthy diet assistant in traditional Chinese medicine culture. Sustainability **10**(11), 4197 (2018). https://doi.org/10.3390/su10114197

---

[8] https://platform.openai.com/docs/models/gpt-4.
[9] https://python.langchain.com/docs/get_started/introduction.html.

8. ElSayed, N.A., et al.: Summary of revisions: standards of care in diabetes—2023. Diabetes Care **46**(1), S5–S9 (2023). https://doi.org/10.2337/dc23-Srev

9. Fan, L., Lafia, S., Li, L., Yang, F., Hemphill, L.: DataChat: prototyping a conversational agent for dataset search and visualization (2023). https://doi.org/10.48550/ARXIV.2305.18358

10. Fan, L., Li, L., Ma, Z., Lee, S., Yu, H., Hemphill, L.: A bibliometric review of large language models research from 2017 to 2023 (2023). https://doi.org/10.48550/ARXIV.2304.02020

11. FAO, FIDA, OPS, PMA, UNICEF: panorama regional de la seguridad alimentaria y nutricional - América latina y el caribe 2022. FAO (2023). https://doi.org/10.4060/cc3859es

12. Fardet, A.: Minimally processed foods are more satiating and less hyperglycemic than ultra-processed foods: a preliminary study with 98 ready-to-eat foods. Food Funct. **7**(5), 2338–2346 (2016). https://doi.org/10.1039/C6FO00107F

13. Freire, W.B., Waters, W.F., Román, D., Jiménez, E., Burgos, E., Belmont, P.: Overweight, obesity, and food consumption in Galapagos, Ecuador: a window on the world. Glob. Health **14**(1), 93 (2018). https://doi.org/10.1186/s12992-018-0409-y

14. Haussmann, S., et al.: FoodKG: a semantics-driven knowledge graph for food recommendation. In: Ghidini, C. (ed.) ISWC 2019. LNCS, vol. 11779, pp. 146–162. Springer, Cham (2019). https://doi.org/10.1007/978-3-030-30796-7_10

15. Herrera, M., Chisaguano, A., Jumbo, J., Castro, N., Anchundia, A.: Tabla de composición química de los alimentos: basada en nutrientes de interés para la población ecuatoriana, *Bitácora Académica USFQ*, vol. 11. USFQ PRESS, Quito (2021). URL https://revistas.usfq.edu.ec/index.php/bitacora/issue/view/191/PDF%20Bit%C3%A1cora%20Acad%C3%A9mica%20Vol.%2011

16. Holmes, S., Moorhead, A., Bond, R., Zheng, H., Coates, V., Mctear, M.: Usability testing of a healthcare chatbot: can we use conventional methods to assess conversational user interfaces? In: Proceedings of the 31st European Conference on Cognitive Ergonomics, pp. 207–214. ACM, BELFAST United Kingdom (2019). https://doi.org/10.1145/3335082.3335094

17. INEC: Estadísticas Vitales - Registro Estadístico de Defunciones Generales de 2021 (2022). URL https://www.ecuadorencifras.gob.ec/documentos/web-inec/Poblacion_y_Demografia/Defunciones_Generales_2021/Principales_resultados_EDG_2021_v2.pdf

18. Martínez-Sánchez, J.M., Balaguer, A.: Universidad saludable: una estrategia de promoción de la salud y salud en todas las políticas para crear un entorno de trabajo saludable. Archivos de Prevención de Riesgos Laborales **19**, 175 – 177 (2016). URL http://scielo.isciii.es/scielo.php?script=sci_arttext&pid=S1578-25492016000300004&nrm=iso

19. Ministerio de Salud Pública del Ecuador: Diabetes mellitus tipo 2 Guía de Práctica Clínica (GPC). Dirección Nacional de Normatización, Quito (2017). URL https://www.salud.gob.ec/wp-content/uploads/2019/02/GPC_diabetes_mellitus_2017.pdf

20. Ministerio de Salud Pública del Ecuador y la Organización de las Naciones Unidas para la Alimentación y la Agricultura: Documento Técnico de las Guías Alimentarias Basadas en Alimentos (GABA) del Ecuador, 1 edn. FAO, Quito (2018). URL http://instituciones.msp.gob.ec/images/Documentos/GABAS_Guias_Alimentarias_Ecuador_2018.pdf

21. Monteiro, C.A., et al.: Ultra-processed foods: what they are and how to identify them. Public Health Nutr. **22**(5), 936–941 (2019). https://doi.org/10.1017/S1368980018003762

22. Morales-Avilez, D., Cruz-Casarrubias, C., Tolentino-Mayo, L., Encalada-Torres, L., Abril-Ulloa, V.: Evaluation of the accurateness of the nutritional labels of processed and ultra-processed products available in supermarkets of Ecuador. Nutrients **12**(11), 3481 (2020). https://doi.org/10.3390/nu12113481
23. Morales-Garzon, A., Gomez-Romero, J., Martin-Bautista, M.J.: A word embedding-based method for unsupervised adaptation of cooking recipes. IEEE Access **9**, 27389–27404 (2021). https://doi.org/10.1109/ACCESS.2021.3058559
24. Phanich, M., Pholkul, P., Phimoltares, S.: Food recommendation system using clustering analysis for diabetic patients. In: 2010 International Conference on Information Science and Applications, pp. 1–8. IEEE, Seoul, Korea (South) (2010). https://doi.org/10.1109/ICISA.2010.5480416
25. Qin, L., Hao, Z., Yang, L.: Question answering system based on food spot-check knowledge graph. In: Proceedings of 2020 6th International Conference on Computing and Data Engineering, pp. 168–172. ACM, Sanya China (2020). https://doi.org/10.1145/3379247.3379292
26. Qin, L., Hao, Z., Zhao, L.: Food safety knowledge graph and question answering system. In: Proceedings of the 2019 7th International Conference on Information Technology: IoT and smart city, pp. 559–564. ACM, Shanghai China (2019). https://doi.org/10.1145/3377170.3377260
27. Rodríguez Delgado, J.: Recomendaciones nutricionales y evidencia científica: ¿hay más dudas que certezas? Pediatría Atención Primaria **21**, 69 – 75 (2019). URL http://scielo.isciii.es/scielo.php?script=sci_arttext&pid=S1139-76322019000100016&nrm=iso
28. Sadler, C.R., Grassby, T., Hart, K., Raats, M., Sokolović, M., Timotijevic, L.: Processed food classification: conceptualisation and challenges. Trends Food Sci. Technol. **112**, 149–162 (2021). https://doi.org/10.1016/j.tifs.2021.02.059
29. Shirai, S.S., Seneviratne, O., Gordon, M.E., Chen, C.H., McGuinness, D.L.: Identifying ingredient substitutions using a knowledge graph of food. frontiers in artificial intelligence **3**, 621766 (2021). https://doi.org/10.3389/frai.2020.621766
30. Vesanto, J., Alhoniemi, E.: Clustering of the self-organizing map. IEEE Trans. Neural Netw. **11**(3), 586–600 (2000). https://doi.org/10.1109/72.846731
31. Zheng, Y., Ley, S.H., Hu, F.B.: Global aetiology and epidemiology of type 2 diabetes mellitus and its complications. Nat. Rev. Endocrinol. **14**(2), 88–98 (2018). https://doi.org/10.1038/nrendo.2017.151

Attack Classification Using Machine Learning Techniques in Software-Defined Networking

Daniel Nuñez-Agurto[1,2]([✉]) [ID], Walter Fuertes[1] [ID], Luis Marrone[2] [ID],
Miguel Castillo-Camacho[1] [ID], Eduardo Benavides-Astudillo[1] [ID],
and Franklin Perez[1] [ID]

[1] Department of Computer Science, Universidad de las Fuerzas Armadas - ESPE,
Av. General Rumiñahui S/N, P.O. Box 17-15-231B Sangolquí, Ecuador
{adnunez1,wmfuertes,macastillo18,debenavides,frperez4}@espe.edu.ec
[2] Faculty of Computer Science, Universidad Nacional de La Plata,
1900 La Plata, Argentina
lmarrone@linti.unlp.edu.ar

Abstract. Software-defined networking represents a novel network model that separates control functionality from data management, significantly enhancing the latter's efficiency and flexibility. Nevertheless, it faces substantial security threats that jeopardize data and service availability. This paper aims to define a model for classifying attacks using machine learning techniques to enhance defense capabilities and bolster data management security in software-defined networking. The classifier was trained with three machine learning algorithms: decision trees, random forests, and support vector machines, applying various feature sets from two public datasets with software-define networking traffic. In the training phase, 99.76%, 99.75%, and 99.50% accuracy rates were achieved for decision trees, random forests, and support vector machines, respectively. Consequently, the results obtained in this study outperform state-of-the-art approaches and demonstrate the successful deployment of a machine learning model in a software-defined networking environment.

Keywords: Software-defined networking · Attacks classification · Machine learning

1 Introduction

Software-defined networking (SDN) has reached a high level of popularity due to its flexibility and scalability, allowing a global view of network traffic and quick configurations, unlike traditional rigid and static networks [7,18]. Despite their impressive functionality, they are attractive to attacks such as denial of service (DoS), distributed denial of service (DDoS), and botnets or botnets. These

---

Supported by Universidad de las Fuerzas Armadas - ESPE.

attacks are the most common attacks on network infrastructures and are growing in volume and sophistication [30]. SDN is currently a highly demanded technology in data centers and carrier networks due to its ability to contribute to innovation in the development of future networks [25]. However, SDN also presents security challenges, as attackers focus on the network's central intelligence component, the controller. This device controls the entire network, including traffic forwarding at the infrastructure layer. Therefore, effective security mechanisms must be implemented to protect the controller and the network.

Traffic classification methods have evolved significantly, starting with categorization based on the application's port [6]. However, this method has become obsolete due to sudden changes in port usage by applications. On the other hand, the deep packet inspection (DPI) method, presented as the most accurate option, gave promising results but eventually became a laborious and computationally inefficient process [13]. Although machine learning (ML) is becoming increasingly popular due to the wide variety of algorithms available for its implementation, and one of its main applications is network traffic detection and classification [16], there are some challenges in applying ML to SDNs, such as the lack of training data, the need to process large amounts of data, and the risk of bias. Despite these challenges, the application of ML to SDNs is an active area of research with the potential to revolutionize how we design and operate networks.

Several security studies have adopted various methods to detect attacks of unknown origin. ML is a practical approach with a wide variety of algorithms and has proven to be widely used in these tasks with remarkable results. In addition, ML can work with network data traffic, allowing it to observe, learn, and make decisions. Therefore, this paper develops an attack classifier based on traffic flow anomalies, using ML techniques to identify attacks that compromise SDN performance and security. The model effectively detects and classifies attacks such as DoS, DDoS, Botnet, and Probe attacks.

The remainder of this paper is organized as follows: Section two presents a literature review. In contrast, section three describes the proposed model and explains the selection of features and the dataset. Section four discusses the evaluation and results. In addition, Section five includes the conclusion of the proposed model and future work.

2   Literature Review

Machine learning is an essential technology for SDNs, as it can significantly improve network resource allocation, traffic classification, malicious traffic detection, and network performance [19]. The following section showcases the different types of machine learning algorithms applied in SDNs for classification or attack detection and the challenges that must be faced when implementing ML.

Sahoo et al. [21] propose the design of a framework for DDoS attack detection using SVM. The developed module receives flow statistics from OpenFlow switches and then extracts the features fed into the ML model. The author created the dataset to train the model, containing 27 characteristics and 224,709 samples of four types of attacks. Kernel Principal Component Analysis (K-PCA) was applied as the feature selection technique. The model Genetic Algorithm (GA) was used, and during the training, K-Fold cross-validation with five iterations was employed. As a result, the model achieves an accuracy of 98.90%, while the KNN and RF models achieve an accuracy of 92.02% and 94.33%, respectively.

Alamri et al. [3] desarrollaron un mecanismo de control de ancho de banda y un clasificador de flujos en la red, utilizando XGBoost, para detectar ataques DDoS. Los autores emplearon un algoritmo de control de ancho de banda para obtener un valor umbral adaptativo (basado en el tiempo y la tasa de bytes) y penalizar los flujos que exceden ese límite. En caso de detectar tráfico anormal, se establece un valor que, si es superado por el contador de violaciones máximas del umbral, se introduce en la clasificación de flujos para determinar si es normal o un ataque DDoS. El conjunto de datos fue creado por los autores en un entorno virtual. El modelo XGBoost se entrenó con 20 características y utilizó la técnica SMOTE para equilibrar las clases minoritarias del conjunto de datos. El modelo alcanza una precisión del 99.90%, un recall del 99.98%, una precisión del 99.98% y un F1-score.

Sudar et al. [23] propose a multilayer classifier to classify traffic in an Intrusion Detection System (IDS). The objective is to apply security mechanisms in the control and data planes. An IDS module based on flows is proposed for the control plane, using ML techniques for feature selection and input classification. The model is trained with 11 features. The NSL-KDD dataset is considered, and the authors' dataset is generated using the Scapy tool. In the data plane, an IDS based on signatures is created, using Snort to inspect various instances of SDN traffic. The multilayer classification model places SVM in the first layer, while NB and C4.5 are in the second layer. Based on the results of the first layer, NB inspects regular traffic; otherwise, C4.5 analyzes attack traffic in its four types. During the individual training phase, SVM achieves an accuracy of 93.50%, NB obtains 94.41%, and C4.5 reaches 95.16%.

Ahuja et al. [2] develop a benign and malicious traffic classification model using ML techniques. It is a hybrid model based on SVM and RF. SVM acts as the first classifier, and RF processes the results from the first one. The model is trained with data generated by the authors, containing 23 features. Mininet, Ryu, an OVS, two hosts, mgen, and hping3 tools are used to obtain the dataset. Data is split with an 80:20 ratio for training and testing. PCA is used to reduce the dataset to 20 dimensions, and stochastic neighbor embedding (t-SNE) is employed to analyze the distribution of the obtained traffic. As the final result, the hybrid SVC+RF model achieves an accuracy of 98.80%.

Ussatova et al. [28] propose a classifier with supervised ML algorithms to detect DDoS attacks in an SDN environment. They use a dataset published by the authors [1], which contains 23 features with two classes: benign and malicious traffic. Additionally, they employ SMOTE to balance the classes and the Min-Max scaler as the data normalization method. The techniques applied for feature selection and reducing the dataset's dimensionality are IG, Chi-Square, and F-test. The models' results in terms of accuracy are as follows: DT, RF, K-NN,

XGBoost, and CatBoost achieve 99.00%, NB reaches 64.00%, while SVM and LR attain 74.00%.

Alzahrani et al. [5] designed a Network Intrusion Detection System (NIDS) using ML algorithms to detect malicious behaviors in the application layer of SDN. The models used were XGBoost, Random Forest (RF), and Decision Tree (DT). They utilized the NSL-KDD dataset, which contains 41 features, to develop the model; however, they considered only five characteristics. For the normalization phase, they employed the Min-Max scaler technique. NIDS comprises three configurable elements: a network rule manager, an attack detector, and the attack type classifier. The results show an accuracy of 95.55% for XGBoost, 94.60% for RF, and 94.50% for DT.

Nadeem et al. [17] develop different ML-based classifiers to detect DDoS attacks, applying various feature selection techniques. To achieve this, they create a feature selection layer using the NSL-KDD dataset and employ three methods: filter, wrapper, and embedded. The first method uses Information Gain (IG), correlation coefficient, and Chi-Square. In the second method, they employ Forward Feature Selection (FFS), Backward Feature Elimination (BFE), and Recursive Feature Elimination (RFE). For the last method, they apply the Least Absolute Shrinkage and Selection Operator (Lasso). The features selected for the SVM, KNN, NB, RF, and DT models vary for each feature selection method. With 28 features and using the Recursive Feature Elimination technique, the SVM, KNN, NB, RF, and DT models achieve an accuracy of 89.18%, 98.57%, 92.12%, 99.97%, and 99.80%, respectively.

Sangodoyin et al. [22] designed a low-cost detection and classification system for DDoS attacks using ML algorithms in SDN. Attack samples were generated with the Low Orbit Ion Cannon (LOIC) tool over an emulated SDN network in Mininet. The data is normalized using the Z-Score method, and the classifier was developed by 3600 data points of HTTP, UDP, TCP flood attacks, and normal traffic. The implemented models are Classification and Regression Trees (CART), Gaussian Naive Bayes (GNB), K-Nearest Neighbors (K-NN), and Quadratic Discriminant Analysis (QDA), achieving accuracies of 98.00%, 96.10%, 95.60%, and 95.90% respectively.

Tonkal et al. [27] propose a DDoS attack detection system in SDN, applying ML algorithms equipped with Neighborhood Component Analysis (NCA). At the input of each model, they introduce a feature selection module. This module is implemented with the NCA algorithm, aiming to extract the most relevant features and reduce the computational cost during the training of each ML model. The implemented models are K-Nearest Neighbors (KNN), Decision Tree (DT), Artificial Neural Network (ANN), and Support Vector Machine (SVM), all of which are trained with 14 features from the "DDOS attack SDN Dataset." The DT model with the Gini criterion achieves an accuracy of 99.17%, while SVM and KNN reach 81.48% and 97.75%, respectively.

Tariq et al. [26] propose a botnet detection method using ML techniques in SDN based on flow data. They develop four modules: trace collection, trace signaling, feature extraction, and trace detection. The treated datasets are CTU-13 and ISOT, and eight features are used to develop the classifier. In the first module, the Time Series Data Repository (TSDR) of the OpenDaylight controller is used to collect current traces and form small batches of flows. The second module groups flow with the same key into a set. For the third module, feature extraction is applied to the previously conglomerated flows, ranging from 10 to 60. Finally, the model processes the extracted statistical data and determines whether it is normal traffic or botnet. The results show a model accuracy of 94.80%.

Janabi et al. [14] desarrolan un IDS basado en ML para identificar flujos normales o de ataques en un entorno SDN. El IDS desarrollado contiene 3 módulos: extracción de características, analizador y decisión. El sistema extrae los datos de la tabla de flujo del switch, para ser enviados al IDS. En el analizador se agrupa cada una de las muestras para formalizar en fila el flujo completo. Finalmente, estos datos son enviados al módulo de decisión que implementa el algoritmo NB, el cual determina si pertenece a un flujo normal o de ataque. El clasificador se entrena con 14 características de muestras del conjunto de datos CSE-CIC-IDS2018 y utiliza el método de T-Test para reducir el número de características innecesarias. Como resultado, obtienen un 98.46% de accuracy.

Dehkordi et al. [8] propose a DDoS attack detection system applying ML methods in SDN. The presented modules are data collection, entropy-based data selection, and classification. The data is collected from flow tables and sent to the controller. In the controller, the flow selector is executed using the entropy method, which calculates, through threshold values, an estimation average to determine whether a particular flow is considered an attack. The previous module's output is the classifier's input, where the flow type is defined as either normal or attack. The model is trained with 14 features using UNB-ISCX, CTU-13, and ISOT datasets. The classification model is trained using algorithms JR8, BayesNet, Logistic Regression, NB, RandomTree, and REPTree, achieving accuracies of 99.93%, 99.71%, 99.79%, 97.75%, 99.95%, and 99.96% respectively.

Kamel et al. [15] develop a model to detect DDoS attacks in SDN, with the DT algorithm as the primary model. The dataset used to train the classifier is the "DDOS-attack SDN dataset," with the selection of 18 features. This model is enhanced using the Genetic Algorithm (GA), which allows finding the most suitable hyperparameter values for its learning. Eventually, this tree is constructed with 49 levels, meaning the maximum depth it reaches among decision nodes. The model achieves an accuracy of 99.46%, classifying normal and attack traffic.

Sumadi et al. [24] develop a system for detecting DDoS attacks using ML algorithms in SDN. The system integrates a honeypot sensor in the control plane to apply mitigation rules. The system consists of two modules: detection and mitigation. An ML algorithm is utilized to detect attacks, and for mitigation, restriction rules are applied, which are issued from a honeypot server to the controller. The dataset used to train the model is generated under a real scenario with the TCPReplay and Scapy tools. The implemented models are SVM, GNB, K-NN, RF, and Classification and Regression Tree (CART), which classify normal and attack traffic.

The control plane employs the Suricata sensor, which identifies anomalies flowing in the network and then directs them to the model to determine an estimated threat average. Finally, the mitigation rules are applied under the integrated honeypot. The model's accuracy is SVM 93.00%, GNB 70.00%, K-NN, CART, and RF achieve 69.00%.

3   The Proposed Method

To construct a classifier, several procedures must be carried out beforehand: data collection, preprocessing, and model training. Firstly, we must obtain traffic samples from various public datasets. Secondly, the collected traffic in the raw format must be converted into computable data and normalized. Each record should share the same input dimensionality. Finally, we design and build the model, set hyperparameters, and train the model with the normalized dataset.

3.1   Data Collection

The data comes from the public InSDN dataset, developed on a specific SDN network to generate normal and attack traffic, which is essential for evaluating performance or developing new intrusion detection systems. The attack traffic covers different elements that are part of the SDN network, and its types are DoS (52,741), DDoS (48,413), Probe (36,372), brute-force attack (1,110), web attacks (192), and Botnet (164). On the other hand, the normal traffic (68,424) is generated with protocols such as HTTPS, HTTP, SSH, email, DNS, FTP, and various popular applications like Facebook and YouTube. The records for each type of traffic are stored in CSV files, with a size of approximately 1.21 GB and 3.58 GB, respectively. The authors used Wireshark to capture the traffic and CICFlowMeter to extract the flows. Additionally, this dataset contains PCAP files [9].

However, upon having flows already extracted, it was determined to use Argus to increase the credibility of the data. This tool allows the extraction of unidirectional and bidirectional flows. Additionally, Argus runs on Linux environments and offers greater flexibility in the configuration options for feature extraction and transformation to various file formats for data storage [20]. Another optional tool is CICFlowMeter, which extracts bidirectional flows, allowing for obtaining 84 features, and is presented as a Python library, although it also has a version in Java [12]. Using Argus, it was configured to extract 120 features. Therefore, all the PCAP files offered by the InSDN dataset were processed to obtain their flows. Additionally, botnet traffic was added from the publicly available CTU-13 dataset containing 13 botnet traffic scenarios. However, only the PCAP files from the first scenario corresponding to the Neris bot type were considered [11]. Table 1 compares the number of flows extracted by both tools.

Based on the previously extracted flows, classes with reduced samples are discarded; namely, Normal, DDoS, DoS, and Probe traffic types are considered. These classes were chosen to achieve a better data balance, although, for normal

Table 1. Comparison of flows extracted in CICFlowMeter and Argus

Classes	Traffic samples	CICFlowMeter	Argus
InSDN			
Normal	68424	53784	111719
DoS	52471	33842	35030
DDoS	48413	398643	3352394
Probe	36372	41980	49452
Brute force	1110	582	886
Web attack	192	120	564
Botnet	164	92	193
CTU13			
Botnet	2753290	132168	192168

and DDoS traffic, the number of extracted flows exceeds 100,000 records. Moreover, it is essential to understand the 120 extracted features based on network identifiers, packets, bytes, flags, time, and flows.

3.2 Data Preprocessing

Missing Values. The presence of missing values is one of the significant anomalies that can occur in datasets, and the reason for their absence is unknown. It is necessary to understand the type of missing values. There are three types of these values: missing completely at random (MCAR), missing at random (MAR), and not missing at random (NMAR) [10]. For the first type, there is a high probability that any value may be missing in different instances and attributes within the dataset. For the second type, missing values are recorded in any attribute. In contrast, for the last type, values are absent because they depend on another value, which is also missing.

During data inspection and visualization, missing values of the NMAR type were detected. The missing values were found in the features related to arrival times in packet intervals, packet active times, fluctuation, and packet size between the source and destination hosts, impacting statistical values such as mean, minimum, and maximum. Therefore, the number of attributes dependent on the main features was verified to address this situation. Likewise, characteristics of the same class but with different operations were identified. For instance, if a sample does not have the maximum or minimum size of packets sent by the source or destination host while the average packet size is zero, these features must also have the same value. Therefore, imputation strategies using mean and constant values were applied using the SimpleImputer() class. Furthermore, the features with a large number of missing data were removed.

Outliers. Outliers, also known as outlier values, differ from others in terms of data value location, distinct behaviors, or uncommon values within the same feature. On the other hand, all data points that fall within the same level or range of visually known values are called inliers. Different methods are used for detecting these values, including those based on statistical techniques, distance between observations, density, clustering, and machine learning [29].

During the data inspection, it was identified that some records had different port designations that did not belong to the known, registered, or dynamic port ranges. Therefore, the protocol used by each flow was analyzed, and based on that, those records were eliminated. This way only flows corresponding to a group of previously mentioned ports were handled. Additionally, characteristics such as total packets, bytes, and packets per second were analyzed. In some instances, these characteristics contained values that could be considered outliers. However, these values reflect the real traffic of each processed class.

Label Encoding. In this section, the encoding process is performed for features that contain non-numeric data. Specifically, protocols and ports are analyzed based on the numbering used by the Internet Assigned Numbers Authority (IANA). Therefore, discrete data encoding is applied. On the other hand, for the target variable, categorical encoding is used.

Data Transformation. At this stage, we are left with 48 features preserved throughout the data cleaning and processing process. Considering this reduced number of features, a thorough analysis is conducted to determine which will be included in the final matrix of independent variables. Subsequently, all these features undergo data scaling through standardization. This approach is employed as it is not sensitive to large values and is ideal for preserving the distribution of outlier values in the network traffic on a different scale. Earlier, outliers were examined, and the reason for their retention in some features was explained. The formula for standardization is as follows:

$$Z = \frac{(xi - mean(x))}{stdev(x)} \tag{1}$$

Standardizing data involves having the average or mean as zero and the standard deviation as one. As a result, it shows how much each observation varies from the mean of that set of features. In this way, one can verify the equality in the original data distribution with the standardized data.

Balanceo de clases. Considering the number of samples for each type of traffic mentioned earlier (see Table 1) and the results obtained during the data cleaning and preprocessing process, an appropriate amount of data must be selected for model training. Figure 1 illustrates the amount of traffic successfully cleaned, where the Botnet and DoS classes do not have the same amount of traffic as the Normal, DDoS, and Probe classes. Although it would be possible to equalize all classes to the same quantity as the DoS class, we have decided to work with 34,200 samples for each class. This approach ensures that the model does not learn in a biased manner toward other classes.

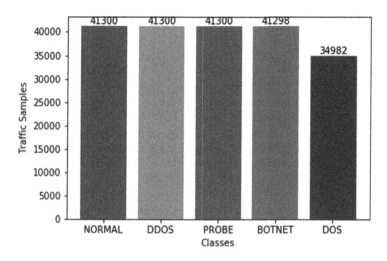

Fig. 1. Traffic samples by class

3.3 Feature Selections

This section aims to identify a predefined feature subset that optimizes the classification models' performance. Initially, it is crucial to comprehend the data and infer the type of information that can be derived from it. To determine the significance of the features, we initially employed a subjective scale of high, medium, and low importance. However, we also utilized the SelectKBest method, provided by Scikit-learn, to select the best features from the dataset. This method yields two sets of results: firstly, the most relevant attributes, and secondly, the least important ones. Nevertheless, a meticulous analysis of the features is essential before applying other techniques for subsequent processes.

Set of Characteristics. Based on the previous sections of data transformation, one of the objectives is to evaluate each variable's impact on the classification results for each type of traffic. Therefore, four sets of features are created, and this step is of utmost importance, considering that it helps identify which variables are crucial in capturing traffic behavior. By selecting the appropriate features, the models' capacity to capture traffic patterns can be enhanced, ensuring they are as accurate as possible when evaluating new data inputs. Table 2 below indicates the grouping of features into sets of 9, 12, 14, and 20 variables.

4 Evaluations and Experiments Results

In this section, the environment configurations are presented, which include the training and testing datasets, as well as the specifications of the software and hardware used. Furthermore, a comparison between the models employed in the study is conducted.

Table 2. Group of Features

Group	Features
FG1	Dur, Proto, Dport, TotPkts, SrcPkts, DstPkts, TotBytes, SrcBytes, DstBytes
FG2	Dur, Proto, Dport, TotPkts, SrcPkts, DstPkts, TotBytes, SrcBytes, DstBytes, Rate, SrcRate, DstRate
FG3	Dur, SrcDur, DstDur, Proto, Dport, TotPkts, SrcPkts, DstPkts, TotBytes, SrcBytes, DstBytes, Rate, SrcRate, DstRate, sMeanPktSz, dMeanPktSz, sMaxPktSz, dMaxPktSz, sMinPktSz, dMinPktSz
FG4	Dur, SrcDur, DstDur, Proto, Dport, TotPkts, SrcPkts, DstPkts, TotBytes, SrcBytes, DstBytes, Rate, SrcRate, DstRate

4.1 Software and Hardware Specifications

In the experimental execution, the RIG server was utilized, which had the following specifications: a 12-core AMD Ryzen Threadripper 2920X CPU, a 500 GB Crucial SSD M.2 NVMe internal storage capacity, 64 GB Crucial Ballistix DDR4-3000 RAM, and a 16 GB Phantom Gaming X Radeon VII GPU accelerator. The experiment was conducted on the Ubuntu 18.04 64-bit operating system, using Python 3.5.2 on Jupyter Notebook 6.0.2 and the NumPy, pandas, and scikit-learn libraries.

4.2 Model Selection

The models are selected based on two algorithms: explanatory and ensemble. In the former, the impact of independent variables on the outcome, i.e., the dependent variable, is determined. In the latter, the results obtained combine predictions from multiple models. Identifying whether these models are suitable for multiclass classification is also essential. Therefore, for the explanatory algorithm, DT is chosen, while for the ensemble-based algorithms, SVM and RF are selected [4]. Table 3 shows the techniques analyzed for attack classification.

Table 3. Selection and evaluation of classification models

ML model	Advantage	Disadvantage	Execution time
Naive Bayes	Easy implementation	Few parameters	Average
Random Forest	High performance	Overfitting	Average
Regresión Logística	Varied output	Supposes	Fast
SVM	Efficient	Low results	Slow
Decision Tree	High performance	Overfitting	Fast
KNN	Quick deduction	Finding N neighbors	Average

Hyperparameter Configuration. Once the models are defined, the data is split into 80.00% for training and 20.00% for testing. Subsequently, the Grid-SearchCV technique selects the best hyperparameters for the machine learning model. This technique is applied to all models and consists of GridSearch and CV. The first component finds the most suitable parameters for the model, while the second component validates the model during its training through cross-validation. Table 4 shows the hyperparameters to be searched in the established models. The hyperparameters found for each model are applied to each feature set in the data transformation.

Table 4. Hyperparameter tuning of classifiers

Model	Hyperparameter	Value
Decision Tree	criterion	entropy
	max_depth	12
	min_samples_split	2
	min_samples_leaf	1
	ccp_alpha	0.0001
	splitter	best
Random Forest	n_estimators	10
	criterion	entropy
	max_depth	12
	min_samples_split	5
	min_samples_leaf	2
	ccp_alpha	0.0001
SVM	C	1000
	kernel	rbf
	gamma	scale
	decision_function_shape	ovo

Evaluation Metrics. Two concepts are considered to evaluate the performance of each model: evaluation metrics, the confusion matrix, and the area under the ROC curve (AUC). The evaluation metrics allow us to understand the performance achieved by a model during its training, which is used to make objective decisions and determine its best applicability. The metrics to be analyzed are:

- **Accuracy:** represents the total of the predictions made correctly over the total data to be predicted.

$$Accuracy = \frac{TP + TN}{TP + TN + FP + FN} \tag{2}$$

- **Precision:** It is the number of samples that have been correctly detected as positive.

$$Precision = \frac{TP}{TP + FP} \tag{3}$$

– **Recall:** portion of positive samples that the model has correctly identified.

$$Recall = \frac{TP}{TP + FN} \tag{4}$$

– **F1-Score:** the average weighting between precision and recall that seeks the model's preference.

$$F1 - Score = 2 * \frac{Precision * Recall}{Precision + Recall} \tag{5}$$

4.3   Experiments Results

This section discusses the significance of the results obtained from the mix of three ML algorithms with four feature groups. These feature groups are listed and described in Table 2. The results of these experiments are shown in Table 5.

Table 5. Cross-validation results

Model	Accuracy	Precision	Recall	F1-Score
FG1				
DT	99.28%	99.29%	99.28%	99.28%
RF	99.31%	99.33%	99.31%	99.32%
SVM	96.83%	96.89%	96.83%	96.83%
FG2				
DT	99.25%	99.26%	99.25%	99.25%
RF	99.30%	99.32%	99.30%	99.30%
SVM	97.09%	97.09%	97.09%	97.04%
FG3				
DT	99.75%	99.75%	99.74%	99.75%
RF	99.76%	99.76%	99.76%	99.76%
SVM	99.50%	99.50%	99.50%	99.50%
FG4				
DT	99.24%	99.25%	99.24%	99.24%
RF	99.25%	99.27%	99.25%	99.26%
SVM	97.06%	97.11%	97.06%	97.06%

Based on the results, the RF model shows better accuracy results with all groups of features. However, it achieves higher accuracy with Feature Group 3. Therefore, we present the graphical analysis performed on the RF model with Feature Group 3 below. Additionally, the training accuracies obtained by the RF model were close to their respective validation accuracies.

The validation curve checks if the model is overfitting and, based on the data, allows us to find the best-fitting model. Each graph contains two curves: one for

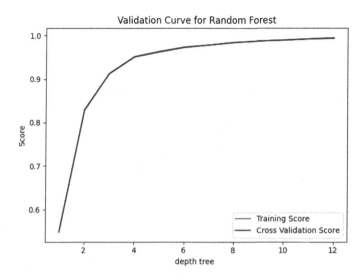

Fig. 2. Validation curve of RF model with FG3 features.

the training set score and the other for the cross-validation performed five times. Figure 2 shows the validation curve for the RF model and FG3 features.

The ROC curve shows the relationship between true positives (TP) and false positives (FP) on the Y and X axes. The area under the ROC curve (AUC) allows us to determine if a classifier model is relatively good. Figure 3 shows the ROC curve for the RF model with feature group FG3.

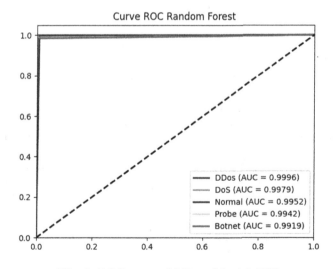

Fig. 3. ROC curve of RF model with FG3

5   Conclusion

In this paper, we developed three supervised machine learning models for classifying normal, DoS, DDoS, probe, and botnet traffic. The selected techniques included DT, RF, and SVM, which were trained using a dataset of 136,800 flow samples. The dataset was a combination of InSDN and CTU-13. Each model was evaluated on a subset of 34,200 samples. The models were carefully chosen based on a prior parameter evaluation, drawing insights from related works in the field. The training results yielded remarkable precision levels of 99.76% for RF, 99.75% for DT, and 99.50% for SVM. It's important to note that these accuracy percentages were obtained from model validation rather than direct training results, as observed in some related studies. Overall, the outcomes demonstrate the effectiveness of the developed models in accurately classifying different types of network traffic. Utilizing distinct feature groups and combining three powerful ML algorithms contributed to the outstanding performance. These results offer promising prospects for enhancing network security through traffic classification, contributing to the broader field of intrusion detection and network management.

One of the potential improvements for future work is the application of deep learning techniques to train the attack classification model, which would allow for more efficient and precise detection of patterns in the data. The use of these techniques could significantly enhance the model's predictive capabilities. However, it is essential to consider the availability of computational resources to process different traffic flows simultaneously.

Acknowledgments. The authors would like to thank the Distributed Systems, Cybersecurity and Content Research Group (RACKLY) at Universidad de las Fuerzas Armadas - ESPE for its scientific and collaborative contribution.

References

1. Ahuja, N., Singal, G., Mukhopadhyay, D.: Detection of DDoS attacks in software defined network using decision tree. In: Mendeley Data, vol. 1 (2020). https://doi.org/10.17632/jxpfjc64kr.1, https://data.mendeley.com/datasets/jxpfjc64kr/1
2. Ahuja, N., Singal, G., Mukhopadhyay, D., Kumar, N.: Automated DDoS attack detection in software defined networking. J. Netw. Comput. Appl. **187** (2021). https://doi.org/10.1016/j.jnca.2021.103108
3. Alamri, H.A., Thayananthan, V.: Bandwidth control mechanism and extreme gradient boosting algorithm for protecting software-defined networks against DDoS attacks. IEEE Access **8**, 194269–194288 (2020). https://doi.org/10.1109/ACCESS.2020.3033942
4. Alojail, M., Bhatia, S.: A novel technique for behavioral analytics using ensemble learning algorithms in e-commerce. IEEE Access **8**, 150072–150080 (2020). https://doi.org/10.1109/ACCESS.2020.3016419
5. Alzahrani, A.O., Alenazi, M.J.E.: Designing a network intrusion detection system based on machine learning for software defined networks. Future Internet **13**(5) (2021). https://doi.org/10.3390/fi13050111

6. Archanaa, R., Athulya, V., Rajasundari, T., Kiran, M.V.K.: A comparative performance analysis on network traffic classification using supervised learning algorithms. In: 2017 4th International Conference on Advanced Computing and Communication Systems (ICACCS), pp. 1–5 (2017). https://doi.org/10.1109/ICACCS.2017.8014634
7. Bannour, F., Souihi, S., Mellouk, A.: Distributed SDN control: survey, taxonomy, and challenges. IEEE Commun. Surv. Tutor. 20(1), 333–354 (2018). https://doi.org/10.1109/COMST.2017.2782482
8. Dehkordi, A.B., Soltanaghaei, M., Boroujeni, F.Z.: The DDoS attacks detection through machine learning and statistical methods in SDN. J. Supercomput. 77(3), 2383–2415 (2021). https://doi.org/10.1007/s11227-020-03323-w
9. Elsayed, M.S., Le-Khac, N.A., Jurcut, A.D.: INSDN: a novel SDN intrusion dataset. IEEE Access 8, 165263–165284 (2020). https://doi.org/10.1109/ACCESS.2020.3022633
10. Garcia, C., Leite, D., Škrjanc, I.: Incremental missing-data imputation for evolving fuzzy granular prediction. IEEE Trans. Fuzzy Syst. 28(10), 2348–2362 (2020). https://doi.org/10.1109/TFUZZ.2019.2935688
11. Garc'ıa, S., Grill, M., Stiborek, J., Zunino, A.: An empirical comparison of botnet detection methods. Comput. Secur. 45, 100–123 (2014)
12. Habibi Lashkari, A.: Cicflowmeter-v4.0 (formerly known as iscxflowmeter) is a network traffic bi-flow generator and analyser for anomaly detection (2018). https://doi.org/10.13140/RG.2.2.13827.20003
13. Hubballi, N., Swarnkar, M.: $bitcoding$: network traffic classification through encoded bit level signatures. IEEE/ACM Trans. Netw. 26(5), 2334–2346 (2018). https://doi.org/10.1109/TNET.2018.2868816
14. Janabi, A., Kanakis, T., Johnson, M.: Overhead reduction technique for software defined network based intrusion detection systems. IEEE Access 10, 66481–66491 (2022). https://doi.org/10.1109/ACCESS.2022.3184722, export Date: 15 November 2022
15. Kamel, H., Abdullah, M.: Distributed denial of service attacks detection for software defined networks based on evolutionary decision tree model. Bull. Electr. Eng. Inform. 11(4), 2322–2330 (2022). https://doi.org/10.11591/eei.v11i4.3835
16. Kumar, R., Swarnkar, M., Singal, G., Kumar, N.: IoT network traffic classification using machine learning algorithms: an experimental analysis. IEEE Internet Things J. 9(2), 989–1008 (2022). https://doi.org/10.1109/JIOT.2021.3121517
17. Nadeem, M.W., Goh, H.G., Ponnusamy, V., Aun, Y.: DDoS detection in SDN using machine learning techniques. CMC-Comput. Mater. Continua 71(1), 771–789 (2022). https://doi.org/10.32604/cmc.2022.021669
18. Nuñez-Agurto, D., Fuertes, W., Marrone, L., Benavides-Astudillo, E., Vásquez Bermúdez, M.: Traffic classification in software-defined networking by employing deep learning techniques: a systematic literature review. In: Valencia-Garcıa, R., Bucaram-Leverone, M., Del Cioppo-Morstadt, J., Vera-Lucio, N., Centanaro-Quiroz, P.H. (eds.) CITI 2023. CCIS, vol. 1873, pp. 67–80. Springer, Cham (2023). https://doi.org/10.1007/978-3-031-45682-4_6
19. Nunez-Agurto, D., Fuertes, W., Marrone, L., Macas, M.: Machine learning-based traffic classification in software-defined networking: a systematic literature review, challenges, and future research directions. IAENG Int. J. Comput. Sci. 49(4) (2022)
20. QoSient, L.: Argus (Year Published). https://openargus.org/
21. Sahoo, K.S., et al.: An evolutionary SVM model for DDoS attack detection in software defined networks. IEEE ACCESS 8, 132502–132513 (2020). https://doi.org/10.1109/ACCESS.2020.3009733

22. Sangodoyin, A.O., Akinsolu, M.O., Pillai, P., Grout, V.: Detection and classification of DDoS flooding attacks on software-defined networks: a case study for the application of machine learning. IEEE Access **9**, 122495–122508 (2021). https://doi.org/10.1109/ACCESS.2021.3109490

23. Sudar, K.M., Deepalakshmi, P.: An intelligent flow-based and signature-based ids for SDNs using ensemble feature selection and a multi-layer machine learning-based classifier. J. Intell. Fuzzy Syst. **40**(3), 4237–4256 (2021). https://doi.org/10.3233/JIFS-200850

24. Sumadi, F., Widagdo, A., Reza, A., Syaifuddin: SD-honeypot integration for mitigating DDoS attack using machine learning approaches. Int. J. Inform. Visual. **6**(1), 39–44 (2022). https://doi.org/10.30630/joiv.6.1.853, export Date: 15 November 2022

25. Tan, L., Pan, Y., Wu, J., Zhou, J., Jiang, H., Deng, Y.: A new framework for DDoS attack detection and defense in SDN environment. IEEE Access **8**, 161908–161919 (2020). https://doi.org/10.1109/ACCESS.2020.3021435

26. Tariq, F., Baig, S.: Machine learning based botnet detection in software defined networks. Int. J. Secur. Appl. **11**(11), 1–11 (2017). https://doi.org/10.14257/ijsia.2017.11.11.01

27. Tonkal, O., Polat, H., Başaran, E., Comert, Z., Kocaoglu, R.: Machine learning approach equipped with neighbourhood component analysis for DDoS attack detection in software-defined networking. Electronics (Switzerland) **10**(11) (2021). https://doi.org/10.3390/electronics10111227

28. Ussatova, O., Zhumabekova, A., Begimbayeva, Y., Matson, E.T., Ussatov, N.: Comprehensive DDoS attack classification using machine learning algorithms. CMC-Comput. Mater. Continua **73**(1), 577–594 (2022). https://doi.org/10.32604/cmc.2022.026552

29. Wang, H., Bah, M.J., Hammad, M.: Progress in outlier detection techniques: a survey. IEEE Access **7**, 107964–108000 (2019). https://doi.org/10.1109/ACCESS.2019.2932769

30. Yungaicela-Naula, N.M., Vargas-Rosales, C., Perez-Diaz, J.A.: SDN-based architecture for transport and application layer DDoS attack detection by using machine and deep learning. IEEE Access **9**, 108495–108512 (2021). https://doi.org/10.1109/ACCESS.2021.3101650

Classification of Toxic Comments on Social Networks Using Machine Learning

María Fernanda Revelo-Bautista(ID), Jair Oswaldo Bedoya-Benavides(ID), Jaime Paúl Sayago-Heredia(ID), Pablo Pico-Valencia(ID), and Xavier Quiñonez-Ku(✉)(ID)

Pontificia Universidad Católica del Ecuador, Esmeraldas, Ecuador
{maria.revelo,jair.bedoya,jaime.sayago,pablo.pico,
xavier.quinonez}@pucese.edu.ec

Abstract. This research addresses the problem of toxic comments in social networks, and how artificial intelligence (AI) and machine learning (Machine Learning) can help. It presents the development of a classification model using AI with machine learning techniques to identify toxic comments on Twitter.

The proposed classifier, developed in Python, was established with 7 different algorithms using approaches or strategies for multi-label classification, preprocessing, cleaning and data visualization. This model was trained with a total of 159571 comments from the Kaggle repository dataset called Jigsaw, which has the comments classified with various features. After the training, evaluation and comparison of the model created, the result was a classifier capable of identifying toxic and offensive words or comments with an accuracy of 92.16%.

Keywords: sentiment analysis · text classification · toxic comments · machine learning · tweets · twitter

1 Introduction

Currently, social networks have become the most popular medium for communicating and expressing feelings. This increase in the use of social networks has led to a massive increase in toxic comments that provoke personal attacks, online harassment, and bullying behaviors [1]. These cases of cyberbullying have generated impacts on many lives since the excessive freedom of unrestricted expression. Toxic comments are defined as those that use strong, rude, disrespectful terms or seek to force users to leave a discussion. Automatic identification of these toxic comments would help to implement safety mechanisms for discussions on various social media platforms.

Today, modern machine learning and natural language processing methods offer effective tools to detect antisocial behaviors from text snippets [2]. The main objective of this research is to build a classification model using artificial intelligence and machine learning techniques to detect toxic comments in social networks [3]. This model is trained using a data set (dataset) and various algorithms and machine learning techniques are

Maestría en Tecnologías de la Información, PUCE Sede Esmeraldas.

employed to improve the efficiency and accuracy of the model. Machine learning, which is a branch of Artificial Intelligence, has the main goal of allowing a computer to acquire knowledge from a model and based on this learning, to make decisions autonomously [4]. Compared to traditional statistical methods, the incorporation of machine learning techniques improves the quality of estimation modeling. This is due not only to the extension of the predictive capacity by using new approaches and strategies to select variables, but also to the optimization of efficiency in the processes thanks to automation [5].

Machine learning allows building and improving software systems by analyzing behavior [6]. A subcategory is supervised machine learning which is characterized using labeled datasets to train algorithms that accurately classify data or predict results [6]. In this context, many works focus on emotion recognition [7, 8].Unsupervised learning and various decision tree-based algorithms have proven useful in addressing classification issues, although capturing nuances and contexts, such as sarcasm and cultural allusions, remains a problem [9]. Machine learning algorithms are inherently complex, as they work with voluminous and possibly unstructured data, such as text, images, and speech [10]. Among the machine learning algorithms used is the Naive Bayes classifier, which is a particular model of Bayesian networks that is applied in the supervised classification task with discrete data [11]. Its main disadvantage is that the predictors or features must be independent, the presence of a particular one does not affect the others [12].

Another algorithm used is the decision tree, which allows expressing mappings by means of tests or attribute nodes linked to two or more subtrees and leaves or decision nodes labeled with a class. This type of algorithm is constructed from a set of training objects using the divide-and-conquer principle [13, 14]. The k-nearest neighbors' algorithm, known as KNN, is a nonparametric supervised learning classifier that uses proximity to make classifications or predictions about the clustering of an individual data point [15]. KNN is also part of a family of "lazy learning" models, which implies that it only stores a training data set rather than going through a training stage [16]. For its part, the Support Vector Machine (SVM) algorithm seeks to find a hyperplane in an N-dimensional space (where N represents the number of features) that allows to clearly classify the data points. Support Vector Machines are a set of supervised learning methods used for classification, regression, and outlier detection [17, 18]. Multi-label classification is a generalization of multi-class classification [19]. A common approach on multi-label classification is problem transformation, where a problem is transformed into one or more single-label problems [20]. These approaches or problem transformation strategies have been employed in algorithms such as SVM, Naive bayes and Logistic regression and can be as follows:

(a) Binary Relevance is the easiest and simplest approach to solve multi-label classification problems by converting n-class multi-label classification into n separate binary class classification tasks [21].

(b) Classifier chains is another technique that preserves the relationship between the various labels, transforms the n-class multi-label classification into different single-label classifications.

The use of evaluation metrics is critical in any machine learning effort. Metrics such as accuracy, precision, and recall are conventional; however, in multi-label classification problems, specialized metrics such as Hamming loss and log loss are used [22, 23]. Hamming loss considers both prediction error and omission error. Several studies have investigated the effectiveness of different methods in the field of machine learning and artificial intelligence to address this problem [6, 21]. An increasing use of online platforms to perpetrate harassment and discrimination has been observed [13, 24]. Classification of toxic comments on online platforms is an active area of research ranging from algorithm development to metrics evaluation and faces challenges ranging from capturing context and nuance to mitigating inherent biases in training data.

The article is distributed as follows. Section 2 explains the methodology used and presents the dataset. Section 3 then discusses the results obtained. Then the conclusions derived from the research are presented, followed by a list of the bibliographical references used.

2 Materials and Methods

2.1 Materials

For the development of the project on the classification model of toxic comments, several algorithms were implemented using Jupiter notebook in Anaconda IDE version 2.4.2 written in the Python 3.10 programming language, on a Dell laptop with a Windows 11 operating system i7 processor and 32 GB RAM. The dataset used for this work was obtained from the Kaggle website provided by Jigsaw. Conventional AI. This data is based on a compilation of many Wikipedia comments tagged as toxic, severely toxic, threats, identity hate, obscene, and insults. The advantage of reusing this type of data is that the information represents a true sample of the content present on the Twitter social network. This set contains 159,571,000 comments that have already been tagged as rude, disrespectful, or likely, cause someone to leave a thread, delete a post, or close an account. The collected tweet dataset was divided into two subsets to train and test the various classifiers. Libraries used to develop the classifier include Pandas for data management, Scikit-learn for building and evaluating machine learning models, matplotlib for imaging, confusion matrix, and NLTK for text preprocessing.

2.2 Analytical Description

The dataset includes many text fields, so the analysis of the comments was performed as follows: First, before starting the cleaning process, it is important to understand what data will be manipulated. This helps to provide more information and background to the dataset. So, after linking the csv file, some functions were performed on the data to have a better understanding with the data.

It is important to know the size of the dataset, the data type of each column, the total of null records, the structure of the different classes. Then, equal rows are excluded if they exist. We employed to the dataset, text preprocessing techniques to clean the tweets, where it includes converting the text to lowercase letters, tokenization and removing username tags, punctuation marks, empty words, retweet symbols, URLs and numbers to clean the comments. Comment analysis was then developed on the cleaned comments as detailed below: The analysis was performed on the dataset collected from the Jigsaw database with 159571 tweets. Composition of the dataset used for training, broken down by different categories of comments. Out of 15294 comments categorized as toxic, they represent 9.58% of the set. Severely toxic comments total 1595, corresponding to 1.0%. Obscene comments amounted to 8449, representing 5.29% of the total. Comments containing threats number 478 and represent 0.30%, while insulting comments total 7877, equivalent to 4.94%. Finally, there are 1405 comments classified as hateful towards an identity, equivalent to 0.88% of the total. In summary, 21.99% of the total data is classified as toxic, and the rest is considered non-toxic. To take a closer look at the text contained in the dataset, a word cloud visualization was designed.

Fig. 1. Cloud of the most common words associated with obscene comments.

The set of words shown in Fig. 1 lists the most common words associated with obscene comments. The set of words is very helpful for understanding what users are commenting on. For the most part, the words are related to comments containing swear words, insults, and hate.

2.3 Methods

The deductive method was used to improve the model parameters and optimally classify toxic comments in any tweet. Likewise, the inductive method was applied to identify toxic words, phrases, and expressions based on data collection. In this study, the steps of the methodology for developing classification models through data exploration were applied using the Cross Industry Standard Process for Data Mining (CRISP-DM) [25]. This process consists of a method and a way to process a dataset, providing any user with a comprehensive approach to successfully complete a data mining project. The CRISP-DM process is valued as one of the leading data mining methodologies according to a survey published in KDnuggets [23]. The CRISP-DM methodology is an approach that is made up of six phases (business understanding, data understanding, data preparation, modeling, evaluation, and deployment) [25].

3   Results

3.1   Understanding the Business

The research aims to classify a dataset whether a comment is toxic or non-toxic through the collection provided the various labeled Jigsaw features. Therefore, from the data a probability of each type of toxicity in a Twitter comment can be classified or predicted.

3.2   Understanding the Data

The data used in this research is obtained from a dataset published by Google Jigsaw from the discussion section of Wikipedia that includes comments tagged by human raters. A comment can be classified as toxic, severe toxic, threatening, identity hatred, obscene, and insulting. The Jigsaw Unintended Bias in Toxicity Classification dataset, published within a Kaggle competition that took place in 2018 [26]. Aiming to explore unintended bias in models across a broad spectrum of online dialogues, the dataset collects content from the Civil Comments platform that allowed starting conversations and posting comments on news sites. Dataset contains 1.56 million text and code pairs, each pair labeled with one of 16 different tasks [27]. The tasks include natural language understanding (NLU), such as language translation, question answering, and text generation, as well as code machine learning tasks, such as code classification, code generation, and code understanding. The Jigsaw dataset is divided into two sets: a training set of 1.2 million pairs and a test set of 360,000 pairs [28]. Link to the dataset: https://www.kaggle.com/competitions/jigsaw-toxic-comment-classification-challenge/data. The proposed framework starts with data collection and preparation as shown in Fig. 2. The models are developed by learning algorithms and the results were used to predict failures.

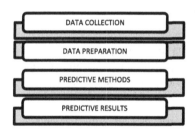

Fig. 2.   Framework to classify toxic comments.

3.3   Data Preparation

In this phase, a pre-treatment technique is first applied to the data obtained to make them suitable for extraction. It is important to ensure that the model produces accurate and reliable results, which is why the model was trained from a ".csv" file that was previously developed by performing cleaning techniques established at the beginning. The training dataset went through a process of counting, cleaning, tokenization that allowed the model

Fig. 3. Preprocessing steps.

to be trained through various algorithms to achieve an efficient classifier suitable for the project. This parameter was carried out through five steps as shown in Fig. 3.

The pre-processing employed for cleaning is as follows: upper-case letters were converted to lower-case letters and special symbols and punctuations were removed [29]. The input text sequences were converted to fixed-sized sequences by shortening or padding. The vocabulary size was reduced to 100 K words and produced good accuracy. Other complex techniques such as stemming, lemmatization and spell correction were also explored. Stemming and lemmatization were not particularly impactful, but other techniques improved the model score [30]. After completing these steps, the file was saved and could be used to train the model without major complications or errors, suitable to be a classifier capable of identifying toxic comments.

3.4 Modeling

Model training: The selected algorithms were four of those that allowed the creation of seven models due to for the training being these:

- Chain Logistic Regression (model 1)
- Logistic Regression with binary relation (model 2)
- Naive Bayes in chain (model 3)
- Naive Bayes with binary relation (model 4)
- Chain SVM (model 5)
- SVM with binary relation (model 6)
- Multiresult XGBoost (model 7)

The dataset used for this model was divided into two parts: train and test. In this research, we used a table of performance measures for the classification of toxic comments and the evaluation of the model trained with the different algorithms. Let's analyze why these metrics are appropriate for this task:

- Hamming Loss: This metric measures the percentage of tags that are incorrectly predicted, i.e., the fraction of tags that the model has incorrectly predicted out of the total tags. In the context of multi-label classification, where each comment may belong to multiple categories (such as toxic, severely toxic, obscene, etc.), the Hamming Loss is particularly useful because it takes into account the prediction accuracy on each individual label. This is important in applications where it is crucial not only to correctly identify relevant categories, but also to avoid false positives in non-relevant categories [31].
- Log Loss: This metric measures the performance of a classification model where the output is a probability between 0 and 1. Log Loss penalizes incorrect classifications, being more severe on those that are further away from the true label. In the case of toxic comment classification, where not only the correct classification but also the

model's confidence in that classification is important, Log Loss is a valuable metric. It helps ensure that the model not only classifies correctly, but is also confident about its predictions, which is crucial in sensitive applications such as content moderation [32].

- Accuracy: Accuracy is the most important indicator for measuring a model's performance [33]. The purpose of the accuracy was to measure the percentage of the total number of correctly classified examples predicted over the total number of examples. The metric equation can be written as.

- $ACC = \frac{TP+TN}{TP+TN+FP+FN}$

- Recall: The recall evaluation metric, also known as the true positive rate (TPR), is used to determine the proportion of correctly classified positive classes [34]. The metric equation can be written as
- $R(TPR) = \frac{TP}{TP+FN}$
- Precision: The primary purpose of precision metrics is to measure the positive patterns from the total predicted patterns in a positive class [33]. The metric equation can be written as
- $P = \frac{TP}{TP+FP}$
- Recovery: It is defined as the ratio of correct labeled positive values to all actual positive values.
- F1 score: Refers to the weighted average of precision and recall being the harmonic mean.

Link to the classifier model in the GitHub repository: https://github.com/JairBedoy a17/ClasificadorComentariosToxicos.

3.5 Evaluation

For model evaluation, different techniques and algorithms are described in this section. Each classification model with the different algorithms was evaluated through the evaluation metrics such as "Hamming Loss", "Log Loss", "Acurracy", "Precision", "recall", "F1 Score" and thus obtaining the most feasible for classification.

From the implementation of the models, it can be seen in Table 1 that the difference in the performance of the classification models is very little: model 3 had the lowest accuracy with 90%, followed by model 4 with 91.4%, model 7 with 91.9% and models 2, 5 and 6 with 92%. The accuracy of model 1 elaborated by chain logistic regression had the best accuracy with a value of 92.19%.

Of the 7 models trained, as shown in Table 1, the Chain Logistic Regression classification model was chosen. The model achieved the highest percentage of accuracy (92.19%) in the course of training and validation (80–20%). The model was managed according to the parameters previously established in the design.

The models behaved according to the results obtained in the code as shown in Table 2, which determined loss metrics distinguishing that the lower the percentage, the higher the effectiveness.

Table 1. Percentage accuracy of trained models

Model	Accuracy
Model 1	92.19%
Model 2	92%
Model 3	90%
Model 4	91.4%
Model 5	92%
Model 6	92%
Model 7	91.9%

Table 2. Percentage of hamming loss and log loss for each model

Model	Hamming Loss	Log Loss
Model 1	0.01858	0.8385
Model 2	0.01867	0.6349
Model 3	0.02459	1.9142
Model 4	0.02164	0.4094
Model 5	0.01827	0.9842
Model 6	0.01787	0.7962
Model 7	0.77292	0.0188

In the statistical graphs in Figs. 4 and 5, we visualize the percentage level that each model reached in the different labels and evaluation metrics according to the training that each model had achieved, visually determining that model 1 was superior to the other classification models.

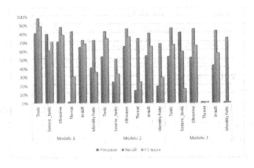

Fig. 4. Comparison of three models.

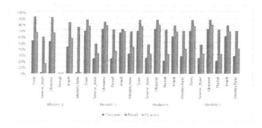

Fig. 5. Comparison of four models.

BATERIA DE PRUEBA	Toxic	Severe toxic	Obscene	Threat	Insult	Identity hate
idiot	1	0	1	0	1	0
fuck	1	1	1	0	1	0
stupid	1	0	1	0	1	0
dumbass	1	0	1	0	1	0
motherfucker	1	0	1	0	1	0
crap	1	0	1	0	0	0
asshole	1	0	1	0	1	0
suck	1	0	1	0	1	0
shit	1	0	1	0	0	0
ass	1	0	1	0	1	0
bullshit	1	0	1	0	0	0
hell	1	0	0	0	0	0
bastard	1	0	1	0	1	0
pussy	1	0	1	0	1	0
bastard	1	0	1	0	1	0
bitch	1	0	1	0	1	0
cock	1	0	1	0	0	0
whore	1	0	1	0	1	0
jerk	1	0	1	0	1	0
piss	1	0	1	0	1	0
black ass	1	0	1	0	1	1

Fig. 6. Toxic Word Test Set.

Figure 6 shows that the model classified 21 toxic words correctly, which depending on the order of the established columns marks one or zero depending on what it means, i.e., it belongs to one or different categories depending on the word to be predicted and its level of toxicity.

BATERIA DE PRUEBA	Toxic	Severe toxic	Obscene	Threat	Insult	Identity hate
love	0	0	0	0	0	0
handsome	0	0	0	0	0	0
beautiful	0	0	0	0	0	0
pretty	0	0	0	0	0	0
felicity	0	0	0	0	0	0
peace	0	0	0	0	0	0
bumblebee	0	0	0	0	0	0
dog	0	0	0	0	0	0
cat	0	0	0	0	0	0
car	0	0	0	0	0	0

Fig. 7. Non-toxic word test set

Figure 7 shows that the model classified 10 non-toxic words correctly, which depending on the order of the established columns marked zero, i.e., it does not belong to any of the categories without having a level of toxicity. With the results, the trained model can be saved so that it can be used later and not have to be trained again or it could be used in a predesigned system or application to classify toxic or non-toxic comments.

3.6 Correlation Matrix

The correlation matrix was generated to identify the correlation between labels as shown in Fig. 8, the matrix according to its correlation range from 0 to 1 that goes from a strong color to a light color show that comments labeled as "toxic" have a higher correlation probability with comments labeled as "obscene" and "insulting"; unexpectedly, "toxic" and "severe toxic" comments are weakly correlated. However, the comments that are highly correlated are those labeled "obscene" and "insulting" which allowed the model to be more effective.

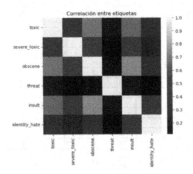

Fig. 8. Correlation matrix.

3.7 Evaluation of Validity

Our proposal innovatively addresses the challenge of identifying and classifying toxic comments in social networks, using advanced algorithms such as KNN and Linear Regression. Despite the inherent difficulties in understanding subtlety and context in comments, the study demonstrates a significant commitment to improving online interaction. The research highlights the importance of addressing biases in datasets and the need for collaboration with experts to create specialized datasets, which is a crucial step towards creating a safer and more respectful digital environment. The next step of improvement is to use a larger training set, which will allow us to increase the accuracy in obtaining toxicity along with a larger dataset.

Moreover, there are other limitations that have not been fully addressed like false positive in toxic comments, target function bias [35] and homogenization bias [36]. To reduce false positives we used expert validation together with the application of evaluation metrics. As for the objective function and homogenization bias, we were unable to validate these biases in our data set because their scope was beyond our scope. In the future, we aim to explore these factors when we extract new data sets that become available. It is important to reinforce negative biases and access to private information, which represents significant risks and consideration should be given to improving training methods, reinforcing data security and educating users [37].

4 Discussion

Toxic comments can have serious consequences for individuals and communities, such as impaired mental well-being, promotion of hate speech, and misinformation. Social media companies often face criticism for failing to adequately address toxic content on their platforms.

To begin with, it is essential to understand what constitutes a toxic comment. According to Jigsaw, an initiative of Alphabet (Google's parent company), a toxic comment can be defined as "a rude, disrespectful, or unreasonable comment that can lead someone to leave a conversation" [21], being clear on the investigation that it is a toxic comment allows the development of the model to be more efficient in its classification.

Supervised machine learning has been the main approach to address this challenge. This involves training a model on a labeled dataset, where comments are marked as toxic or non-toxic [22]. Once the model has been trained, it can predict the toxicity of new comments. For example, the "Perspective API" developed by Jigsaw uses this technique and has shown impressive performance in identifying toxic comments [24]. This research contributes to the proposed article since it used a data set where the model that It was developed to identify the algorithm that best classifies toxic comments.

Algorithms often face challenges understanding subtlety and context, particularly in scenarios where sarcasm or cultural references are common. If the data set used to train the model contains biases against certain groups or topics, the resulting model could manifest discrimination [38]. This is a crucial aspect to consider during the dataset investigation phase. Specifically, if the data set is exclusively focused on a certain group or topic, the model might not be effective in classifying comments as toxic or non-toxic.

KNN is an instance-based classification algorithm that classifies a comment based on how its nearest neighbors are tagged. In a study [39], it was found that KNN can be effective in classifying toxic comments when the data set has a balanced distribution. However, its performance can be affected by unbalanced data sets and choosing an inappropriate "k".

On the other hand, although Linear Regression is an algorithm generally more suitable for regression problems, there are investigations that have explored its application in classification tasks. In a study referenced as [40], researchers applied linear regression techniques to classify toxic comments. The results showed that linear regression can serve as a useful baseline in these tasks. Although it may not be the best tool for the job, its simplicity and efficiency make it an option to consider, especially as a starting point for comparison with more complex algorithms.

Each algorithm has its own advantages and limitations when it comes to classifying toxic comments. While KNN is simple and can be effective with the proper setup, its performance can vary depending on the data set. Linear regression, while not the most natural approach to classification, can offer a useful insight. For its part, SVM has shown promise given its adaptability and handling of high-dimensional data. It is essential, when choosing an algorithm, to consider the characteristics of the data set and the specific context in which the classification will be applied.

5 Conclusions

The Chain Logistic Regression model proved to be the most effective with an accuracy of 92.195% in classifying Twitter comments into various categories such as is toxic, severely toxic, threatening, obscene, insulting and identity hate, it not only had the highest accuracy, but also performed well on additional metrics such as Hamming Loss, Log Loss, precision and recall, suggesting a healthy balance between sensitivity and specificity, it was selected after comparing it with six other machine learning algorithms, proving to be the most suitable for the dataset used.

The hamming loss and log loss metrics suggest that the model performance is robust. The loss metrics are relatively low for the selected model, indicating higher effectiveness, for a more complete evaluation of the model multiple metrics are used (Hamming Loss, Log Loss, Accuracy, Recall, F1 Score).

Additionally, the model can effectively classify words into relevant categories. For example, the word "love" is classified as non-toxic in all categories, while the word "fuck" is classified as toxic, severely toxic, obscene, and insulting.

The correlation matrix reveals that comments labeled "toxic" are most strongly correlated with "obscene" and "insulting" comments, which is valuable for understanding the nature of toxic language. Surprisingly, "toxic" and "severely toxic" comments have a weak correlation, which may require further study.

Machine Learning models can be trained to recognize different forms of toxicity, including offensive, discriminatory, sexist, sexist, racist, and other types of inappropriate behavior. In addition, these models can be scaled to work in different languages and cultural contexts.

For future work, the creation of a specialized dataset in collaboration with experts in the area is suggested, given its fundamental importance. In addition, the development of a model capable of continuously improving its learning performance after being trained is proposed. The incorporation of feedback from different approaches and languages would contribute significantly to the development and adaptability of the dataset.

References

1. Andročec, D.: Machine learning methods for toxic comment classification: a systematic review. Acta Univ. Sapientiae, Informatica **12**, 205–216 (2020). https://doi.org/10.2478/ausi-2020-0012
2. Brassard-Gourdeau, É., Khoury, R.: Using sentiment information for preemptive detection of harmful comments in online conversations. In: Proceedings of the Canadian Conference on Artificial Intelligence (2021).https://doi.org/10.21428/594757db.08d5c187
3. Ibrahim, M., Torki, M., El-Makky, N.: Imbalanced toxic comments classification using data augmentation and deep learning. In: Proceedings - 17th IEEE International Conference on Machine Learning and Applications, pp. 875–878. ICMLA 2018 (2019)

4. Chelmis, C., Zois, D.-S.: Dynamic, incremental, and continuous detection of cyberbullying in online social media. ACM Trans. Web **15**(3), 1–33 (2021). https://doi.org/10.1145/3448014

5. Calvo, J., Guzmán, M., Ramos, D.: Machine learning, una pieza clave en la transformación de los modelos de negocio. Manage. Solutions (2018)

6. Bishop, M.: Acknowledgments and bibliographical note. In: A History of Cornell (2017)

7. Simeone, O.: A brief introduction to machine learning for engineers. Found. Trends Signal Process. **12**(3–4), 200–431 (2018). https://doi.org/10.1561/2000000102

8. Arevalillo-Herráez, M., Ayesh, A., Santos, O.C., Arnau-Gonzáalez, P.: Combining supervised and unsupervised learning to discover emotional classes. In: UMAP 2017 - Proceedings of the 25th Conference on User Modeling, Adaptation and Personalization, pp. 355–366 (2017)

9. Dalal, K.R.: Analysing the role of supervised and unsupervised machine learning in IoT. In: Proceedings of the International Conference Electronics Sustainable Communication System ICESC (2020)

10. Tare, P.: toxic comment detection and classification. In: 31st Conference on Neural Information Processing Systems (NIPS 2017), pp. 1–6 (2017)

11. Vaidya, A., Mai, F., Ning, Y.: Empirical analysis of multi-task learning for reducing identity bias in toxic comment detection. In: Proceedings of the 14th International AAAI Conference on Web and Social Media, ICWSM (2020).https://doi.org/10.1609/icwsm.v14i1.7334

12. Gutiérrez, A.M., Pacheco, P.A., Gutiérrez, J.C., Bressan, G.: Development of a naive bayes classifier for image quality assessment in biometric face images. In: Proceedings of the 25th Brazillian Symposium on Multimedia and the Web Web Media (2019)

13. Lynch, G., Moreau, E., Vogel, C.: A naive bayes classifier for automatic correction of preposition and determiner errors in ESL text. In: Proceedings of the 7th Workshop on Innovative Use of NLP for Building Educational Applications, BEA 2012 at the 2012 Conference of the North American Chapter of the Association for Computational Linguistics: Human Language Technologies, NAACL-HLT (2012)

14. Papageorgiou, E., Stylios, C., Groumpos, P.: A combined fuzzy cognitive map and decision trees model for medical decision making. In: Annual International Conference of the IEEE Engineering in Medicine and Biology – Proceedings, pp. 6117–6120 (2006)

15. Albu, A.: From logical inference to decision trees in medical diagnosis. In: 2017 E-Health and Bioengineering Conference, EHB, pp. 65–68 (2017)

16. Sun, B., Du, J., Gao, T.: Study on the improvement of K-nearest-neighbor algorithm. In: 2009 International Conference on Artificial Intelligence and Computational Intelligence, no. 4, pp. 390–393. AICI (2009)

17. Ni, K.S., Nguyen, T.Q.: An adaptable k-nearest neighbors algorithm for MMSE image interpolation. IEEE Trans. Image Process. **18** (2009).https://doi.org/10.1109/TIP.2009.2023706

18. Mohan, L., Pant, J., Suyal, P., Kumar, A.: Support vector machine accuracy improvement with classification. In: Proceedings of the 2020 12th International Conference on Computational Intelligence and Communication Networks, CICN, pp. 477–481 (2020)

19. Ertekin, Ş, Bottou, L., Giles, C.L.: Nonconvex online support vector machines. IEEE Trans. Pattern Anal. Mach. Intell. **33**, 368–381 (2011). https://doi.org/10.1109/TPAMI.2010.109

20. Sorower, M.: A Literature Survey on Algorithms for Multi-Label Learning. Oregon State University, Corvallis (2010)

21. Read, J., Pfahringer, B., Holmes, G., Frank, E.: Classifier chains for multi-label classification. Mach. Learn. **85**, 333–359 (2011). https://doi.org/10.1007/s10994-011-5256-5

22. Wulczyn, E., Thain, N., Dixon, L.: Ex machina: personal attacks seen at scale. In: 26th International World Wide Web Conference, WWW, pp. 1391–1399 (2017)

23. Schapire, R.E., Singer, Y.: BoosTexter: a boosting-based system for text categorization. Mach. Learn. **39**, 135–168 (2000). https://doi.org/10.1023/a1007649029923

24. Fiuza Perez, M.D., Rodriguez Perez, J.: La regresión logística : una herramienta versátil. Nefrología **20**(6), 495–500 (2000)
25. Dixon, L., Li, J., Sorensen, J., et al.: Measuring and mitigating unintended bias in text classification. In: AIES 2018 - Proceedings of the 2018 AAAI/ACM Conference on AI, Ethics, and Society. Association for Computing Machinery, Inc., pp. 67–73 (2018)
26. Kolyshkina, I., Simoff, S.: Interpretability of machine learning solutions in public healthcare: the CRISP-ML approach. Front Big Data **4**, 660206 (2021). https://doi.org/10.3389/fdata.2021.660206
27. Sahoo, N., Gupta, H., Bhattacharyya, P.: Detecting unintended social bias in toxic language datasets. In: CoNLL 2022 of the 26th Conference on Computational Natural Language Learning, Proceedings of the Conference (2022)
28. Zhai, Z.: Rating the severity of toxic comments using BERT-based deep learning method. In: 2022 IEEE 5th International Conference on Electronics Technology, ICET, pp. 1283–1288 (2022)
29. Manerba, M.M., Guidotti, R., Passaro, L., Ruggieri, S.: Bias discovery within human raters: a case study of the jigsaw dataset. In: 1st Workshop on Perspectivist Approaches to Disagreement in NLP, NLPerspectives 2022 as part of Language Resources and Evaluation Conference, LREC 2022 Workshop, pp. 550–572 (2022)
30. Johnson, R., Zhang, T.: Convolutional neural networks for text categorization: Shallow Word-level vs. Deep Character-level (2016)
31. Deshmukh, S., Rade, R.: Tackling Toxic Online Communication with Recurrent Capsule Networks (2019)
32. Butucea, C., Ndaoud, M., Stepanova, N.A., Tsybakov, A.B.: Variable selection with hamming loss. Ann. Stat. **46**, 1837–1875 (2018). https://doi.org/10.1214/17-AOS1572
33. Gao, Y., Hasegawa, H., Yamaguchi, Y., Shimada, H.: Malware detection using gradient boosting decision trees with customized log loss function. In: International Conference on Information Networking, pp. 273–278 (2021)
34. Hossin, M., Sulaiman, M.N.: A review on evaluation metrics for data classification evaluations. Int. J. Data Min. Knowl. Manag. Process. **5**, 01–11 (2015). https://doi.org/10.5121/ijdkp.2015.5201
35. Hassan, H., Abdel-Fattah, M.A., Ghoneim, A.: Risk Prediction Applied to Global Software Development using Machine Learning Methods (2023)
36. Chakraborty, J., Majumder, S., Menzies, T.: Bias in machine learning software: Why? How? What to do? In: ESEC/FSE 2021 of the Proceedings of the 29th ACM Joint Meeting European Software Engineering Conference and Symposium on the Foundations of Software Engineering. Association for Computing Machinery, Inc., pp. 429–440 (2021)
37. Das, S., Donini, M., Gelman, J., et al.: Fairness Measures for Machine Learning in Finance (2020)
38. Weidinger, L., Mellor, J., Rauh, M., et al.: Ethical and social risks of harm from Language Models (2021)
39. Risch, J., Krestel, R.: Toxic Comment Detection in Online Discussions, pp. 85–109 (2020) https://doi.org/10.1007/978-981-15-1216-2_4
40. Schnappinger, M., Osman, M.H., Pretschner, A., Fietzke, A.: Learning a classifier for prediction of maintainability based on static analysis tools. In: IEEE International Conference on Program Comprehension. IEEE Computer Society, pp. 243–248 (2019)
41. Huang, S.M., Yang, J.F.: Linear discriminant regression classification for face recognition. IEEE Sig. Process. Lett. **20**, 91–94 (2013). https://doi.org/10.1109/LSP.2012.2230257

Author Index

M. Botto-Tobar et al. (Eds.): ICAT 2023, CCIS 2050, pp. 271–273, 2024.
https://doi.org/10.1007/978-3-031-58953-9

Printed in the United States
by Baker & Taylor Publisher Services